T0156006

Lecture Notes in Artificial Intelligence 11710

Subseries of Lecture Notes in Computer Science

More information about this series at http://www.springer.com/series/1244

Vladimír Mařík · Petr Kadera ·
George Rzevski · Alois Zoitl ·
Gabriele Anderst-Kotsis ·
A Min Tjoa · Ismail Khalil (Eds.)

Industrial Applications of Holonic and Multi-Agent Systems

9th International Conference, HoloMAS 2019
Linz, Austria, August 26–29, 2019
Proceedings

Editors
Vladimír Mařík
Czech Technical University in Prague
Prague, Czech Republic

Petr Kadera
Czech Technical University in Prague
Prague, Czech Republic

George Rzevski
The Open University
Milton Keynes, UK

Alois Zoitl
Johannes Kepler University of Linz
Linz, Austria

Gabriele Anderst-Kotsis
Johannes Kepler University of Linz
Linz, Austria

A Min Tjoa
Software Competence Center Hagenberg
Hagenberg im Mühlkreis, Austria

Ismail Khalil
Johannes Kepler University of Linz
Linz, Austria

ISSN 0302-9743 ISSN 1611-3349 (electronic)
Lecture Notes in Artificial Intelligence
ISBN 978-3-030-27877-9 ISBN 978-3-030-27878-6 (eBook)
https://doi.org/10.1007/978-3-030-27878-6

LNCS Sublibrary: SL7 – Artificial Intelligence

This Springer imprint is published by the registered company Springer Nature Switzerland AG
The registered company address is: Gewerbestrasse 11, 6330 Cham, Switzerland

Preface

It is a real pleasure to declare that the research activities around holonic and multi-agent systems for industrial applications have continued and even increased their importance during the last two decades. The number of both the scientific topics and the achievements in the subject field is growing steadily, especially as the ideas quickly penetrate into industrial practice, being stimulated by the Industry 4.0 visions.

This year's conference is the 12th in the sequence of HoloMAS events. The first three (HoloMAS 2000 in Greenwich, HoloMAS 2001 in Munich, and HoloMAS 2002 in Aix-en-Provence) were organized as workshops under the umbrella of DEXA. As of 2003, HoloMAS achieved the status of independent conference organized bi-yearly in the odd years, still under the DEXA patronage (HoloMAS 2003 in Prague, HoloMAS 2005 in Copenhagen, HoloMAS 2007 in Regensburg, HoloMAS 2009 in Linz, HoloMAS 2011 in Toulouse, HoloMAS 2013 in Prague, HoloMAS 2015 in Valencia, HoloMAS 2017 in Lyon). The HoloMAS line of scientific events created a community of researchers who are active in the subject field. They have started to cooperate in large EU projects. One of the largest projects is the RICAIP project leading to the development of the Research and Innovation Center for Advanced Intelligent Production, shared by CIIRC CTU Prague, BUT Brno, DFKI Saarbruecken, and Zema Saarbruecken, which aims to plant a seed of European infrastructure for Distributed Manufacturing. Many more projects have been submitted or are under preparation.

The research of holonic and agent-based systems invokes stronger and stronger interest of industry and receives increasing support from both public sector and private institutions. There are a number of impacted journals that provide space for articles dealing with industrial agents like *IEEE Transactions on SMC: Systems, IEEE Transactions on Industrial Informatics, Journal of Production Research, Journal of Intelligent Manufacturing or JAAMAS*. Despite this fact, we feel that conferences as a means for personal meetings of the engaged researchers are quite important and stimulating for further development in the field. Alongside HoloMAS, which has been the pioneering event in the subject field, there are multiple conferences like IEEE SMC annual conference, ETFA, INDIN, or INCOM that focus their attention on advanced industrial solutions based on intelligent agents. However, the HoloMAS conference keeps its orientation, character, and flavor, and remains strongly industry oriented.

It is our pleasure to inform you that for HoloMAS 2019 there were 14 papers selected, as well as 2 papers invited by the Program Committee, to be included in this volume. The papers are organized into five sections. Two invited talks presented by leading researchers in the subject field, Robert Brennan (University of Calgary) and Thomas Strasser (AIT Vienna), are included in the first section. This is followed by the sections entitled Methodologies and Frameworks (three papers), Agent-based Production and Scheduling (four papers), and Data and Knowledge (four papers). As usual, the last section is dedicated to MAS technology applications, and this is titled MAS in Various Areas (three papers). In general, we appreciate that the papers included in this volume follow the main innovation trends in the field and display the current state-of-the-art interdisciplinarity of the research in the given area keeping the industrial orientation of the research in mind. Thus, HoloMAS 2019 reflects the progress in the field and its diversity, but keeps its original character and focus.

The MAS technology represents an excellent and promising theoretical background for developing a Industry 4.0 solution. The MAS theory can be used with advantage to support research activities and to bring new features to these solution explorations e.g. AI principles, machine learning, data mining, and data analytics in general. But the implementations explore – as a rule – the SOA (Service Oriented Architecture) approaches on an even broader scale. These are critically simplifying real-life solutions.

The HoloMAS 2019 conference represented another successful scientific event in the HoloMAS history and created a highly motivating environment, challenging the future research and fostering the integration of efforts in the subject field.

We are very grateful to the DEXA Association for providing us with this excellent opportunity to organize the HoloMAS 2019 Conference within the DEXA event. We would like to express many thanks to Prof. Gabriele Kotsis, Mr. Ismail Khalil, and Mrs. Michaela Horáková for all their organizational efforts, which were of key importance for the success of our conference.

June 2019

Vladimír Mařík
Petr Kadera
George Rzevski
Alois Zoitl

HoloMAS 2019

9th International Conference on
Industrial Applications of Holonic and Multi-Agent Systems
Linz, Austria, August 26–29, 2019

Conference Co-chairs

Petr Kadera	Czech Technical University in Prague, Czech Republic
Vladimír Mařík	Czech Technical University in Prague, Czech Republic
George Rzevski	The Open University, UK
Aloi Zoitl	Johannes Kepler University Linz, Austria

Program Committee

Jose Barata	Universidade Nova de Lisboa, Portugal
Robert Barelkowski	West Pomeranian University of Technology, Poland
Maria Letizia Bertotti	Free University of Bolzano, Italy
Theodeor Borangiu	University of Bucharest, Romania
Armando W. Colombo	University of Applied Sciences Emden-Leer, Germany
Amro M. Farid	Dartmouth University, USA
Adriana Giret	Universidad Politechnica de Valencia, Spain
Zdeněk Hanzálek	Czech Technical University in Prague, Czech Republic
Václav Jirkovský	Czech Technical University in Prague, Czech Republic
Matthias Klusch	German Research Center for Artificial Intelligence (DFKI), Germany
Jose L. M. Lastra	Tampere University of Technology, Finland
Paulo Leitao	Polytechnic Institute of Braganca, Portugal
Wilfired Lepuschitz	PRIA, Austria
Francisco Maturana	Rockwell Automation, USA
Duncan McFarlane	Cambridge University, UK
Munir Merdan	PRIA, Austria
Thanh Nguyen Ngoc	Polytechnic University of Wroclaw, Poland
Marek Obitko	Rockwell Automation, Czech Republic
Stuart Rubin	SPAWAR Systems Center, USA
Nestor Rychtyckyj	Ford Motor Company, USA
Arndt Schirrmann	Airbus Group, Germany
Tim Schwartz	German Research Center for Artificial Intelligence (DFKI), Germany
Weiming Shen	National Research Council, China
Petr Skobelev	Smart Solutions, Russia
Alexander Smirnov	SPIIRAS, Russia

Organizers

scch
software competence center
hagenberg

JKU
Institute for
Telecooperation

@WAS
www.iiwas.org

Contents

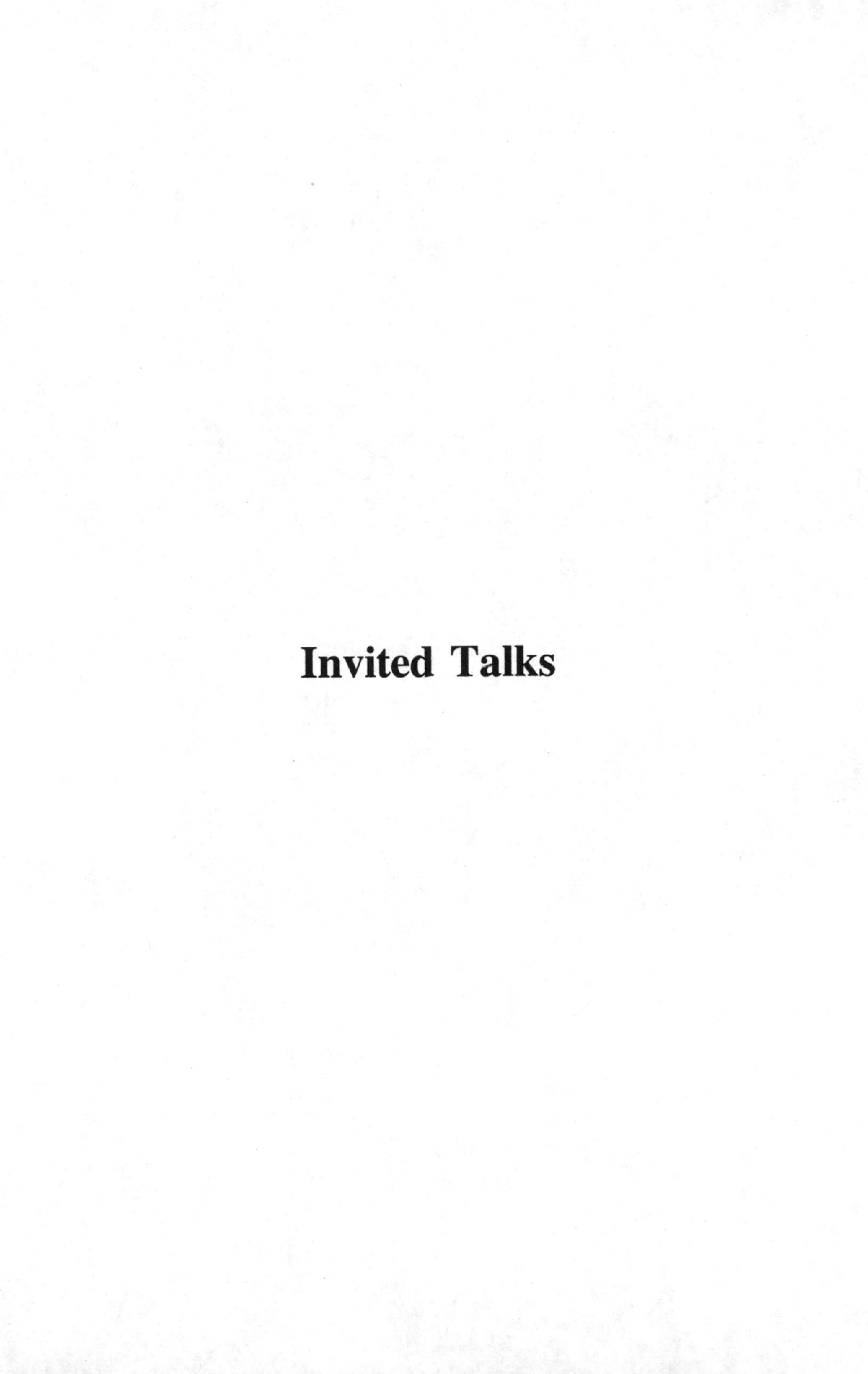

Invited Talks

IEC 61499 and the Promise of Holonic Systems

Robert W. Brennan(✉) and Guolin Lyu

Schulich School of Engineering, University of Calgary, Calgary, Canada
rbrennan@ucalgary.ca

Abstract. This paper provides a review of the IEC 61499 standard for industrial automation from the perspective of holonic manufacturing systems. This standard played a central role since the beginnings of the Holonic Manufacturing Systems (HMS) movement, and by many, was considered the enabling approach to realize holonic systems. In this paper, we ask if, after 20 years of research and development, this promise has been realized.

Keywords: IEC 61499 standard · Holonic manufacturing systems

1 Introduction

The concept of holonic systems has its roots in the goal of developing a distributed intelligent control paradigm for manufacturing. Unlike multi-agent systems (MAS), which is a broader software approach that can be also used for distributed intelligent control, a holonic manufacturing system (HMS) is, by definition, a manufacturing-specific approach to distributed intelligent control.

The concept was first introduced in 1989 by Suda [1] to address the shortcomings of extant industrial systems to address the pressures faced by manufacturers in the 1990s: i.e., increasingly stringent customer requirements for high-quality, customizable, low-cost products that can be delivered quickly, as well as the increasing levels of system complexity due to the distributed, concurrent, and stochastic nature of manufacturing systems.

During this time, research in distributed control led many to the realization that an "autonomous, distributed and co-operative" approach was required to address these issues. This new control software and hardware approach appeared to hold the most promise of realizing manufacturing systems that are both flexible (capable of reconfiguration) and responsive (capable of recovering from disturbances). However, past experiences with "green field" approaches like Flexible Manufacturing Systems (FMS) left a bad taste in the mouths of many manufacturers. Clearly, an incremental approach was required if new techniques of flexible automation were to be accepted by industry.

Central to this work on holonic manufacturing systems was concurrent work on the IEC 61499 standard for distributed intelligent control [2]. Although focused on the lower, real-time control level of the manufacturing control hierarchy, IEC 61499 appeared to show considerable promise for realizing holonic control (e.g., [3]).

Since early 2000, the IEC 61499 standard has gained more and more attention from academia and industry. However, it is still not clear if IEC 61499 has realized the goal

V. Mařík et al. (Eds.): HoloMAS 2019, LNAI 11710, pp. 3–12, 2019.
https://doi.org/10.1007/978-3-030-27878-6_1

of holonic manufacturing. In this paper we ask the question, after 20 years of research and development, has IEC 61499 realized its promised objectives and expected results? We begin by placing IEC 61499 in the context of its enabling technologies (Sect. 2), then focus on the efforts to implement the standard in industry (Sect. 3). We conclude this paper with a brief discussion of our perspectives on the IEC 61499 standard.

2 Realizing Intelligent Automation

In this section we focus on how IEC 61499 has been integrated with its enabling technologies to realize distributed intelligent industrial automation. Two perspectives are provided: design paradigms including object-oriented design, component-based design and service-oriented architecture, and computing paradigms including distributed intelligence, autonomic computing and cloud computing.

2.1 Design Paradigms

Object-oriented extensions (i.e., methods, inheritance, and interfaces) were first introduced to function blocks (FB) for automation programming in IEC 61131-3 [4], and made their way to IEC 61499. FBs encapsulate data structures and internal algorithms and can be instantiated working copies by type definitions. Polymorphism and inheritance are not often used in automation programming due to issues raised by computation cost and execution determinism, except that adapters provide kind of inheritance for similar FBs to share common interfaces.

Vyatkin et al. [5] proposed a conceptual object-oriented design (OOD) framework for modeling automation software based on IEC 61499 for potential benefits of intellectual property encapsulation and reuse. Dai and Vyatkin [6] proposed an object-oriented approach, including conversion of PLC code into an ECC and reuse of PLC code in an algorithm, to redesign distributed PLC control systems using IEC 61499 FBs. Two cases, modern building management systems [7] and airport baggage handling systems [8], were studied by using OOD to model IEC 61499 based system architectures.

The *component-based design paradigm* (CBD) uses coarse-grained and loose-coupled components with certain well-defined functionalities and pre-defined communication interfaces from a cohesive set of fine-grained objects. Compared with object-oriented modeling, component-based design models systems by functional components rather than physical objects, and multiple functions share a single algorithm with one generic event input instead of using dedicated events and algorithms for each method call [8]. Proposed frameworks in research for component-based design are mainly based on the Automation Component or Automaton Object (AC or AO) concept and then toward intelligent control [9–12].

Finally, the *service-oriented architecture (SOA) paradigm* approaches software system as a network of loose-coupled and discoverable services with formal defined interfaces communicating through messages [13]. Research projects of SOA in IEC 61499 based industrial automation systems were reviewed by Thramboulidis [14].

From a broad view, OOD, CBD and SOA can be considered as the same story. Designs are modeled through IEC 61499 FBs with mapping, creation, composition and execution of FBs as objects/components/services on different modeling levels. Some key points can be concluded as: (a) layered or multi-layer architecture is employed; (b) communication or interface design is focused; (c) reconfiguration, reuse, and flexibility is aimed.

2.2 Computing Paradigms

Distributed intelligence is a major step for distributed and intelligent automation, usually realized through *multi-agent systems* (MAS). With this computing paradigm, distributed and intelligent automation can be achieved through autonomous and cooperative agents that are capable of operating by themselves or collaborating with others to decide what actions to take, how and when to act in dynamic environments [15, 16]. More recently, MAS and SOA are increasingly considered as key enabling technologies to model IEC 61499 based industrial CPS with cloud and autonomous computing capabilities [17–19].

IEC 61499 based industrial automation systems are not only designed with fundamental features (e.g., distributed to be flexible, configurable, portable, and interoperable) but also envisioned for advanced ones (e.g., intelligent to incorporate self-managing capabilities) indicative of *autonomic computing* [20]. Intelligent behaviors require next generation industrial automation systems have flexible architectures (i.e., hardware and software) and adaptable strategies (i.e., rules and knowledge). The goal is to support real-time self-configuration (i.e., configure and reconfigure functions, structures, and processes), self-healing (i.e., detect and recover from disturbance and faults), self-optimization (i.e., improve and optimize what has been affected), and self-protection (i.e., identify and protect against safety and security attacks) for responsiveness to changes [15, 21]. More recently, the focus has been on formal mapping between IEC 61499 and service-oriented architectures (SOA) [22–24].

Cloud computing has also emerged as a new computing paradigm for industrial Cyber-physical Systems (CPS) [25]. As defined by the National Institute of Standards and Technology (NIST), cloud computing enables ubiquitous, convenient, on-demand network access to a shared pool of configurable computing resources that can be rapidly provisioned and released with minimal management effort or service provider interaction [26]. For modeling industrial CPS, integration of the cyber (i.e., cloud) and the physical (i.e., devices) are enabled by encapsulating services in design entities (e.g., IEC 61499 FBs). Recent work in this area includes that of Karnouskos et al. [27], Dai et al. [6], and Demin et al. [28].

In summary, the key idea of above research is to introduce SOA and MAS, cloud and autonomic computing in the design modeling of industrial CPS to support flexibility and interoperability, and to realize part of self-management capabilities.

3 Implementing IEC 61499 Based Systems

The implementation of IEC 61499 based industrial automation systems requires first the development of IEC 61499 compliant engineering environments and then the application of them in research examples and industrial cases. This section is focused on how IEC 61499 engineering environments have been implemented.

3.1 Development of IEC 61499 Compliant Engineering Environments

Since the publication of the IEC 61499 standard, academic activities and industrial practices on developing engineering environments to implement IEC 61499 FB models have been conducted. Table 1 lists some typical projects for the development of IEC 61499 compliant engineering environments.

Table 1. IEC 61499 compliant engineering environments.

Product	Type[a]	Grade[b]	Capability[c]	Status	Technology
Holobloc [29]					
FBDK	ST	ACA	PIC	A	Oracle Java SE Platform;
FBRT	RP				XML Document Type Definition
4DIAC [30]					
4DIAC-IDE	ST	ACA	PIC	A	Eclipse Framework;
4DIAC-RTE	RP				C++ Programming Language
4DIAC-LIB	EL				
nxtControl [31]					
nxtSTUDIO	ST	IND	PIC	A	Microsoft .NET Framework;
nxtIECRT	RP				XML Document Type Definitions;
nxtLIB	LB				ST Programming Language;
nxtHMI	RP				Hardware Independent Engineering
ICS Triplex/ISaGRAF [32]					
Workbench	ST	IND	C	A	Microsoft Visual Studio Shell;
Runtime	RP				Virtual Machine
ISaVIEW	RP				
Fuber [33]					
FUBER	RP	ACA	n/a	A	Java; BeanShell
O3neida [34]					
Workbench	ST	ACA	n/a	I	Java; NetBeans; Eclipse
FBench	ST	ACA	n/a	I	Originates in O^{3}neida Workbench
Software Engineering Group, University of Patras [35]					
CORFU	EB	ACA	C	I	UML
Archimedes	RP	ACA	C	I	Model Integrated Mechatronics

[a] ST: Software Tool; RP: Runtime Platform; LB: Library of software components; EB: Runtime Embedded Tool

[b] ACA: Academic; IND: Industrial

[c] P: Portability; I: Interoperability; C: Configurability

Engineering environments usually include the following three components [36], in which some implementations integrate one or more components into one environment (e.g., Corfu) while others are with more function components (e.g., nxtHMI): (i) an integrated development environment to model designs (i.e., software tools), (ii) a runtime environment to execute programs (i.e., runtime platforms), (iii) a library to store elements (i.e., libraries of software components). Furthermore, these implementations can be classified into three categories. However, in this section we consider all as IEC 61499 compliant for simplicity although the utmost goal is to develop IEC 61499 based ones. More specifically, we consider IEC 61499 based implementations (e.g., Holobloc FBDK/FBRT), IEC 61131-3 based but IEC 61499 supported implementations (e.g., ISaGRAF Workbench/Runtime), and IEC 61499 and/or IEC 61131 based (hybrid) implementations (e.g., nxtControl nxtSTUDIO/nxtIECRT).

As proposed in IEC 61499-4, three key features are expected in developing IEC 61499 based systems, devices and software tools [37]. In this section, multi-source is defined as the described objects (i.e., devices, libraries, software tools, runtime platforms) are provided by different suppliers and/or developed through different techniques: i.e., configurability of multi-source devices by multi-source software tools, portability of multi-source libraries between multi-source software tools, and interoperability of multi-source devices in multi-source runtime platforms.

As the first IEC 61499 feasibility demonstration, the Function Block Development Kit (FBDK) is developed and maintained to support fundamental features and incorporate new updates of IEC 61499 [29]. It is widely used in academic research, experiment design, technical training, and commercial product test. The currently released version FBDK 3.3 in August 2018 enables one to build and test IEC 61499 library elements including data types, function block types, resource types, device types, network segment types, adapter types, functions and system configurations [29]. One of the key characteristics is to support design patterns, including Layered MVC, Local Multicast, Proxy, Tagged Data, Matrix Framework, Time-Stamped Messaging. The new version also supports many enhanced features for generation of HTML documentation and experimental features of transient EC states and compact encoding of management commands and responses.

The ISaGRAF is the first commercial software environment for industrial implementation of both IEC 61131-3 and IEC 61499 (IEC 61131-3 based but IEC 61499 supported) to develop distributed automation and control systems. It includes the software tool built on Microsoft Visual Studio Shell (i.e., ISaGRAF Workbench) that provides plug-in functions such as editor, documentation, library management, and a runtime platform based on a Virtual Machine (i.e., ISaGRAF Runtime) that executes target independent code (TIC) generated by control applications [32].

A more comprehensive industrial solution package for efficient and intelligent automation of distributed control systems comes from nxtControl. It includes the software tool nxtSTUDIO to integrate all automation tasks, the library nxtLIB to offers pre-fabricated software objects (CATs, Composite Automation Types), the runtime platform nxtIECRT to support hybrid control paradigms (i.e., IEC 61131-3 and/or IEC 61149 based), and the user interface nxtHMI together with SCADA to enable multi-client/multi-server visualization [31].

The Eclipse 4DIAC provides open source solutions to the development of IEC 61499 based industrial automation and control solutions in research activities and industrial adoption. It includes the software tool 4DIAC-IDE based on the Eclipse framework, the runtime platform 4DIAC-RTE supporting online reconfiguration of applications and real-time execution of function block types, the library 4DIAC-LIB containing function blocks, adapters and sub-applications [30].

In summary, the above four projects are widely recognized in academia and industry. Portability of library elements between software tools, configurability of devices by software tools, and interoperability of devices in runtime platforms have been formally and/or informally tested [37]. Generally, solutions from Holobloc, Eclipse 4DIAC, and nxtControl meet these requirements in which nxtControl provides more configurability classes [37]. ISaGRAF provides only portability through its Workbench, interoperability by its Runtime, and configurability between its Workbench and Runtime [32].

There are also some other projects providing IEC 61499 compliant engineering environments. Fuber (FUnction Block Execution Runtime, last updated October 2017) is an interpreter developed in Java and BeanShell and runs IEC 61499 based applications [33]. O3neida Workbench and FBench are pioneered by Christensen for experimental use in the development and test of Automation Objects (AOs) for industrial automation and control [5, 34]. The CORFU framework developed by Thrambouldis consists of an IEC 61499 compliant Engineering Support System (ESS) based on UML modeling approach, a 4-layer architecture to facilitate the application of FB model, and a development process based on model transformation [35]. Thrambouldis also proposed Archimedes system platform based on Model Integrated Mechatronics (MIM) architecture to support the development of complex mechatronic manufacturing systems that enable runtime reconfiguration by using IEC 61499 FB model. Most of these projects have not been active in recent years, but are still valuable reference implementations for developing IEC 61499 based automation and control systems.

3.2 Applications of IEC 61499 Compliant Engineering Environments

Wide adoption of IEC 61499 by industry has been a challenge. However, there are still some early adopters to build automation and control systems through applying previous discussed engineering environments. Table 2 provides an overview of these applications from different software vendors. As discussed in previous sections, engineering environments from Holobloc and 4DIAC are mainly used in academic research for case studies. For example, the case of airport baggage handling systems is thoroughly studied by Dai and Vyatkin for their research on IEC 61499. Industrial-grade applications from nxtControl and ISaGRAF can be found from their official websites. The main application domain includes smart grids, smart factories, smart buildings, etc.

Table 2. Applications of the IEC 61499 standard.

IEC 61499 application	Software
Meat processing plant and fertilizer production plant [38, 39] Airport baggage handling systems [40] Smart grids [41, 42] Transportation line for shoe manufacturing [43]	Holobloc [29]
Smart grids [30] Pick & Place station [30]	4DIAC [30]
HVAC and lighting control [31] Fertilizer production plant [31]	nxtControl [31]
Food processing embedded control [44] Research centre data acquisition and control on a drying test bench [44] Control of hydraulic parameters of district heating region in Sofia [45] High-speed train monitoring and control [46] Railway safety functions in mining transport system [47] I-8000 waste water treatment system [47] Smart grids [48]	ISaGRAF [32]

4 Summary and Perspectives

The IEC 61499 standard has advanced considerably since its introduction: i.e., from the early work on the reference architecture, to more recent work on function block execution and semantics. As noted previously, in recent years we have seen increasing interest in academic and industrial applications. However, compared with widely used IEC 61131-3 standard in industrial practices, IEC 61499 is mainly promoted in academia and seldom accepted by industry. If the adoption of this new technology is viewed in the context of the well-known three-phase S-shaped "logistic curve" [49], IEC 61499 was in the first phase of *Launch* promoted by innovators in 2012 for the second edition and is now in the transition to the second phase of *Takeoff* with some early adopters [50]. Arguably, there is still be a long way to go to reach the third phase of *Maturity* unless some key issues are not be reasonably solved.

Three main types of challenges for industrial adoption of IEC 61499 are prevalent: industrial concerns on business development, technical issues related to standard itself, and societal aspects of trained personnel. A summary of these challenges is provided in Table 3.

Considering these critical factors, much effort has been put into realizing successful industrial adoption of IEC 61499. Some reasonable solutions have been suggested such as providing feasible methods, techniques, and guidelines for designing new IEC 61499 based systems, applications and components; redesigning existing IEC 61131-3 based systems so they are compliant with IEC 61499; and providing qualified courses and hands-on training to learn and use IEC 61499. Efforts in the design of new IEC 61499 based systems must continue to focus on execution models and semantics (e.g., [9, 13]) as well as more recent work on autonomic and cloud computing discussed in Sect. 2. Although the work on redesigning existing IEC 61131-3 based systems has led to opportunities for industrial implementations of IEC 61499, this approach is still an intermediate step of full transition from existing IEC 61131-3 based systems to IEC 61499 based ones.

Table 3. Main challenges for industrial adoption of IEC 61499.

Main challenge	Detailed explanation
Industrial concerns	Large amount of existing IEC 61131-3 based systems Little demand for a completely new design approach Huge cost incurred by introducing new technologies Much effort required without significant performance improvement
Technical issues	Lack of system development and implementation guidelines and tools Few proved methods for migration from IEC 61131-3 to IEC 61499 Same execution semantics may result in different system behaviors Long way to realize its promised objectives and expected results
Societal aspects	New qualification requirements for control engineers New course design for teaching and learning IEC 61499 New industrial training for applying and using IEC 61499 Unwilling to be the first to use unmatured new technologies

Acknowledgments. The authors wish to thank the Natural Sciences and Engineering Research Council of Canada, Spartan Controls, and the Suncor Energy Foundation for their generous support of this research through grant CDE 486462-15.

References

1. Suda, H.: Future factory automation system formulated in Japan. Techno Japan **22**, 15–25 (1989)
2. Christensen, J.: HMS: initial architecture and standards directions. In: Proceedings of the 1st European Conference on Holonic Manufacturing Systems, Hannover, pp. 1–20 (1994)
3. Fletcher, M., Garcia-Herreros, E., Christensen, J., Deen, S., and Mittmann, R.: An open architecture for holonic cooperation and autonomy. In: Proceedings of the 11th International Workshop on Database and Expert Systems Applications, pp. 224–230 (2000)
4. Werner, B.: Object-oriented extensions for IEC 61131-3. IEEE Ind. Electron. Mag. **3**(4), 36–39 (2009)
5. Vyatkin, V., Christensen, J.H., Lastra, J.L.M.: OOONEIDA: an open, object-oriented knowledge economy for intelligent industrial automation. IEEE Trans. Industr. Inf. **1**(1), 4–17 (2005)
6. Dai, W., Vyatkin, V.: Redesign distributed PLC control systems using IEC 61499 function blocks. IEEE Trans. Autom. Sci. Eng. **9**(2), 390–401 (2012)
7. Vyatkin, V.: Software engineering in industrial automation: state-of-the-art review. IEEE Trans. Industr. Inf. **9**(3), 1234–1249 (2013)
8. Dai, W., Vyatkin, V., Christensen, J.H.: Applying IEC 61499 design paradigms: object-oriented programming component-based design and service-oriented architecture. In: Zoitl, A., Strasser, T. (eds.) Distributed Control Applications: Guidelines, Design Patterns, and Application Examples with the IEC 61499. CRC Press, Boca Raton (2017)

9. Vyatkin, V.: Intelligent mechatronic components: control system engineering using an open distributed architecture. In: Proceedings of 8th IEEE Conference on Emerging Technologies and Factory Automation, Lisbon, pp. 277–284 (2003)
10. Cengic, G., Ljungkrantz, O., Akesson, K.: A framework for component based distributed control software development using IEC 61499. In: Proceedings of 11th IEEE Conference on Emerging Technologies and Factory Automation, Prague, pp. 782–789 (2006)
11. Lepuschitz, W., Zoitl, A.: An engineering method for batch process automation using a component-oriented design based on IEC 61499. In: Proceedings of 13th IEEE International Conference Emerging Technologies and Factory Automation, Hamburg, pp. 207–214 (2008)
12. Zoitl, A., Prähofer, H.: Guidelines and patterns for building hierarchical automation solutions in the IEC 61499 modeling language. IEEE Trans. Industr. Inf. **9**(4), 2387–2396 (2013)
13. Jammes, F., Smit, H.: Service-oriented paradigms in industrial automation. IEEE Trans. Industr. Inf. **1**(1), 62–70 (2005)
14. Thramboulidis, K.: Service-oriented architecture in industrial automation systems - the case of IEC 61499: a review, arXiv preprint (2015)
15. Marik, V., McFarlane, D.: Industrial adoption of agent-based technologies. IEEE Intell. Syst. **20**(1), 27–35 (2005)
16. Brennan, R.W.: Toward real-time distributed intelligent control: a survey of research themes and applications. IEEE Trans. Syst. Man Cybern. - Part C: Appl. Rev. **37**(5), 744–765 (2007)
17. Leitão, P., Colombo, A.W., Karnouskos, S.: Industrial automation based on cyber-physical systems technologies: prototype implementations and challenges. Comput. Ind. **81**, 11–25 (2016)
18. Dai, W., Dubinin, V.N., Christensen, J.H., Vyatkin, V., Guan, X.: Toward self-manageable and adaptive industrial cyber-physical systems with knowledge-driven autonomic service management. IEEE Trans. Industr. Inf. **13**(2), 725–736 (2017)
19. Dai, W., Riliskis, L., Wang, P., Vyatkin, V., Guan, X.: A cloud-based decision support system for self-healing in distributed automation systems using fault tree analysis. IEEE Trans. Industr. Inf. **14**(3), 989–1000 (2018)
20. IBM: An architectural blueprint for autonomic computing. IBM White Paper (2006)
21. Mubarak, H., Göhner, P.: An agent-oriented approach for self-management of industrial automation systems. In: Proceedings of 8th IEEE International Conference on Industrial Informatics, pp. 721–726 (2010)
22. Lepuschitz, W., Zoitl, A., Vallée, M., Merdan, M.: Toward self-reconfiguration of manufacturing systems using automation agents. IEEE Trans. Syst. Man Cybern. Part C Appl. Rev. **41**(1), 52–69 (2011)
23. Strasser, T., Froschauer, R.: Autonomous application recovery in distributed intelligent automation and control systems. IEEE Trans. Syst. Man Cybern. Part C Appl. Rev. **42**(6), 1054–1070 (2012)
24. Kaindl, H., Vallée, M., Arnautovic, E.: Self-representation for self-configuration and monitoring in agent-based flexible automation systems. IEEE Trans. Syst. Man Cybern.: Syst. **43**(1), 164–175 (2013)
25. Givehchi, O., Trsek, H., Jasperneite, J.: Cloud computing for industrial automation systems - a comprehensive overview. In: Proceedings of 18th IEEE Conference on Emerging Technologies and Factory Automation, Cagliari, pp. 1–4 (2013)
26. Mell, P., Grance, T.: The NIST definition of cloud computing. National Institute of Standards and Technology, Gaithersburg, Maryland (2011)

27. Karnouskos, S., et al.: A SOA-based architecture for empowering future collaborative cloud-based industrial automation. In: Proceedings of 38th Annual Conference of the IEEE Industrial Electronics Society, Montreal, pp. 5766–5772 (2012)
28. Demin, E., Patil, S., Dubinin, V., Vyatkin, V.: IEC 61499 distributed control enhanced with cloud-based web-services. In: Proceedings of 10th IEEE Conference on Industrial Electronics and Applications, Auckland, pp. 972–977 (2015)
29. Holobloc, April 2019. https://www.holobloc.com/
30. Eclipse 4DIAC, April 2019. https://www.eclipse.org/4diac/
31. nxtControl, April 2019. https://www.nxtcontrol.com/en/references/
32. ICS Triplex ISaGRAF, April 2019. http://www.isagraf.com/index.htm
33. Fuber, April 2019. https://sourceforge.net/projects/fuber/
34. O3neida FBench, April 2019. https://www.controleng.com/articles/new-iec-61499-function-block-programming-safety-energy-systems-resources-from-isa-o3neida/
35. SEG Corfu, April 2019. http://seg.ece.upatras.gr/Corfu/dev/index.htm
36. Vyatkin, V.: IEC 61499 as enabler of distributed and intelligent automation: state-of-the-art review. IEEE Trans. Industr. Inf. **7**(4), 768–781 (2011)
37. Christensen, J.H., Strasser, T., Valentini, A., Vyatkin, V., Zoitl, A.: The IEC 61499 function block standard: software tools and runtime platforms. ISA Automation Week, Orlando (2012)
38. Tait, P.: A path to industrial adoption of distributed control technology. In: Proceedings of 3rd IEEE International Conference on Industrial Informatics, Perth, pp. 86–91 (2005)
39. Zoitl, A., Strasser, T., Hall, K., Staron, R., Sünder, C., Favre-Bulle, B.: The past, present, and future of IEC 61499. In: Mařík, V., Vyatkin, V., Colombo, A.W. (eds.) HoloMAS 2007. LNCS (LNAI), vol. 4659, pp. 1–14. Springer, Heidelberg (2007). https://doi.org/10.1007/978-3-540-74481-8_1
40. Black, G., Vyatkin, V.: Intelligent component-based automation of baggage handling systems with IEC 61499. IEEE Trans. Autom. Sci. Eng. **7**(2), 337–351 (2010)
41. Vyatkin, V., Zhabelova, G., Higgins, N., Schwarz, K., Nair, N.: Towards intelligent smart grid devices with IEC 61850 interoperability and IEC 61499 open control architecture. In: Proceedings of IEEE PES Transmission and Distribution Conference and Exposition, New Orleans, pp. 1–8 (2010)
42. Zhabelova, G., Vyatkin, V.: Multiagent smart grid automation architecture based on IEC 61850/61499 intelligent logical nodes. IEEE Trans. Industr. Electron. **59**(5), 2351–2362 (2012)
43. Colla, M., Brusaferri, A., Carpanzano, E.: Applying the IEC-61499 model to the shoe manufacturing sector. In: Proceedings of 11th IEEE Conference on Emerging Technologies and Factory Automation, Prague, pp. 1301–1308 (2006)
44. Centris Technologies, April 2019. https://www.centristech.com/en/
45. KIBERNETIKA, April 2019. http://www.kibernetika-bg.com/
46. EKE Electronics, April 2019. https://www.eke-electronics.com/
47. ICP DAS USA, April 2019. https://www.icpdas-usa.com/, (April 2019)
48. Brusaferri, A., Ballarino, A., Carpanzano, E.: Reconfigurable knowledge-based control solutions for responsive manufacturing systems. Stud. Inform. Control **20**(1), 31–42 (2011)
49. Shapiro, C., Varian, H.R.: Information Rules: a Strategic Guide to the Network Economy. Harvard Business Press, Boston (1999)
50. Strasser, T., et al.: The IEC 61499 function block standard: launch and takeoff. ISA Automation Week, Orlando (2012)

Engineering and Validating Cyber-Physical Energy Systems: Needs, Status Quo, and Research Trends

Thomas I. Strasser[1,2(✉)] and Filip Pröstl Andrén[1]

[1] Center for Energy, AIT Austrian Institute of Technology, Vienna, Austria
thomas.i.strasser@ieee.org

[2] Institute of Mechanics and Mechatronics, Vienna University of Technology, Vienna, Austria

Abstract. A driving force for the realization of a sustainable energy supply is the integration of renewable energy resources. Due to their stochastic generation behaviour, energy utilities are confronted with a more complex operation of the underlying power grids. Additionally, due to technology developments, controllable loads, integration with other energy sources, changing regulatory rules, and the market liberalization, the system's operation needs adaptation. Proper operational concepts and intelligent automation provide the basis to turn the existing power system into an intelligent entity, a cyber-physical energy system. The electric energy system is therefore moving from a single system to a system of systems. While reaping the benefits with new intelligent behaviors, it is expected that system-level developments, architectural concepts, advanced automation and control as well as the validation and testing will play a significantly larger role in realizing future solutions and technologies. The implementation and deployment of these complex systems of systems are associated with increasing engineering complexity resulting also in increased engineering costs. Proper engineering and validation approaches, concepts, and tools are partly missing until now. Therefore, this paper discusses and summarizes the main needs and requirements as well as the status quo in research and development related to the engineering and validation of cyber-physical energy systems. Also research trends and necessary future activities are outlined.

Keywords: Cyber-physical energy systems · Engineering · Research infrastructure · Smart grids · Systems of systems · Testing · Validation

1 Introduction

Renewables are key enablers in the plight to reduce greenhouse gas emissions and cope with anthropogenic global warming [16]. The intermittent nature and limited storage capabilities of renewables culminate in new challenges that power

V. Mařík et al. (Eds.): HoloMAS 2019, LNAI 11710, pp. 13–26, 2019.
https://doi.org/10.1007/978-3-030-27878-6_2

system operators have to deal with in order to regulate power quality and ensure security of supply [7]. At the same time, the increased availability of advanced automation and communication technologies provides new opportunities for the derivation of intelligent solutions to tackle the challenges [11,24]. Previous work has shown various new methods of operating highly interconnected power grids, and their corresponding components, in a more effective way. As a consequence of these developments, the traditional power system is being transformed into a Cyber-Physical Energy System (CPES) [31]. The electric energy system is therefore moving from a single system to a system of systems.

While reaping the benefits that come along with those intelligent behaviours, it is expected that system-level developments, architectural concepts, advanced automation and control, innovative Information and Communication Technology (ICT) as well as the validation and testing will play a significantly larger role in realizing future solutions and technologies [11,24]. The implementation, validation, and deployment of these complex systems of systems are associated with increasing engineering complexity resulting also in increased total life-cycle costs. Proper engineering and validation approaches, concepts, and tools are partly missing until now [26].

The aim of this paper is to discuss and summaries the main needs and requirements as well as the status quo in research and development related to the engineering and validation of CPES. Also research trends and necessary future activities are outlined.

The remaining parts of the paper are organized as follows: Sect. 2 provides a brief overview of the desired engineering and validation process of CPES-based applications whereas in Sect. 3 the main problems and needs are identified. Afterwards, the status quo in research and development is analysed in Sect. 4 followed by a discussion of future research trends in Sect. 5. Finally, the main conclusions are provided in Sect. 6.

2 Desired CPES Engineering and Validation Process

As already mentioned above, the development of new application for CPES is associated with increasing engineering complexity. One main issue with this is that traditional engineering methods for power system automation were not intended to be used for applications of this scale and complexity. By combining the outcome of several publications in the last few years, a desired engineering and validation process can be proposed containing four main phases: *(i)* specification and use case design, *(ii)* automated engineering, *(iii)* validation, and *(iv)* deployment [3,4,8,13,21]. The proposed process is based on a model-driven approach and is illustrated in Fig. 1 with the main focus on providing the user with automated support throughout the whole process.

The process starts with a specification and use case design. Based on use case description methods such as the Smart Grid Architecture Model (SGAM) and IEC 62559 (also known as the IntelliGrid approach), a structured description and visualization of use cases can be defined. However, to fully take advantage

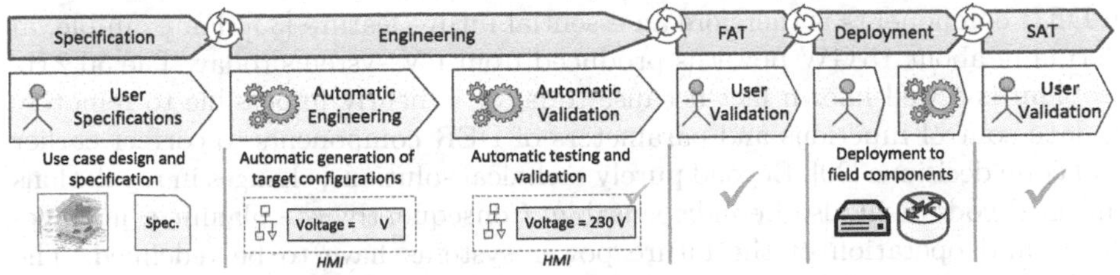

Fig. 1. Overview of a desired engineering and validation process of CPES [22].

of the high amount of information in the modelled use cases these description methods must be transformed into machine-readable and formal formats [2]. Formal specifications together with the high-level use case description act as the main input and thus form the basis for the following automated steps of the development process [22].

The following automated steps in the process are based on the formal specifications and use case descriptions. First of all, it is possible to generate different types of configurations. This can be executable code for field devices, configurations for ICT equipment or generated setups for Supervisory Control And Data Acquisition (SCADA). Model-based or ontology based approaches from software engineering are examples of methods that can provide this kind of automation [22,32]. Optimally it should also be possible to automatically validate the resulting generated output configurations. Automated testing for software development has already existed since several years. However, similar approaches for CPES are currently missing. When testing CPES, multiple system aspects need to be validated, such as ICT, automation/control, and security and privacy topics apart from the power system itself [3,25]. For system tests the advantage of automated testing would be even greater than for single components.

Once validation has been successfully accomplished the last phase is deployment of the software and configurations to field devices. When the power system relies on more and more software systems for a secure and safe operation, the deployment and update process of this software gets more complicated. If updates are not applied in the correct order, or if an update is unsuccessful, this can cause the power system to operate incorrectly or even damage it or people working with it. To support the user with this stage, the development process should be able to analyze the power system state and create rollout schedules that minimizes the risk of disruptive events and errors [5,13,27].

3 Main Problems and Needs

A characteristic feature of renewable sources and customer side solutions is that they are mostly available in a decentralized way as DER [16]. From today's point of view it is nearly impossible to address all future needs and requirements in CPES and DER components. The flexible addition of new control functionalities in DER components is therefore an essential future feature [33]. For example, in Germany about 15 GW power is produced from PV systems today. The 50.2 Hz problem is a well-known fact because today it is nearly impossible to remotely update control functions and parameters of DER components to correct earlier grid code decisions [30]. Beyond purely technical solutions, changes in regulations and grid codes will also be indispensable. Consequently, the planning, management, and operation of the future power systems have to be redefined. The implementation and deployment of these complex systems of systems are associated with increasing engineering complexity resulting in increasing engineering costs.

The usage of proper methods, automation architectures, and corresponding tools offers a huge optimization potential for the overall engineering process. The starting point is detailed use case and requirements engineering. This has led to a number of recent smart grid projects where use case descriptions of corresponding applications are in the focus [9,23]. Some promising approaches have already been developed like the IntelliGrid method [12] or SGAM [10,28,29] but they are mainly lacking of a formalized and computer-readable representation for engineering and validation automation. The same is true for other input specifications that are typically provided as an input to the engineering process. Also, there is no standardized way of representing the objects, e.g., controllers and power grid components, neither in the way they are depicted, nor in the semantics used in the description.

A significant amount of work has to be spent a repeated number of time *(i)* in the specification, *(ii)* the implementation, *(iii)* the validation and testing but also *(iv)* in the deployment phase. This is a very time-consuming and error-prone approach to design and test CPES applications. To conclude, the following main problems related to the engineering of CPES exist today [15,25,26]:

- *Rigorous engineering:* Rigorous model-based engineering concepts for CPES applications are missing or only partly available.
- *Rapidness and effort:* CPES solutions are becoming more and more complex, which results in increasing engineering efforts and costs. Therefore, it is important to improve the rapidness of traditional engineering methods.
- *Correctness:* Due to the multidisciplinary character of CPES applications this also requires the engineer to have an expert knowledge in each discipline. This is often not the case, which increases the risk of human errors.
- *Handling legacy systems:* Power grid operators expect a long service life of all components in their systems. Available proprietary automation solutions in smart grid systems prevent efficient reuse of control software.
- *Geographical dispersion:* The distribution of components over large geographical areas requires special attention. New ICT approaches and wide-area communication are needed.
- *Interoperability:* Interoperability is a critical issue in CPES applications. This must be assured on all levels, from specifications over implementation, to deployment and finally during operation. Also components from different manufacturers must be handled, which requires a manufacturer independent method.

- *Real-time constraints:* Some applications may enforce real-time constraints on hardware, software and networking. Performance management is often not adequately addressed in existing engineering processes.
- *Scalability:* Current engineering methods are focusing on the development for a single system. With the introduction of new intelligent grid components and DER these methods must be able to handle not only a single system, but a system of systems.
- *Reference scenarios:* Common and well understood reference scenarios, use cases, and test case profiles for CPES need to be provided to power and energy systems engineers and researchers; also, proper validation benchmark criteria and key performance indicators as well as interoperability measures for validating CPES solutions need to be developed, extended, and shared with engineers and researchers.
- *Deployment support:* An easy, secure, and trustable deployment of CPES applications to a large amount of corresponding components and devices is necessary.
- *Standardization:* A harmonization and standardization of multi-domain CPES-based engineering and validation approaches as well as corresponding and testing procedures is required.

If the information gathered during the use case description phase can also be used directly in an automated method, the development effort can substantially be decreased. By collecting the use case information in a formal model this can be used for direct automatic code generation. The result can be executable code for field devices, communication configurations as well as HMI configurations. Moreover, an automated approach also has the potential to de-crease implementation errors and at the same time increase the software quality [18].

The availability of both a formal specification of CPES use cases and the possibility to automatically generate target configurations also enables the use of automated testing. For CPES this can be pure software tests but can also be a combination of software, hardware and simulations. When automatic validation errors can be detected at an early stage, this will increase the overall quality and mitigate the development risk. The quality of CPES applications is also very much dependent on the experience and knowledge of the responsible engineer(s). Furthermore, the electric energy system is becoming a multi-domain system. This requires knowledge not only about the power system but also about ICT, control, and automation issues. In order to benefit from the knowledge of experienced engineers, machine learning can be used to reason about user design experience.

In the following sections the status quo in research and development is analysed and an outlook about potential future research directions are provided.

4 Status Quo in Research and Development

Promising approaches and research results categorized according to the above outlined process (i.e, see Fig. 1) related to the engineering and validation of CPES applications and solutions are briefly summarized and discussed below.

4.1 Specification Phase

An approach for specifying and modelling CPES was introduced first with IntelliGrid [12] and later refined by SGAM [17]. In principle, SGAM provides a set of concepts, viewpoints, and a mapping method and thus a structured approach for smart grid architecture development. It allows depicting various aspects of smart grid artefacts (information, communication, etc.) and supports identification and coordination of elements on different levels. It also facilitates the identification of interoperability issues [10,28,29]. The basis for SGAM is a three-dimensional frame consisting of domains, zones and layers. The use of the SGAM modelling approach combined with the IntelliGrid use case template provides a powerful methodology for smart grid use case and application development. The design steps as outlined in Fig. 2 define the structured approach [17]:

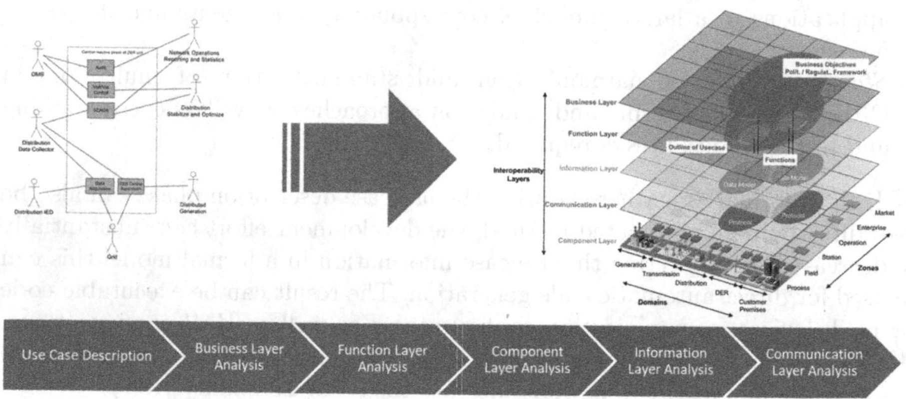

Fig. 2. SGAM-based design process for smart grid use cases and applications [17].

4.2 Engineering Phase

Model-Based Engineering: In order to provide tool support for the methodology illustrated in Fig. 2, Dänekas et al. developed the "SGAM Toolbox", which is an extension to the Enterprise Architect (EA) software [6]. This has the advantage that standard UML modelling tools, such as sequence or activity diagrams can be used by the engineering since these are standard parts of the EA tool. With the SGAM Toolbox, support is provided to cover modeling of all steps in the SGAM use case methodology. Additionally, due to the already included code generation capabilities of EA, it is also possible to generate certain code components based on the models made by the SGAM Toolbox. One drawback, is that the code generation is intended for general-purpose applications and thus no extended generation support for other configurations (e.g., communication or HMI configurations) is provided [21].

Another work, also based on the SGAM Toolbox, by Knirsch et al. implements a model-driven assessment of privacy issues [14]. To do this, the analysis is based on modeled data flows between actors and secondly, an assessment can be made during design time to study what impact it has on the modeled use case. A related approach was also developed by Neureiter et al. [19], where they use the SGAM models together with the "Guidelines for Smart Grid Cybersecurity" from the National Institute of Standards and Technology (NIST) [1]. By including cybersecurity issues directly into the modeling of smart grid use cases they show how this be used to study potential security implications, which can serve as a basis for further implementations.

Another holistic approach for rapid development of intelligent power utility automation applications was presented by Andrén et al. [2,21]. In [2], the outline of a Model-Driven Engineering (MDE) approach for automated engineering of smart grid applications was presented. This was later complemented with a Domain-Specific Language (DSL) for SGAM compliant use case design [21]. Compared to the SGAM Toolbox this work also focuses on code generation as well as generation of communication configurations. The result of these two publications is a model-based rapid engineering approach for smart grid automation applications.

Ontology-Based Engineering: Ontologies are a way to abstract domain specific information, usually with the aim to represent objects, types, and their semantic relations in a formal machine-readable way. Additionally, a set of inference rules and restrictions on relations can be defined to support semantic interpretation. An approach based on ontologies was used by Zanabria to model multi-functional Energy Storage System (ESS) applications and to handle inconsistencies derived from the overlapping of corresponding applications [32]. Focus was put on handling Energy Management System (EMS) application and for this, the EMS Ontology (EMSOnto) was created [32]. An overview of the main EMSOnto concepts are shown in Fig. 3.

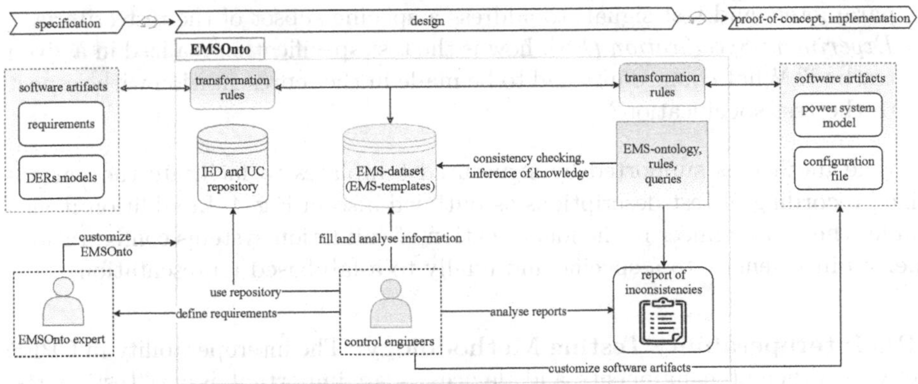

Fig. 3. Overview of the EMSOnto engineering process [32].

The core ontology defines the structure of a database (EMS-database) used to gather relevant information for the design of the EMS functions. This information can be available at the specification stage or it can be provided manually by control engineers. The whole database is checked and validated against terminological axioms contained in the EMS-ontology. A reasoner engine uses the validated database to execute complex axioms and logical rules in order to deduce new information. This reasoning is used on the information in the database in order to identify inconsistencies and also generate handling proposals of any identified conflicts. This information is included within reports that are presented to the user, who analyses the reports and can decide on improvements and modifications within the EMS design. The referred process is recursively executed in order to achieve an error-free design [32].

4.3 Validation and Testing Phase

ERIGrid Holistic Validation Procedure: The specification and execution of tests or experiments is central to any assessment approach. The holistic testing procedure proposed in ERIGrid [25] aims to unify the approach to testing across different research infrastructures, different testbed types and to facilitate multi-domain testing. A central element of the ERIGrid approach is the Holistic Test Description (HTD) method [3]; it defines a number of specification elements for any test, to be identified independently of the particular assessment methodology. The specification elements comprise three main levels of specification as outlined in Fig. 4:

- *Test Case (TC):* a concise formulation of the overall test objectives and purpose of investigation, specifying the object under investigation, separating system structure from functions (system under test vs. functions) and identifying test criteria.
- *Test Specification (TS):* a detailed description of the test system, control parameters and test signals to address a specific subset of the test criteria.
- *Experiment Specification (ES):* how is the test specification realized in a given testbed? What compromise had to be made in the representation with respect to the test specification?

The method is supported by structured templates to facilitate the harmonized recording of test descriptions as outlined also in Fig. 4. In addition it also guides the test engineer in the identification of validation systems configurations (i.e., from a generic to a specific and finally to a lab-based representation).

JRC Interoperability Testing Methodology: The interoperability in CPES between different components and devices is an important issue. Testing the interoperability in this domain requires producing detailed test cases describing how the different players, services, and components are intended to interact with each other. A systematic approach for developing CPES-based interoperability

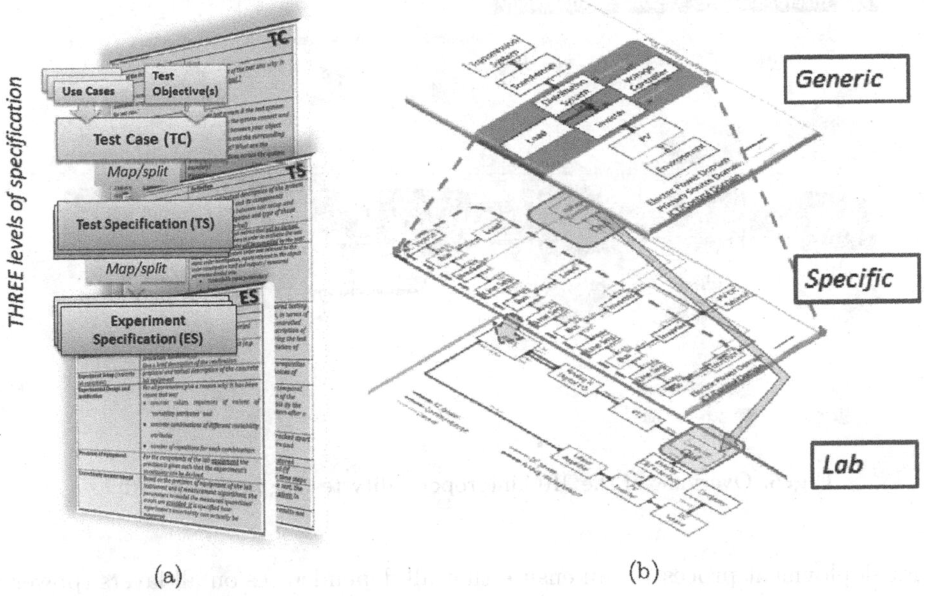

Fig. 4. Overview of the ERIGrid holistic test description: (a) holistic testing methodology and corresponding templates, (b) validation system configurations on different levels (adapted from [3]).

tests has the potential to facilitate the development of new solutions and applications. Therefore, the Joint Research Center (JRC) of the European Commission (EC) has developed a corresponding methodology.

It helps the CPES engineer in a structured way to create interoperability testing Use Cases, Basic Application Profiles (BAP) and Basic Application Interoperability Profiles (BAIOP) and it is used mainly as a common framework for interoperability testing. Five main steps have been identified which are *(i)* Use Case creation, *(ii)* Basic Application Profile (BAP) creation, *(iii)* Basic Application Interoperability profile (BAIOP) creation, *(iv)* Design of Experiments (DoE) as well as the *(v)* Testing and Analysis of Experiments (AE). Figure 5 provides a brief overview of the overall approach.

Each stage allows the engineer to select certain features then used in the subsequent stage. During the completion of all stages, the developer can select relevant standards, their options, test beds with all qualified and test equipment as well their attributes or functions used during the testing.

4.4 Deployment Phase

Especially for future CPES, where a large number of functions and services interact with each other within a complex dynamic system, processes for deployment and software update become more important and more complex. It is important

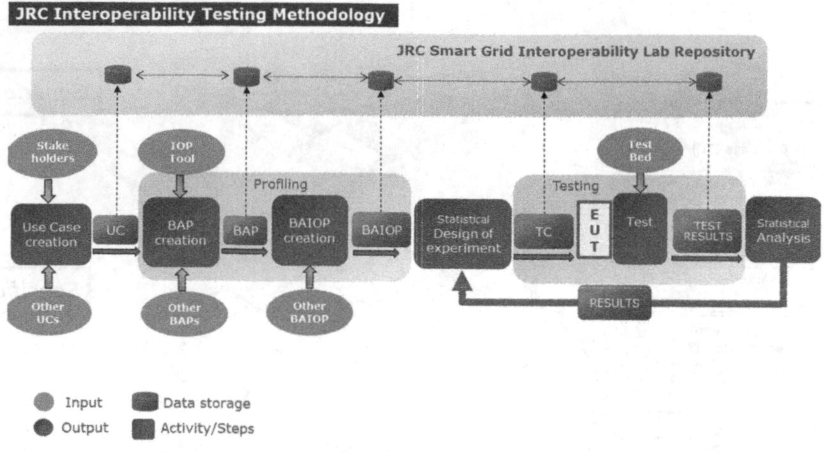

Fig. 5. Overview of the JRC interoperability testing approach [20].

that deployment processes can ensure that all dependencies on all layers (power system, communication, information) are fulfilled. Furthermore, these processes also must be resilient against faults and attacks (internal and external). The LarGo! project aims at enabling mass roll-out of smart grid applications for grid and energy management by defining a seamless, safe and secure application deployment process for the grid and customer domain [13].

In the LarGo! project two main approaches are followed. First, a new and inter-domain software deployment process is designed to monitor multiple conditions (e.g., timing, power system state, business and customer issues, weather conditions) to ensure that the deployment of software results in the desired overall system behavior. To enable the operator to create an optimal rollout schedule, a tool helps the operator with a guided and assisted process. This is combined with a knowledge-based systems to provide and resolve necessary conditions and requirements [13]. The second part of LarGo! complements the deployment process with secure and resilient system design. This includes developments of resilient control applications that can handle disruptive events, such as faults and attacks, and also cyberssecurity concepts with the goal to detect root-causes of errors after a software update (i.e., was the error caused by an attack during the deployment process) [5,27].

5 Discussion of Future Research Needs

In fact, current research show that already many aspects needed for a better engineering and validation of CPES are available. Nevertheless, many issues are still open and since the advancement of CPES technologies is still ongoing, new needs are constantly appearing. In Sect. 3 several problems and needs were pointed out. Some of these can already—at least partly—be solved by using the approaches presented in this paper. The following list is an attempt to summarize the above presented approaches, show how the identified problems and needs can be solved, and to point out possible research directions that still needs to be explored:

- *Harmonization of existing approaches*: As already shown in this paper, there are already quite many approaches that attempt to improve the engineering and validation of CPES. However, it is also clear that these approaches all have their own focus and cannot cover the whole development process, as it is depicted in Fig. 1. Therefore, one important midterm goal for future research will be to harmonize already existing approaches. This will directly provide better support for *rigorous engineering*, *rapidness and effort*, *correctness*, and *deployment support* of CPES applications since many approaches already focus on these. Furthermore, through a harmonization a better *interoperability* can be reached. A logical continuation, and a more longterm goal, will be to integrate the harmonized approaches within international *standardization* organizations.
- *Large-scale examples and scenarios*: Many of today's approaches from research are still to be proven on large-scale real world examples. More research is needed were the different methods are applied to larger use cases. This is important to solve any remaining issues regarding *scalability*. Associtated is also the development of *reference scenarios* that can help to test and benchmark future engineering and validation approaches as they emerge.
- *Integration with traditional engineering approaches*: Components and systems for the power system domain are known for their long lifespan. Due to this, it will also be necessary for any new and future development process to integrate with already existing traditional engineering approaches. This is one the one hand necessary in order to increase the acceptance of the new development approaches On the other hand it will also be needed to *handle legacy systems* and to ensure *interoperability* with older components.
- *Introducing new abstractions and modeling options*: Following the continuous development of CPES, the associated engineering and validation methods need to evolve as well. In order to handle increasingly complex systems development, new abstractions and modeling options will be needed to support engineers. *Real-time constrains*, timing [15], *geographical dispersion*, and *scalability* are examples of abstractions that are currently not supported by any of the discussed approaches. The more complex the CPES gets, the more computer-aided support—for example through machine-learning—will be needed in order to handle these issues.

Summarizing, engineering and validation support will be critical for successful development of future CPES applications. Without the proper tool support many of the tasks will require immense manual efforts and will require engineers educated in multiple domains (e.g., energy system physics, ICT, automation and control, cybersecurity). The tools available today and currently in development all provide small steps in the right direction, but more research efforts are still needed in the years to come.

6 Conclusions

The current electric energy system is moving towards CPES. Integration of more and more renewable energy sources require a change of tactics for the planning and operation today's power systems. New technologies, such as ICT, automation, and control systems are needed together with changing regulatory rules and a market liberalization. The implementation and deployment of these complex systems of systems are associated with increasing engineering complexity resulting also in increased engineering costs. Proper engineering and validation approaches, concepts, and tools are partly missing until now.

In this paper the most major needs for future CPES engineering and validation approaches have been discussed. Furthermore, the current state of research in this are today have been presented. The development of CPES applications has been divided into four main phases: specification, engineering, validation, and deployment. For each phase corresponding approaches have been presented, highlighting advantages and disadvantages. This is followed by a discussion on future research needs.

As a conclusion, engineering and validation support will be critical for successful development of future CPES applications. Some needs are already covered by today's approaches, but even more can be covered by harmonization of those that already exist. Current approaches will also need to introduce new abstractions and modeling possibilities once future CPES applications increase in complexity. Examples are real-time constraints and timing, which are not yet properly covered. In summary, more support can still be provided.

Acknowledgments. This work is partly funded by the Austrian Ministry for Transport, Innovation and Technology (bmvit) and the Austrian Research Promotion Agency (FFG) under the ICT of the Future Program in the MESSE project (FFG No. 861265), by the European Community's Horizon 2020 Program (H2020/2014-2020) in the ERIGrid project (Grant Agreement No. 654113), and by the framework of the joint programming initiative ERA-Net Smart Energy Systems' focus initiative Smart Grids Plus, with support from the European Union's Horizon 2020 research and innovation programme under grant agreement No. 646039 in the LarGo! project (national funding by the Austrian Climate and Energy Fund FFG no. 857570).

References

1. NISTIR 7628 Revision 1: Guidelines for Smart Grid Cyber Security (2014)
2. Pröstl Andrén, F., Strasser, T., Rohjans, S., Uslar, M.: Analyzing the need for a common modeling language for smart grid applications. In: Proceedings of the 2013 11th IEEE International Conference on Industrial Informatics (INDIN), pp. 440–446. IEEE (2013)
3. Blank, M., Lehnhoff, S., Heussen, K., Bondy, D.M., Moyo, C., Strasser, T.: Towards a foundation for holistic power system validation and testing. In: 2016 IEEE 21st International Conference on Emerging Technologies and Factory Automation (ETFA), pp. 1–4 (2016)
4. Brunner, H.: DG DemoNet - Smart LV Grid (2015)

5. Chong, M.S., Sandberg, H.: Secure patching of an output-feedback controller for a class of nonlinear systems under adversarial attack. In: 2018 IEEE Conference on Decision and Control (CDC), pp. 7255–7260, December 2018
6. Dänekas, C., Neureiter, C., Rohjans, S., Uslar, M., Engel, D.: Towards a model-driven-architecture process for smart grid projects. In: Benghozi, P.J., Krob, D., Lonjon, A., Panetto, H. (eds.) Digital Enterprise Design & Management. AISC, vol. 261, pp. 47–58. Springer, Cham (2014). https://doi.org/10.1007/978-3-319-04313-5_5
7. Farhangi, H.: The path of the smart grid. IEEE Power Energy Mag. **8**(1), 18–28 (2010)
8. Faschang, M.: Rapid control prototyping for networked smart grid systems based on an agile development process. Ph.D. thesis, Vienna University of Technology (2015)
9. Frascella, A., et al.: Looking for the unified classification and evaluation approach of SG interface standards for the purposes of ELECTRA IRP. In: 2015 International Symposium on Smart Electric Distribution Systems and Technologies (EDST), pp. 318–323, September 2015
10. Gottschalk, M., Uslar, M., Delfs, C.: The Use Case and Smart Grid Architecture Model Approach: The IEC 62559-2 Use Case Template and the SGAM applied in various domains. Springer, Heidelberg (2017). https://doi.org/10.1007/978-3-319-49229-2
11. Gungor, V., et al.: Smart grid technologies: communication technologies and standards. IEEE Trans. Ind. Inf. **7**(4), 529–539 (2011)
12. Hughes, J.: Intelligrid architecture concepts and IEC61850. In: 2005/2006 IEEE/PES Transmission and Distribution Conference and Exhibition, pp. 401–404, May 2006
13. Kintzler, F., et al.: Large scale rollout of smart grid services. In: 2018 Global Internet of Things Summit (GIoTS), pp. 1–7. IEEE (2018)
14. Knirsch, F., Engel, D., Neureiter, C., Frincu, M., Prasanna, V.: Model-driven privacy assessment in the smart grid. In: International Conference on Information Systems Security and Privacy (ICISSP), pp. 1–9. IEEE (2015)
15. Lee, E.A.: Cyber physical systems: design challenges. In: 2008 11th IEEE International Symposium on Object Oriented Real-Time Distributed Computing (ISORC), pp. 363–369. IEEE (2008)
16. Liserre, M., Sauter, T., Hung, J.Y.: Future energy systems: integrating renewable energy sources into the smart power grid through industrial electronics. IEEE Ind. Electron. Mag. **4**, 18–37 (2010)
17. Mandate M/490, European Commission: Standardization mandate to European Standardisation Organisations (ESOs) to Support European Smart Grid Deployment (2011)
18. Mellor, S.J., Scott, K., Uhl, A., Weise, D.: MDA Distilled: Principles of Model-Driven Architecture. Addison-Wesley Professional, Boston (2004)
19. Neureiter, C., Engel, D., Uslar, M.: Domain specific and model based systems engineering in the smart grid as prerequesite for security by design. Electronics **5**(2), 24 (2016)
20. Papaioannou, I., et al.: Smart grid interoperability testing methodology. Technical report, Joint Research Center (JRC) of the European Commission (EC) (2018)
21. Pröstl Andrén, F., Strasser, T., Kastner, W.: Engineering smart grids: applying model-driven development from use case design to deployment. Energies **10**(3), 374 (2017)

22. Pröstl Andren, F., Strasser, T., Seitl, C., Resch, J., Brandauer, C., Panholzer, G.: On fostering smart grid development and validation with a model-based engineering and support framework. In: Proceedings of the CIRED Workshop 2018 (2018)
23. Santodomingo, R., et al.: SGAM-based methodology to analyse smart grid solutions in discern European research project. In: 2014 IEEE International Energy Conference (ENERGYCON), pp. 751–758, May 2014
24. Strasser, T., et al.: A review of architectures and concepts for intelligence in future electric energy systems. IEEE Trans. Ind. Electron. **62**(4), 2424–2438 (2015)
25. Strasser, T.I., et al.: An integrated research infrastructure for validating cyber-physical energy systems. In: Mařík, V., Wahlster, W., Strasser, T., Kadera, P. (eds.) HoloMAS 2017. LNCS (LNAI), vol. 10444, pp. 157–170. Springer, Cham (2017). https://doi.org/10.1007/978-3-319-64635-0_12
26. Strasser, T., Pröstl Andrén, F., Lauss, G., et al.: Towards holistic power distribution system validation and testing—an overview and discussion of different possibilities. Elektrotech. Inftech. **134**(1), 71–77 (2017)
27. Umsonst, D., Sandberg, H.: A game-theoretic approach for choosing a detector tuning under stealthy sensor data attacks. In: 2018 IEEE Conference on Decision and Control (CDC), pp. 5975–5981, December 2018
28. Uslar, M., et al.: Applying the smart grid architecture model for designing and validating system-of-systems in the power and energy domain: a European perspective. Energies **12**(2), 258 (2019)
29. Uslar, M., et al.: Standardization in Smart Grids: Introduction to IT-Related Methodologies, Architectures and Standards. Springer, Heidelberg (2012). https://doi.org/10.1007/978-3-642-34916-4
30. Verband Deutscher Elektrotechniker (VDE): Technical minimum requirements for the connection to and parallel operation with low-voltage distribution networks (2011)
31. Yu, X., Xue, Y.: Smart grids: a cyber-physical systems perspective. Proc. IEEE **104**(5), 1058–1070 (2016)
32. Zanabria, C.: Adaptable engineering support framework for multi-functional battery energy storage systems. Ph.D. thesis, Vienna University of Technology, Institute of Mechanics and Mechatronics (2018)
33. Zhu, L., Shi, D., Duan, X.: Standard function blocks for flexible IED in IEC 61850-based substation automation. IEEE Trans. Power Deliv. **26**(2), 1101–1110 (2011)

Methodologies and Frameworks

Intelligent Multi-agent Platform for Designing Digital Ecosystems

George Rzevski(✉)

The Open University, Milton Keynes and Digital Ecosystems Ltd., London, UK
georgerzevski@digital-ecosystems.net

Abstract. The concept of Digital Ecosystem is defined, examples given and the idea that a Digital Ecosystem is, in fact, a Complex Adaptive System is introduced and elaborated. The paper then describes how to use ontology and multi-agent technology as a platform for designing digital ecosystems. A design of an urban digital ecosystem is presented as an illustration.

Keywords: Digital ecosystem · Complexity · Multi-agent platform · Adaptability · Selforganization

1 What Is Digital Ecosystem?

A trend to think about business as an ecosystem began as early as 1993, triggered by the James Moore's article in Harvard Review [1]. By now, complexity of the environment in which we live and work, has increased to such a degree that we would be well advised to adopt ecosystem approach to all aspects of our lives.

In the 21st century, a business, group of businesses, administration, nation, union of nations or, indeed, the whole Global Village, can be organized as an ecosystem only with substantial use of digital technology. It is therefore justified to underline the key role of digital technology by adopting the term Digital Ecosystem.

1.1 A Definition

According to Wikipedia [2], "A digital ecosystem is a distributed, adaptive, open socio-technical system with properties of self-organization, sustainability and scalability inspired from natural ecosystems. Digital ecosystem models are informed by knowledge of natural ecosystems, especially for aspects related to competition and collaboration among diverse entities".

The Wikipedia definition of digital ecosystems is good because it captures the key element of the new concept. According to this definition, a digital ecosystem is:

- Socio-technological system (rather than purely technological or social) - constituent agents have either human intelligence (HI) or artificial intelligence (AI)
- Characterised by distributed decision making (rather than centralised) - constituent agents are empowered to make certain decisions and may cooperate or compete with each other

V. Mařík et al. (Eds.): HoloMAS 2019, LNAI 11710, pp. 29–40, 2019.
https://doi.org/10.1007/978-3-030-27878-6_3

- Adaptive (rather than rigid, hierarchical, command and control) – capable of autonomously eliminating, or at least reducing, consequences of unpredictable disruptive events
- Self-organising (rather than organised and, from time to time, reorganised by managers)
- Sustainable – capable of coevolving with its environment over a long period of time
- Scalable – capable to grow in size and/or performance

Clearly, this definition places digital ecosystems into category of *complex adaptive systems*, as defined in this paper in Sect. 6.1 and in [3].

Gartner's definition [4] is compatible: "A digital ecosystem is an interdependent group of enterprises, people and/or things that share standardized digital platforms for a mutually beneficial purpose (such as commercial gain, innovation or common interest). Digital ecosystems enable you to interact with customers, partners, adjacent industries - even your competition".

Mckinsey article "Management's next frontier: making the most of ecosystem economy" [5], focuses on the need for businesses to develop new managerial skills required to manage highly connected, interacting ecosystem-like business.

1.2 Social Usefulness

The main value of digital ecosystems could be that they help to make business outputs socially useful and thus build close links between business and society.

How would this be done?

Whilst, in general, businesses may have many different objectives, including, the accumulation of the personal wealth of owners, the objectives of businesses engaged in operating digital ecosystems should be *to build connected, sustainable society, which is capable of cost-effectively feeding, watering, housing, educating, keeping in good health, moving and employing its members without endangering its environment.*

1.3 Global Impact

Converting all conventional businesses into digital ecosystems based on multi-agent technology in the UK would mean transferring estimated 40% of all current jobs to multi-agent systems. Since new technologies always create new jobs, the problem is not as bad as it seems, notwithstanding the need for retraining, rehousing and compensation. The author has researched the division of labor between human and artificial intelligence and reported findings in [6].

1.4 Examples

Examples of digital ecosystems include Smart City, Smart Community, Smart Agriculture, Smart Housing, Smart Transport and Smart Manufacturing. Two of these examples are outlined below.

Smart City – An Urban Digital Ecosystem. Consider an urban settlement such as a town, a city, a megacity or a city state. At present, every vital service to citizens is managed individually, and coordination is done intermittently through a set of meetings. As a result, there is a considerable waste of resources.

Urban environments are very complex – they are characterized by frequent disruptive events (such as changes in demand, failures of resources or delays of deliveries caused by accidents, traffic jams, shopping sprees, festivities, tourist seasons, epidemics, etc.). Consequences of these disruptions can be eliminated, or at least reduced, only by rapid rescheduling of disrupted services without disturbing services that are not affected by the disruption.

No centralized planner could possibly handle this complexity.

In contrast, an urban digital ecosystem consisting of a network of co-operating and/or competing real-time schedulers would ensure that constituent services adapt to every change in demand or availability of resources for the benefit of society.

In addition to a network of real-time schedulers, ensuring adaptability of services, a digital ecosystem contains a network of knowledge discovery systems whose role is to dynamically extract knowledge from data.

Smart Factory – A Car Production Digital Ecosystem. Cars are currently manufactured using rigid production lines, which are very expensive to design and build, and have a short lifespan.

The author and his research team have developed technology for replacing rigid and expensive car production lines with self-organizing and evolving car production ecosystems, which are particularly suitable for the production of electric cars.

The production infrastructure consists of (1) Assembly Points, where components are assembled into subassemblies and subassemblies are assembled into cars; (2) Assembly Robots, which assembly cars in co-operation with assembly workers; (3) Stores, where components and subassemblies are stored while waiting to be assembled; and (4) Mobile Robots, which load, unload and transport components and subassemblies between stores and assembly points. Assembled electric cars are driven from assembly points to (4) Pre-Delivery Stores.

Every car component and every subassembly are equipped with an electronic tag with sufficient processing capacity to maintain a Component/Subassembly Agent and Local Ontology. Digital Agents communicate with each other via Production Digital Network connected to the Internet. Assembly Points have extended digital processing facility for handling, storing, modifying and displaying car designs.

The production progresses by Agents sending messages to each other triggering delivery of components/subassemblies to assembly points.

Such a production ecosystem has all the advantages, as listed in Sect. 1.1, over current mass-production lines.

2 Why Do We Need Digital Ecosystems?

Digital ecosystems are needed only under conditions of market complexity. In the past, when the economic environment within which we lived and worked, was stable, and demand and supply were reasonably predictable, more conventional business and administration organizations, designed for the Economy of Scale, were preferred.

The diagram below shows how co-evolution of technology, business and society leads to the increase in connectivity and, consequently, in complexity. Currently, the increase is exceedingly steep and high (Fig. 1).

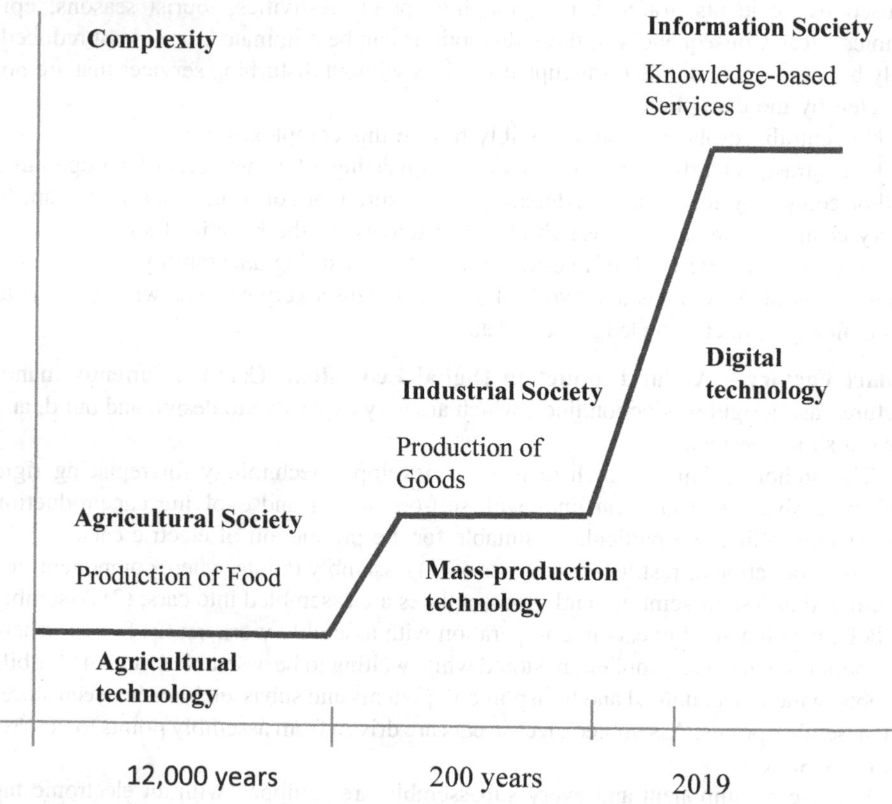

Fig. 1. Co-evolution of technology, business and society drives the increase in complexity

2.1 21st Century Is the Century of Complexity

In a very short period of time since the beginning of the 21st century, we have built a huge global digital network, connecting documents (the Internet of Documents), people (the Internet of People), things (the Internet of Things) and digital currency (the Internet of Values) into a giant Global Village of considerable complexity [7]. The consequences of the exponential growth of the Internet-based global market are of two kinds:

- Frequent, unpredictable disruptive events affect conventionally organised businesses and administrations
- Massive opportunities for the entrepreneurs are available to open new web-based business and for leading administrators to improve supply of services to the citizens

To cope with frequent unpredictable disruptions, businesses must be adaptive [8], which means, able to (1) instantly detect a disruptive event, (2) rapidly identify which business processes will be affected and (3) reschedule the affected processes with a view to eliminating, or at least reducing, consequences of disruption in real time, before the next disruption occurs.

Under conditions of complexity, which now prevail, the key success factor is Adaptability, rather than Economy of Scale [9].

3 Architecture of a Digital Ecosystem

A system architecture defines the interfaces between the system and its environment as well as interconnections between key subsystems.

The architecture and the method for designing digital ecosystems presented in this paper, is to the best of author's knowledge, original and very practical. During the past 20 years, it has produced a large number of digital ecosystems that have considerably increased their client values.

As Fig. 2 shows, author's digital ecosystems contain three key subsystems: Real World, Virtual World and Knowledge Base (Ontology + Data). Virtual World and Knowledge Base constitute an Intelligent Multi-Agent Platform.

3.1 Real World

In essence, the Real World consists of Human Decision Makers, Demands (orders) and Resources (human, physical and financial). Under current conditions of market complexity, The Real World cannot cope with frequent unpredictable disruptive events, on its own. It requires help from the Multi-Agent Platform consisting of the Virtual World and Knowledge Base.

3.2 Virtual World

Virtual World consists primarily of digital Demand Agents, representing real demands, and Resource Agents representing real resources. Agents are the decision makers and they arrive at decisions through a process of negotiation among themselves and, occasionally, involving human decision makers.

When a disruptive event occurs, agents rapidly detect the event, identify parts of the Real World that will be affected, reschedule affected parts, without disrupting the operation of unaffected parts, and send instruction to the Real World how to neutralize the disturbance. All this is done in real time, often in seconds, or even microseconds.

3.3 Knowledge Base (Ontology + Data)

Knowledge Base contains domain knowledge required to run the ecosystem. It consists of two distinctive parts: (1) ontology, which contains conceptual knowledge organized as a semantic network and (2) data.

Ontology can be updated whenever rules, regulations or policy of the ecosystem change, without interrupting the Ecosystem operation.

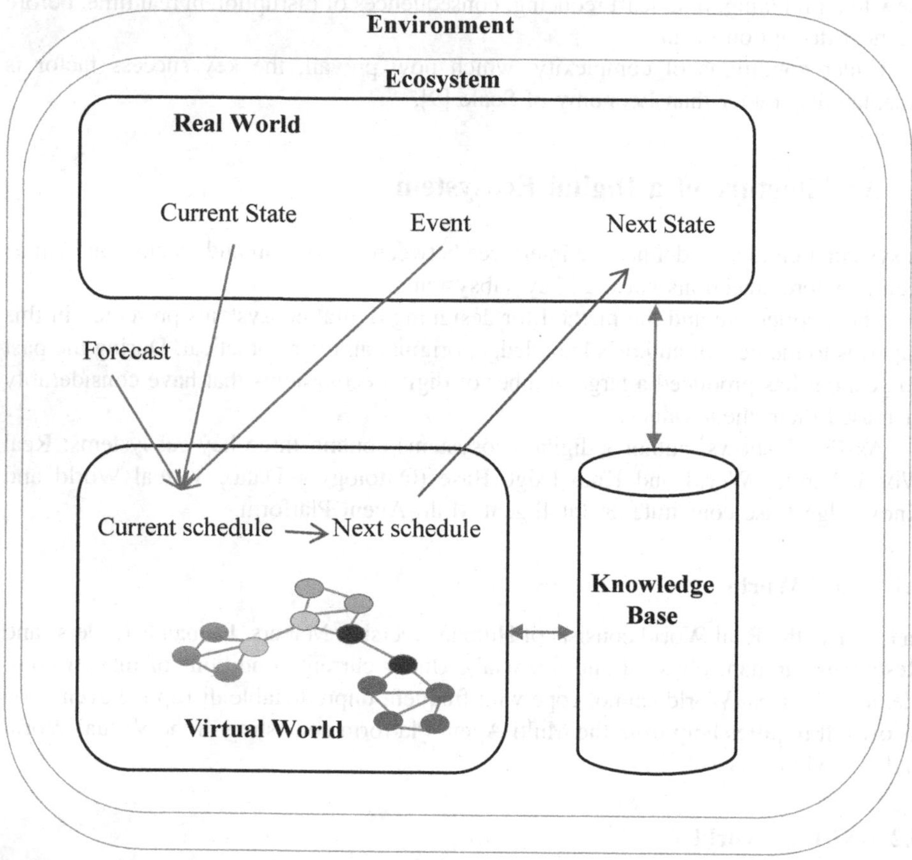

Fig. 2. Digital ecosystem architecture

For large digital ecosystems the Virtual World may consists of several "swarms" of agents, each allocating resources to demands for a different product or service.

It is important to understand that digital agents, at present, exclusively make decisions on the resource allocation at operational level.

4 A Design Case Study

Let us consider a typical urban settlement governed by the council and managed by the town administration responsible for services to citizens, such as:

- education
- social services

- roads and transport
- waste disposal
- economic development
- planning
- protecting the public (from crime, fire, elements, etc.)
- libraries
- rubbish collection
- environmental health
- tourism
- leisure and amenities
- planning permission
- housing-needs services
- collection of council tax

And let's assume that the Council has decided to substantially improve each service to citizens and at the same time reduce the costs of service provision.

The above services may be delivered by the town administration or outsourced to private companies, in which case, we would deal with an ecosystem containing both public and private sectors.

4.1 Requirements Specification

The conventional wisdom is to approach the problem top-down by attempting to perform requirements specification for the whole town before starting the work on design.

Such approach would be unacceptable under current dynamics of the political, social, economic and technological town environment. The dynamics is such that requirements would be obsolete before completed.

An evolutionary design method is advocated by the author, as described below.

4.2 Evolutionary Design Method

Under conditions of frequently changing requirements, it is advisable to adopt an evolutionary design method, as follows:

1. Consider all services with a view to identifying one whose improvement would bring the highest value to the client
2. Complete a requirements specification for the improvement of the selected service
3. Design a part of a digital ecosystem consisting of the selected service only
4. Evaluate and update the solution demonstrating the achieved increase in the client value
5. Select the next service and repeat steps 2, 3, 4, ensuring that the newly added service cooperates or competes with the previously improved services, as required
6. As the number of improved services increases, continuously monitor and, if necessary, adjust the overall ecosystem design

In theory, the evolutionary improvement of services should never stop. In practice, contractual arrangements between clients and digital ecosystem designers cannot be indefinite and will have to be limited to the improvement of one or more services at a time.

A wise client would ensure that they have priority access to a skilled team for continuously maintaining and improving the new digital ecosystem. And that would represent an extension of the urban ecosystem with additional self-maintenance and self-improvement services.

4.3 Concurrent Design Mode

In addition to approaching the design in an evolutionary manner, the ecosystem designers should be organized in three teams working concurrently on (1) requirements specifications, (2) the design, and (3) the commissioning of improved services, timing the work in such a way that

- Whenever the design of the improvement of a service is completed, the requirements specification for the improvement of the next service is ready for design
- Whenever the commissioning of the improved service is completed, the design for the improvement of the next service is ready for commissioning.

4.4 The First Few Steps

Let's assume that the critical service selected for the improvement is ambulance service.

Designing Ontology. The design begins with outlining ontology for the ambulance service, which involves:

- Selecting Object Classes (Ambulance Vehicle, Ambulance Crew, Crew Member, Ambulance Equipment, Rout, Road, Hospital, Patient, Relative)
- Identifying Relations (Crew belongs to Vehicle, Equipment belongs to Crew, Vehicle follows Route)
- Defining Properties of Object Classes (for Crew Member: id, qualifications, availability)

It is prudent at this stage to write scripts for agents, which should be also stored in ontology as properties of Object Classes, and ready for agents to pick them up when given a task to perform.

All policies, rules and regulations guiding the delivery of services should be also stored in ontology.

A Peak into the Design of Virtual World. To design the Virtual world means to design the whole digital infrastructure that supports the exchange of meaningful messages among, potentially, hundreds of thousands of agents. The choice of technology is vital and our recent switch to Python and Microservices brought considerable gains: the development time has been almost halved!

Virtual world is a place where agents negotiate among themselves how to allocate resources to demands. The process is rapid and, in principle, not repeatable. The conditions, under which negotiations between agents are conducted, often change during the negotiations. In this respect, Virtual world is like Heraclitus' river: no agent can enter the sane Virtual World twice.

In the Ambulance Service Virtual World, the matching of crew members to crews, crews to ambulance vehicles, ambulance vehicles to hospitals, roads to routs, patients to hospitals, etc. is done by exchange of messages between relevant agents.

To achieve adaptability, the matching of demands to resources is done by agent communication rather than by computation. If, for example, a road to selected hospital is blocked by excessive traffic, Road Agent of the blocked road will immediately let other Road Agents know of a problem and trigger a wave of renegotiations between affected agents to determine a new route to the hospital. If a new route is too long, agents may try to negotiate a different hospital.

The key advantage of this type of rescheduling is that parts of the Ambulance Service Ecosystem not affected by the road closure, continue functioning as though no disruption occurred.

All scheduling decisions made in the Virtual World have to be rapidly conveyed to the Real World, the preferred method being messaging to smart phones, or directly to relevant "things".

What is described here is just a minute part of the design process, hopefully sufficient to demonstrate how multi-agent technology offers a considerable advantage over conventional batch-mode optimizers. Many more design details may be found in [3].

4.5 Extending the Initial Design

Scheduling of ambulance vehicles is easily extended to cover, for example, the scheduling of hospital staff and facilities that are required by patients brought in by ambulance vehicles. We just need an additional swarm of agents to do this job. And then, of course, we can add more swarms of agents to schedule other hospital resources such as operating theatres, etc. The design should advance step by step, each step proven in practice before the next one is commissioned.

5 Experience

During the last 20 or so years, the author's team has designed and commissioned a large number of digital ecosystems [3]. The several systems, designed in the year 2000, are still working, bringing to their clients considerable competitive edge. Among them, the most important are our Taxi Ecosystem and Crude Oil Transportation Ecosystem, which are still unique. The most prestigious accomplishment is, perhaps, the Adaptive Logistics for the Delivery of Crew and Cargo to the International Space Station.

6 Context

The concept of Digital Ecosystems was conceived as a new paradigm in the theory of organizations when complexity of the technological, social and economic environment in which we live and work increased to such as an extend that the old paradigm of a rigid, hierarchical organization with centralized decision making began to show its weaknesses. As predicted by Kuhn [10], before the old, dominant paradigm disappears, many new candidate paradigms fight among themselves for the privilege of becoming dominant. Here are some of the pretenders.

6.1 Complex Adaptive Systems

A system, or a situation, is said to be *complex* if it is *open* (exchanges information with its environment), consists of many *diverse*, partially *autonomous* and richly *connected* components, called *Agents*, and if it has *no central control*. Behavior of complex systems is uncertain without being random. The global behavior *emerges* from the interaction of constituent agents. The autonomy of agents is limited by constraints imposed on them by the system to which they belong. *Emergent* properties of complex systems are properties of the system as a whole, which cannot be found in constituent components; they emerge from the interaction of constituent components.

The word "complex" derives meaning from the word *plex* (interwoven or interconnected) and should not be confused with words like "complicated" (as a jet engine), "cumbersome" (as bureaucracy), "unwieldy" (as an aged empire), "chaotic" (as a disorderly administration) or "difficult to understand" (as a verbose document).

Since the key feature of a complex system is that it is *Adaptive,* it is customary to call such a system, a *Complex Adaptive System*. Examples include: human brain [11, 12], natural ecology and the Internet-based global market [13]. Complex adaptive systems are discussed in detail in [3]. Recommended further reading are: [14–18].

The most fascinating complex adaptive system is, of course, human brain, consisting of 100 billion neurons, each incorporating a copy of human genome, potentially interconnected into a vast *neural network* exhibiting emergent properties such as *intelligence* and *creativity*. Artificial neural networks are many orders of magnitude smaller and their design as a "clean slate" (tabula rasa) require them to be trained before can be used.

The author considers digital ecosystems to be a subclass of complex adaptive systems.

6.2 Industry 4.0

Industry 4.0 is the name given to the current trend in automation and data exchange in manufacturing. It includes Cyber-Physical Systems, the Internet of Things and Cloud Computing. Industry 4.0 technology is intended to embrace all technologies needed to create a Smart Factory. Within the modular structured smart factory, cyber-physical systems monitor physical processes, create a virtual copy of the physical world and make decentralized decisions. Over the Internet of Things, cyber-physical systems communicate and cooperate with each other and with humans in real time, and via the Internet of Services both internal and cross-organizational services are offered and used by participants of the value chain. All very much as in an digital ecosystem.

What is missing in Industry 4.0 is an explicit blueprint how to achieve adaptation to and coevolution with the complex manufacturing social and economic environment.

The concept of Ecosystem not only include such a blueprint, it's scope is far broader and covers any economic, social or political system, not just manufacturing.

6.3 Multi-agent Systems

Conventional multi-agent systems have been used for straightforward industrial applications for many years, often designed as deterministic systems performing batch-mode optimization tasks. The potential of agent-based technology is, however, vast, primarily as technology for building complex adaptive systems and digital ecosystems. The author's research focuses specifically on this aspect of agents: achieving adaptability, coevolution and emergent intelligence. Empowered with emergent intelligence, agent-based technology is likely to replace conventional computing algorithms as the key technology for building digital ecosystems.

7 New Developments

The most important new development has matured sufficiently to be announced. It is a digital ecosystem for designing digital ecosystems.

It consists of (1) the Real World of human designers, (2) Ontology containing knowledge how to design ecosystems, and (3) Virtual World of digital agents that build, through a process of negotiations, Ontology and Virtual World of the new ecosystem. One can argue that such a system represents a primitive reproduction.

Acknowledgement. It is the author's pleasure to acknowledge the contribution of Professor Petr Skobelev, Samara State University, and Smart Solutions Ltd, Samara, Russia, to the work described in this paper throughout a twenty-year long collaboration with the author.

References

1. Moore, J.F.: Predators and prey: a new ecology of competition. Harvard Bus. Rev. **71**, 75–86 (1993)
2. Wikipedia. https://en.wikipedia.org/wiki/Digital_ecosystem
3. Rzevski, G., Skobelev, P.: Managing Complexity. WIT Press, Southampton, Boston (2014)
4. Gartner.com: Drive innovation from digital ecosystems
5. Mckinsey.com/Management's next frontier: Making the most of ecosystem economy (2017)
6. Rzevski, G.: Human versus artificial intelligence: competing or collaborating? In: Keynote at the International Conference on Artificial Intelligence, Colombo, Sri Lanka (2018)
7. Rzevski, G.: Coevolution of technology, business and society. Int. J. Design Nat. Ecodyn. **13**(3), 231–237 (2018)
8. Rzevski, G.: A practical methodology for managing complexity. Emerg. Complex. Organ. – Int. Transdisc. J. Complex Soc. Syst. **13**(1–2), 38–56 (2011)

9. Rzevski, G.: Harnessing the power of self-organization. Int. J. Design Nat. Ecodyn. **11**(4), 483–494 (2016)
10. Kuhn, T.: The Structure of Scientific Revolutions, 2nd edn. The University of Chicago Press, Enlarged (1970)
11. Edelman, G.: Bright Air, Brilliant Fire: On the Matter of the Mind. Allen Lane the Penguin Press, London (1992)
12. Noble, D.: The Music of Life. Oxford University Press, Oxford (2006)
13. Beinhocker, E.: The Origin of Wealth: Evolution. Complexity and the Radical Remaking of Economics. Random House Business Books, New York (2007)
14. Prigogine, I.: The End of Certainty: Time. Chaos and the new Laws of Nature. Free Press, New York (1997)
15. Prigogine, I.: Is Future Given?. World Scientific Publishing Co., Singapore (2003)
16. Kaufman, S.: At Home In the Universe: The Search for the Laws of Self-Organization and Complexity. Oxford Press, Oxford (1995)
17. Holland, J.H.: Hidden Order: How Adaptation Builds Complexity. Addison Wesley, Boston (1995)
18. Holland, J.: Emergence: From Chaos to Order. Oxford University Press, Oxford (1998). ISBN 0-19-850409-8

Contribution to the Theory of Uncertain Systems Alliances

Mirko Novák, Petr Vysoký, and Zdeněk Votruba(✉)

Faculty of Transportation Sciences, CTU in Prague, Prague, Czech Republic
{mirko, vysoky, votruba}@fd.cvut.cz

Abstract. Basic concepts and ideas of uncertain systems alliances are briefly overviewed. Then the strength of the alliance joints is analyzed via medium mutual information measure. This approach can help to estimate the value/importance of respective bonds within the alliance, which is important in alliances with significant uncertainty.

Keywords: Systems alliance · Uncertainty · Interface · Fuzzy approach · Medium mutual information

1 Introduction

The concept of systems alliances proposed already in 2001 Vlček [1]. He introduced it on the idea that an alliance of two or more parts/modules originates as:

- a product of random encounter
- an outcome of processes of contamination and immunity
- a construct.

Generally, the systems alliance does not hold common characteristics of species (genetic code), or common goals, or common identity, i.e. it can hardly be identified as a system. Components of the alliance have to be well distinguishable; they must contain well-defined interfaces. They also do not require identification as systems or automata. The membership of components within the alliance is typically dynamic one. Their members generally mediate holistic goals in alliances, if any.

The principles of the alliance forming have been explained via the concepts of information power (IP) and of multilingual translation efficiency respectively. An illustration of basic phenomena resulting in the emergence of alliance could be based on the concepts of interface sharing (IS), and of irregularities conjugation (IC) as well [2–6].

Many alliances can be represented in suitable language model. The language model of the alliance makes possible quantitative evaluation of its processes.

Basic ideas of this construct are as follows:

- Any module/system, which takes part in the alliance, is expressed in respective multi-grammar language. The relations within these modules are expressed via mutual translations of particular languages of modules elements.

V. Mařík et al. (Eds.): HoloMAS 2019, LNAI 11710, pp. 41–51, 2019.
https://doi.org/10.1007/978-3-030-27878-6_4

- The relations of any module participating in alliance against the super – system (SS) are performed in mutual translation of boundary elements languages into the language of the respective SS.
- The mutual relations of the modules taking part in alliance are reflected in mutual translation of the languages of the respective boundary systems elements.
- The alliance manifests itself in more complete and/or more efficient translation of the alliance language into the language of SS in comparison with the independent translations of the languages of modules taking part in alliance.

Problems arise due to incompleteness of grammars of respective languages.

Synergic phenomena of IS and IC are so significant that they could be used as the definition characteristics of the alliance [5, 6]. An emergence of these phenomena results in the improvement of the regularity of the interfaces either mutually among the modules/systems which take part in the alliance or between the alliances as a whole and its neighborhood (environment, forming together with considered alliance the super – system SS). The secondary effect is an improvement of the efficiency of the resources utilization.

Interfaces (IF) are in fact the only parts of alliances which one has firmly keep under the control and which are almost identified in detail. Among interfaces, the significant position is hold by so-called critical interfaces (IFs). Critical interfaces within the alliance can be modeled via finite deterministic automata, or hard subsystems. These models make possible to take into consideration uncertainties which could be linked with irregularities of interfaces. The same models are capable to present the irregularities conjugation as well. Similar models can also represent the effects of alliance control.

More sophisticated and more powerful model of alliance interfaces stem from the concept of quantum–like subsystems [4, 7]. Quantum superposition of states or even the concept of entanglement are suitable tools how to record non - orthogonal interface parameters and resulting phase sensitivity of the respective IF (Fig. 1).

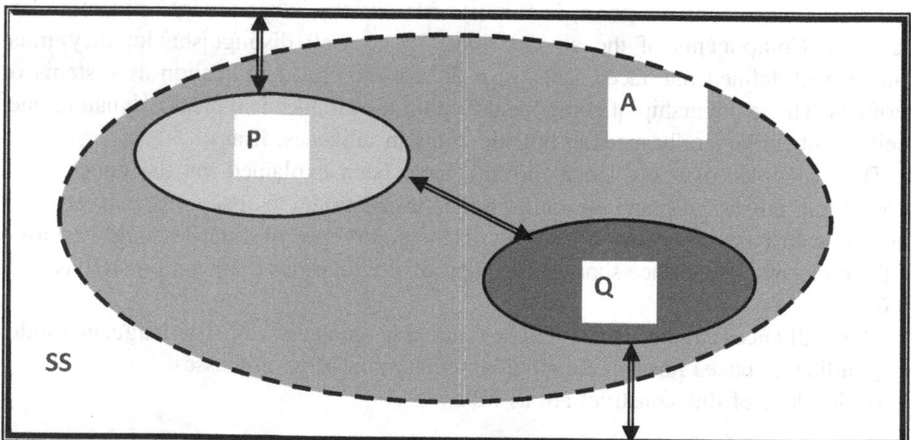

Fig. 1. Simplified presentation of systems alliance, consisting of two parts - "Amoeba model"; (P and Q are constituent elements - modules of alliance A; SS represents super – system, i.e. the environment the alliance exists within, the arrows indicate various types of relations between parts)

- The forming and existence of alliance is causally joined with the receiving and processing of information. In the dissipative environment it is the condition sine qua non for the plain existence of alliance.
- The impact of the information received can be measured utilizing the concept of IP, which is defined as the integral response of the alliance “systems time” to the information received [5].
- At this level, we cannot distinguish if the resulting effect is the randomizing or ordering one. In alliances, it means whether or not the sharing of interface increases or decreases its regularity. (It can be distinguished at the higher level of abstraction and within the frame of constructive approach only) [5, 11].
- The results of experiments on various real processes (laser cooling; traffic control; social preferences…) support the idea that the ordering can easily be flipped into chaos, et vice versa. The results are very sensitive on “phase” i.e. on the actual time delay with which information received is transformed into the sequence of events (run of system time).
- This knowledge resulted in the trials to construct “phase sensitive” systems modeling methodology, which could be able to respect this effect. There is probably not a matter of chance that this methodology has some significant similarities with the models of quantum physics.

2 Uncertainty in Alliances

Let turn the attention to more general situations when some systems alliances consist from parts being in principle either nonlinear or uncertain (or both). Such cases appear almost ever, when the complexity of alliance exceeds certain limit. This is typical namely for alliances consisting of a mixture of various kinds of components and involving as the elements living bodies e.g. human. In this case, one has to face strong uncertainty factor resulting from the extremely high complexity of human brain and unability to define firmly its actual state and properties. Actually, nobody is able to define actual state and structure of any human brain and there are (and never had been) two identical brains (in structure and in behavior). Moreover, one is not able to recognize perfectly not only the state of certain human brain, but also the stage of interaction in certain human group. Therefore, one must consider the interaction of human intelligence with technical components of some alliance as highly uncertain. Anyway, the uncertain within the alliance have to be considered also other factors, like the impacts of environmental influences, some functional dependences on impacts of various independent variables (namely the time).

As an example of one important factor appeared considerably newly found circa-dial dependence of the system controlling daily biological rhythms regulating the activity of more than 40% of human genes, which orchestrates the activity of eating, blood temperature and blood pressure. Now there is known, that almost any cell in the human body contains its own circa-dial clock machinery, the master circa-dial clock system then synchronizes almost all of them. A tiny brain region called the supraciasmatic nucleus controls the level of hormones responsible for the control of sleep – wake cycles. These Chrono - types differ so widely, that no two people have identical intervals of activity distribution. They differ about 8 h or even more. The sleep can cause numerous ill effects e.g. disturbances in distribution of the sleep hormone, melatonine.

3 Systems Alliance Cohesion

A grouping of components/systems creating an alliance has certain necessary attributes, particularly these:

- It forms a meta-structure
- Its parts/subsystems communicate with each other on a level of symbolic information
- Its parts are often complex systems showing “intelligent behavior”

Within the framework of intelligent behavior of the systems that create an alliance, one should hold the following typical features in mind:

- The subsystems have their own identity
- They create a model of the world
- They create a system of values for themselves
- They have goal-oriented behavior.

To use the term alliance most of these attributes have to be valid. One cannot say that a car is an alliance of mechanical, hydraulic and electrical systems. On the other hand, a pack of wolves hunting alone stag is an alliance. The particular members of the pack can live individually, they have common behavior and the particular members of the pack have to communicate with each other while hunting (of course nonverbally in this case).

The fundamental criteria for judging, whether the agreement of independent systems’ behavior with the same goals is coincidental, or whether it is an alliance’s coordinated behavior lies in the strength of bonds (joints) among a particular subsystems, i.e. in an exchange of information among them. The co-ordination means exchanging information. The strength of bonds among particular subsystems is in fact the rate of co-ordination - from zero co-ordination of mutually independent systems to the strongest co-ordination, when the particular subsystems are tied via deterministic function relations. In this case, we do not speak about the alliance but about the system built up from original alliance’s members.

The question arises whether one cannot explicit the vague definition of the term being discussed with the help of formal methods measuring the strength of the bonds among particular subsystems creating the “possible alliance”, in other words whether one can identify the alliance with certain method?

4 Co-ordination Measure Quantification

Suppose that one has two systems and that one will evaluate the activities of both systems by observing or measuring the two quantities. The quantity X describes the behavior of the system A, while the quantity Y describes the behavior of the system B.

One can judge their coordinated synergy according to the behavior of both quantities. Of course, the number of quantities can be higher.

If the behaviors of the quantities are somehow similar, there will be some kind of co-ordination. Mostly the basic statistic methods are used and one measures the rate of similarity by the correlation coefficient. If it is small, one can say that the quantities are non-correlated, if it is close to one, one says that the quantities are strongly correlated. However, the term non-correlated does not mean independent. The often-mentioned correlation coefficient can be zero and the quantities are in a deterministic function relation. The situation introduced above can take place if the described relations are non-linear.

The principle of independence is defined precisely by the means of distribution of the quantities mentioned above.

If the quantities are independent, then it holds true:

$$P(X, Y) = P(X)P(Y),$$

where P(X), P(Y) are marginal probabilities of both quantities and

P(X, Y) is their joint combined probability.

If the relation:

$$P(X, Y) < P(X)P(Y),$$

is valid, then there is some kind of dependence between the quantities.

One can determine the strength of this dependence (the strength of the mutual bond) accurately if one determines what information of Y the X quantity bears, and vice versa. The fact, what information of Y the X quantity bears, is determined by the medium mutual information set by the relation:

$$T(X : Y) = H(X) + H(Y) - H(X, Y)$$

where H(X) and H(Y) are marginal entropies

$$H(X) = -\sum_{i=1}^{n} P(x_i) \log P(x_i)$$

and

$$H(X, Y) = -\sum_{i=1}^{n} \sum_{k=1}^{m} P(x_i, y_j) \log P(x_i, y_j)$$

is the combined joint entropy.

The medium mutual information can be extended on a multi-dimensional case of more variables. The medium mutual information is a non - negative symmetric but unfortunately it does not meet the triangle inequity and thus it does not have property of metrics and one cannot directly use it as a distance between the particular possibilities of the alliances' ordering. As one will see below, it is possible to get around this disadvantage by means of a proper procedure.

How can one use the rate of mutual dependence for discovering mutual bonds among such subsystems that one would consider being an alliance? One can use a method that was developed in the general theory of systems many years ago for the detection or identification of the structure of a system [7–9].

Imagine a very simple system consisting of three variables X, Y, Z. One could call the system of these three quantities an alliance if all of them are bound with strong bonds, if the three of them all are mutually dependent. If the three of them all are independent or two of them are dependent and the third one independent, then one will not be able to speak about the alliance of three systems described by these quantities.

Let all of the possible orderings of dependencies among the mentioned quantities – the possible structures of the system be created.

$$
\begin{aligned}
K_0 &= (X, Y, Z),\\
K_1 &= (X, Y; Y, Z),\\
K_2 &= (X, Z; Y, Z),\\
K_3 &= (X, Z; X, Y),\\
K_4 &= \{X, Y; Z\},\\
K_5 &= \{X, Z; Y\},\\
K_6 &= \{Y, Z; X\},\\
K_7 &= \{X; Y; Z;\}.
\end{aligned}
$$

K_0 is the most complex system in this case; the system of three independent variables K_7 is the simplest system. One can order the particular possible structure in such a way that the elements of a more simple structure are subsets of the elements of a more complex structure. This means that element K_0 will have the highest rate of ordering while element K_7 will have the lowest one.

The ordered set with the biggest and the smallest element creates a union. If one demonstrates the ordering by means of a chart, one will get the so-called Hasse diagram of the union mentioned above (Fig. 2).

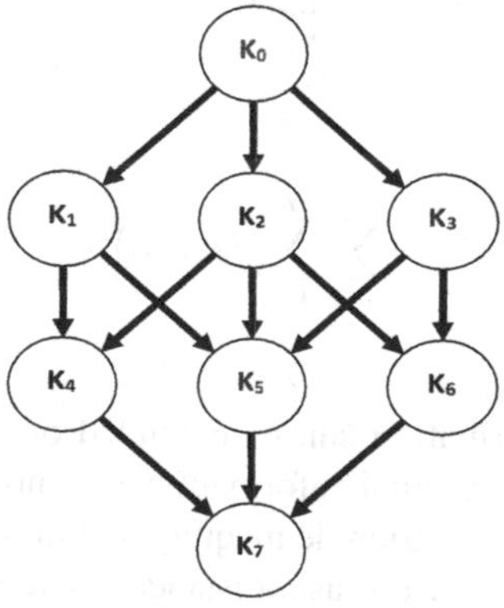

Fig. 2. Hasse diagram of the union of the candidates of structure

In this case, K_1 is a subset of K_0, K_4 is a subset of K_1 and K_7. If one moves along any edge of the Hasse diagram in the direction of the arrows, the following element will be always the subset of the preceding element. This feature of the union enables us to use medium mutual information for discovered structures. When moving along the edge of the Hasse diagram the medium mutual information will also meet - apart from the features mentioned above - the triangle inequity and has, therefore, the features of a metric. The difference between the medium mutual information, providing all three quantities are mutually independent, and a genuinely measured medium mutual information will show which candidate of the structure is closest to the candidate K_0 and thus one can consider this structure to be the searched structure of the system.

In practice it is processed in this way: one finds out the values of the combined joint probabilities $P(x_i, y_j, z_k)$, where x_i, y_j, z_k are particular classes of the values of these variables. If one summarizes over all i one will get the joint probability $P(y_j, z_k)$, so:

$$P(y_j, z_k) = \sum_{i=1}^{n} P(x_i, y_j, z_k)$$

Analogously one attains the marginal probabilities $P(y_j)$, $P(z_k)$

$$P(y_j) = \sum_{k=1}^{r} P(y_j, z_k)$$

and

$$P(z_k) = \sum_{j=1}^{m} P(y_j, z_k)$$

In such a way, one can find all of the necessary marginal and joint probabilities so that one could set the medium mutual information for the particular candidates of the structure. From the measured joint probability, one set the medium mutual information for the candidate of the structure K_0. The difference between the medium mutual information $T(K_0)$ and medium mutual information of any further candidate of the structure will be the distance of this candidate from the system with the structure being searched. Let remark that this way of looking for a structure is one of the oldest but also most illustrative. It is suitable for the identification of systems with a relatively small number of variables. In the course of time a large number of other methods has been developed that use somewhat different approaches and that are more effective in the case of a larger number of variables.

The essential question deals with the variables themselves. By now, one had silently assumed that the variables of the system are in metrological terminology metric variables. One deals with those variables mostly in physical disciplines. However, one can unambiguously assign numeric values to values of variables based on some measuring procedure and a specific unit is defined. (One is not going to deal with a precise definition of a specific unit - the specific unit is for example weight, electric charge, power etc.). The measured values of these quantities can be easily selected according to their size into classes and one can estimate the probabilities of their incidence.

5 A Task of Empirical Data Evaluation

Here however another problem occurs. With the exception of theorizations, if one works with empirical data, one never knows their actual probabilities. One only estimate the probabilities based on empirically established relative frequencies. How the estimation of probability will differ from the real probability and how the estimation will be deflected depends on many circumstances: how many samples one will have for disposal, into how many classes one will divide the range of possible values that the relevant variable acquires, how many dimensional probabilities one will estimate etc. The deflection of the estimation for a small number of samples can cause quite large errors, which can lead to very incorrect images of the system's structure.

It is interesting that these methods were at first used in practice in the scientific disciplines like psychology, where the experimenters struggled with shortage of sufficient experimental data all the time. The problem of an accurate comparison of medium mutual pieces of information set based on inaccurate estimations of probabilities was transferred onto testing statistic hypotheses. E.g. "the quantities are independent" type towards the alternative "the quantities are not independent" ones by means of statistic tests (c2 – test, F-test) which one has a lot of experience with within the experimental research. This enables to decide how many samples one will need at a certain anticipated complexity of the system and a number of possible quantum levels of particular quantities.

These information measures based on probabilities are of a big advantage in that they are not limited only to metric quantities, which can be unambiguously quantified. In many economic systems, biological, psychological and similar systems, one encounters quantities whose values are only able to be ordered – ordinal quantities where for example, one of the most important quantities in economics – utility belongs.

One can say that this activity will bring a bigger utility than the other one but one is not able to say "by how much". There is no unit for utility. In humanistic and socio-economic systems are frequently encountered quantities, whose values one is not even able to order. Mostly one assigns mere verbal designation to the values and one speaks them as about the nominal quantities.

For example, in various sociological systems alliances the mood of the subject plays a role. If one has three degrees of mood "I am angry", "I am nervous", "I am weary", it is hard for us to find any ordering. (If one assigns numbers to these values, they mostly have meaning of mere designation. It is of no use making any mathematical operations with them. For instance, inventory numbers, numbers of health insurance etc.) Also in these cases, the entropic rates for searching for relations among the alliance's members work satisfactorily. They would work very well if one is able to place the values of the mentioned nominal quantities into respective classes. These quantities, e.g. type of mood play an important part in the creation of electoral alliances of citizens, in market research etc. Nevertheless, classification of a certain mood into a proper class is on the one hand very subjective and on the other hand very vague.

Here one encounters a different type of uncertainty than statistic uncertainty, the certainty of vagueness type. One terms the values verbally but the uncertainty lies in the semantics of a verbal label. The uncertainty lies in what all one terms with the given word. In other words, the classes into which one classifies the particular values of nominal quantities do not have sharp limits. This type of uncertainty can be detected by means of fuzzy sets and one will show that the relations among variables can be searched for in the same way as was done by now. The basic idea of detection of vagueness by means of fuzzy sets lies in the fact that the uncertainty of belonging into a class is defined via the function of affiliation. One can formalize the semantics of a respective value of a nominal variable by means of a suitable function of affiliation. Then one works with the so-called linguistic variable.

6 Fuzzy Approaches

For example, the relation among the elements of alliances of stock market speculators, who by means of artificial demand or sale influence prices of shares, are among such variables. The relations are in the form of regulations (logic implications) of the type: "if the A company shares are rising and the B company shares are sluggish then let us buy the C company shares". One can illustrate how it is possible to identify the existence of such relations and consequently the existence of alliances.

One will proceed from a classic definition of probability. The probability of the E phenomenon is defined as:

$$P(E) = \int_{\Omega} \chi_E(\omega) dP$$

where χ_E is a characteristic function of the set of E phenomena. Ω is a selective space and P is a probability rate.

At sharp phenomena, one assumes that the phenomenon with a certainty either belongs or does not belong into respective set (class of values). The characteristic function therefore gains values "0" or "1".

The probability of the fuzzy phenomenon is:

$$P(F) = \int_{\Omega} \mu_F(\omega) dP$$

where the characteristic function for the fuzzy set is created by the function, which gains values from the interval (0, 1). The probability of the fuzzy value gives us the probability of a random gaining uncertain value. For the discrete selective space $\Omega = \{\omega_1, \omega_2, \dots \omega_n\}$ one will get for the probability of the fuzzy phenomenon

$$P(A) = \sum_{i=1}^{n} \mu_A(\omega_i) P(\omega = \omega_i)$$

Similarly as for sharp quantities, one can only estimate the probability from data. At crisp data, one has to estimate to be based on frequencies; at fuzzy data one estimates to be based on the so called pseudo-frequencies.

The pseudo-frequency fuzzy value incidence is defined as:

$$N(\omega_1) = \sum_{i=1}^{n} \mu_A^i(\omega_1)$$

The pseudo-frequency of values belonging into the fuzzy set A is a sum of degrees of pertinence with which the particular values belong into the fuzzy set. It will not be a problem to find the estimation for a one-dimensional pseudo-frequency. For searching for relations identifying a possible alliance one need to estimate the joint probabilities.

7 Discussion

The results of alliance behavior are very sensitive on "phase" i.e. on the actual time delay with which information received is transformed into the sequence of events (run of system time). This knowledge resulted in the trials to construct "phase sensitive" systems modeling methodology, which could be able to respect this effect. There is probably not a matter of chance that this methodology has some significant similarities with the models of quantum physics [10].

Now let turn the attention to more general situations, when some alliances consist of parts being either nonlinear or uncertain (or both). As it was already mentioned, such situations appear in the case the complexity of alliance exceeds (e.g. in number of its elements) certain limit. This is typical situation namely for alliances consisting of specific elements – human beings with their highly complex information systems based on neural systems/brains. Here one has to face strong uncertainty factor resulting from the extremely high complexity of each human brain and un-ability to define firmly its actual properties, inner states respectively.

However, as uncertain for systems alliance operation have to be considered also other factors, like the impacts of environmental influences, some functional dependences or impacts of various independent variables (namely the time) and also the change of requirements on alliance properties and behavior. The last aspect can be considered as typical especially for alliances involving the living components as their properties and behavior can change in the course of gaining their experience and level of their knowledge, which of course can be for each such component different [11].

New tools/models utilizing synergy of Computer Science (Big data, Internet of things), Artificial Intelligence (Holonic or neural networks) and Systems Theory (Complex Systems/Alliances behavior) can help solving these complex tasks of tackling omnipresent uncertainty.

The authors are convinced that the ideas, concepts and methodologies of uncertain systems alliances could be fruitful also for the studies and applications of agent/holonic nets.

References

1. Vlček J.: Fabric of constructive theory of hybrid systems (in Czech: Návrh struktury konstruktivní teorie hybridních systémů). Vlcek's Seminars CTU, Faculty of Transportation Sci, CTU, Prague, May 2001
2. Novák, M., Votruba, Z.: Complex uncertain interfaces. In: Conference on ACMOS 2005, Prague, 13–15 March 2005
3. Votruba, Z.: Systems ideas for transportation, invited plenary lecture. In: WSEAS, Malta, 15 September 2005
4. Svítek, M., Votruba, Z., Zelinka, T., Jirovský, V., Novák, M.: Transport telematics - systemic view. 1st edn. 305 p. WSEAS Press, New York (2013). ISBN 978-1-61804-144-9
5. Votruba, Z: Reliability of information power. CTU in Prague, 32 p. (2005). ISBN 80-01-03186-1
6. Votruba, Z., Novák, M.: Alliance approach to the modelling of interfaces in complex heterogenous objects. Neural Netw. World. **20**(5), 609–619 (2010)
7. Broekstra, G.: On the representation and identification of structure systems. Int. J. Syst. Sci. **9**(11), 1271–1427 (1978). https://doi.org/10.1080/0020727808941775
8. Klir, G.J.: Fuzzy Sets, Uncertainty and Information. Prentice Hall, Engelwood Cliffs (1988)
9. Klir, G.J.: Uncertainty and Information – Foundation of Generalized Information Theory. Wiley, Hoboken (2006). https://doi.org/10.1002/0471755575
10. Svítek, M.: Towards complex system theory. Neural Netw. World (2015). https://doi.org/10.14311/NNW.2015.25.001
11. Novák, M., Votruba, Z.: Theory of System Complexes Reliability, pp. 46–67. Ed. Aracne editrice, Roma (2018). ISBN 978-88-255-0807-7

The Framework for Designing Autonomous Cyber-Physical Multi-agent Systems for Adaptive Resource Management

V. I. Gorodetsky[1], S. S. Kozhevnikov[2], D. Novichkov[3], and P. O. Skobelev[4(✉)]

[1] InfoWings Ltd., Lev Tolstoy str., 1/3, 197022 Saint Petersburg, Russian Federation
vladim.gorodetsky@gmail.com
[2] CIIRC CTU, Jugoslávských Partyzánů 1580/3, 160 00 Prague, Czech Republic
koz@kg.ru
[3] Business Center "Vertical", office 1201, Smart Solutions, Ltd., Moskovskoye Shosse 17, 443013 Samara, Russian Federation
novichkov@smartsolutions-123.ru
[4] Samara State Technical University, Molodogvardeyskaya str., 244, 443100 Samara, Russian Federation
petr.skobelev@gmail.com

Abstract. The paper contributes to design of autonomous cyber-physical multi-agent systems for adaptive resource management providing increase of efficiency of business operating in uncertain and dynamic environment. Evolution of multi-agent systems from purely decision-making support and simulation tool to cyber-physical system including Digital Twins and fully autonomous systems is analyzed. The main paper contribution is the proposed conceptual framework for designing autonomous cyber-physical multi-agent systems for adaptive resource management. It is shown in the paper that, in cyber-physical multi-agent systems for adaptive resource management, the ontology-customized multi-agent engine and ontology-based model of enterprise are forming ontology-driven "Digital Twin" of the enterprise providing opportunity to combine operational scheduling of resources with ongoing real-time simulations and evolutional re-design of configuration of enterprise resources. The functionality and architecture of the autonomous cyber-physical multi-agent systems for adaptive resource management are developed to support for the full cycle of autonomous decision making on resource management. Time metrics for measuring event-based response time and level of adaptability of autonomous cyber-physical multi-agent systems for adaptive resource management are proposed. Results of developments can be applied for smart transport and smart manufacturing, smart agriculture, smart logistics, smart supply chains, etc.

Keywords: Resource management · Autonomous systems · Model-driven · Cyber-physical multi-agent systems · Performance metrics

V. Mařík et al. (Eds.): HoloMAS 2019, LNAI 11710, pp. 52–64, 2019.
https://doi.org/10.1007/978-3-030-27878-6_5

1 Introduction

Cyber-physical systems (CPS) is a new concept of systems integrating computation, communication and control components, including cloud resources and services, sensors and actuators, as well as tools for interacting with users [1, 2].

Starting from automatic control and embedded systems, modern CPSs are being transformed into a powerful tools supporting for fusion of distributed information and interaction of real, social and virtual worlds, which can provide new opportunities for developing autonomous systems in different applications areas with intensive system-to-system and user-centric collaboration.

Multi-agent systems (MAS) are formerly applied mainly as decision making, planning and simulation tools [3, 4]. However, now they tend to become a natural part of CPS for operational management. As it stated in [4], "MAS technologies share common ground with CPS and can empower them with multitude capabilities in their efforts to achieve complexity management, decentralization, intelligence, modularity, flexibility, robustness, adaptation, and responsiveness".

One of the promising application areas of cyber-physical MAS (CP MAS) is adaptive resource management (ARM), where CP MAS are capable to increase client service level, efficiency of resources utilization, to reduce costs and risks caused by high uncertainty and dynamics of environmental event flow.

In our previous research, a number of planning and scheduling MAS implementing ARM were developed. They related to the areas of smart transport and manufacturing, supply chains, mobile field services, railways, etc. [5]. In a step-by-step way, MAS were transformed in CP MAS integrated with GPS and other real-time external sensors, as well as with handheld devices capable to send real-time updates for plans and new instructions to users which are able now to stay 24/7 online and be accessible for real time decision making.

As a next step in MAS developments, we are developing new conceptual framework for designing autonomous CP MAS for ARM supporting partially or fully autonomous decision-making applications. As a core part of such CP MAS, we are involving the "Digital Twin" technology that can help not only to connect agents with real world objects, but also to provide ongoing real-time simulations combined with operational management of resources and evolutional co-design for reconfiguration of enterprise resources. In result, Digital Twin technology helps to avoid bottlenecks, peaks of utilization or idle run of resources. The developed framework is now under implementation as digital platform of eco-system of smart services intended support for a wide range of smart applications in manufacturing, agriculture, logistics, etc.

In this paper, we start with short overview of CPS in different applications to analyze requirements for designing CP MAS for ARM (Sect. 1) and propose the conceptual framework for designing autonomous CP MAS for ARM (Sect. 3). It is also shown that the ontology-customized multi-agent engine (computational procedures) and ontology-based scene (data) in CP MAS ARM are forming ontology-driven "digital twin" (ODDT) of the enterprise, which can be separated from other source codes (Sect. 4). Such ODDT helps to combine operational scheduling of resources with the forecasting and real-time simulations of unpredictable event flows – in order to make system smarter via predicting and resolving bottlenecks, load peaks and idle runs of resources in advance thus improving key performance indicators of the operational management. As a next step of our efforts, the functionality and architecture of autonomous CP MAS for ARM is developed. In it, key temporal metrics for measuring event-based response time and adaptability of autonomous CP MAS for ARM are introduced (Sect. 5). In conclusion (Sect. 6) the potential applications are shown for transportation and manufacturing, logistics, mobile field services, supply chains, etc.

2 State of the Art

The potential applications of CPS cover potentially all types of human activity, including diversity of industrial systems, agricultural, transport, energy and military systems, many types of life support systems, starting from medicine to smart homes and cities, as well as economic and other systems.

The key feature of CPS is integrations of computation, networking, and physical processes. Embedded computers and networks with cloud-based computations monitor and control the physical processes with the further feedback loops from physical processes to affect computations and, vice versa, from computations to affect physical processes.

The idea to use different kinds of mathematical models to control objects in CPS is not new – a number of different deterministic models is considered in [1, 2] based on differential equations, synchronous digital logic and single-threaded imperative programs, etc. When possible, these models help to automatically compare expected results with actual information and generate signals for control parameters of physical processes.

For example, in agriculture CPS provide key technology for precise farming [6] being aimed for monitoring soil moisture for planning plowing, monitoring mineral content in soil for planning fertilization, monitoring weather for preventing freezing, monitoring crop growth for controlling diseases and pests, and managing yield. Full integration of CPS with smart devices in the Internet of Things is considered as an important step in automatic control of all processes of agricultural production, which ensures stability and adaptability to environmental and market changes [7].

As a next step in developing CPS, the concept of "Digital Twin" (DT) was introduced for Smart manufacturing 4.0 [8–10]. For a smart manufacturing shop floor, real-time monitoring, simulation and prediction of manufacturing operations are vital to improve the production efficiency and flexibility. CPS and DT technologies are introduced to build the interconnection and interoperability of a physical shop floor and corresponding cybershop floor. A "Digital Twin-based Cyber-Physical Production System (DT-CPPS)" is introduced as a configuring mechanism, operating mechanism and real-time data-driven operation control.

DT technology enables real objects (products, machines, humans, etc.) to link the current state of their processes and behavior in interaction with their computer models by using CPS and cloud computing. It gives opportunity to convert real objects into smart products that incorporate self-management capabilities based on connectivity and computing technology. In this case, simulation as a proven approach for analyzing of system behavior can be applied for conducting numerical experiments at a low cost. DT can be used not only during system design but also during runtime to predict system behavior online [11].

As a brief summary, today DT is usually considered as a number of "digital objects" with various available digital information about all stages of their life cycle mirroring the life of its corresponding "flying" real objects. Most of DT studies focused on the modelling concepts and frameworks of a CPS digital twin, but for autonomous managing of resources it requires development of the specific DT simulators, decision-making support systems, expert systems or recommendation or other services working on their own.

In this paper, we propose the new conceptual framework for developing autonomous CP MAS for ARM, which can work as an "Augmented Intelligence" for users in supporting their everyday decision making in operational resource management.

3 Ontology-Based DT in Autonomous CP MAS for ARM

Intensive flow of disruptive events of different positive or negative kinds (e.g. new order arrived or resource is unavailable, etc.) are becoming usually the norm rather than an exception and under these requirements CP MAS for ARM can solve critical issues for business efficiency, growth and sustainability [12].

The future of ARM is associated with highly connected "autonomous things" [13]. For example, in agriculture, an autonomous drone operating in the air will need to cooperate with a fully autonomous farming robot in a field and cloud-based real-time schedulers of humans, machines and fertilizers, finance resources, etc.

The autonomous CP MAS for ARM pretend to be able to manage fleet of any resources (humans or robots) in unmanned way without participation of dispatchers or specialists in management or logistics: orders are processed, scheduled, optimized, confirmed to clients and sent to workers or robots as instructions automatically.

This future vision is in agreement with the current trends in MAS developments [14] associating software agents with any physical, virtual or abstract objects. In this context, MAS tend to become a real time decision-making technology to provide adaptability of resource management on the top of CPS and DT technologies.

However, our practical experience proves that designing MAS requires digitalization of domain-specific knowledge strongly affecting the quality and the efficiency of decisions. During last decades, this issue addresses the ontology as becoming the key semantic component of MAS and as a tool for digitalizing domain-specific knowledge needed to agents for decision-making.

In our approach to adaptive resource management, we introduce basic ontology of resource management problem, which specify the main classes of concepts and relations relevant to adaptive resource management. Examples of concepts include such as "order", "task" and "process", "product", "resource" and some others, and examples of relations like process "consists" of tasks, task "requires" resource, task is "previous-next" for another one, etc. [15]. These concepts and relations are pre-built in associated basic classes of software agents, which can make "clones" (copies) of concept instances and customize their behavior based on these specifications.

The basic ontology gives possibility for specifying main aspects of any enterprise relevant for resource management, for instance:

- Organizational structure of enterprise;
- Products and their parts or components;
- Technology or business processes including tasks (operation);
- Resources including humans, machines, materials, finance, etc.

With the use of basic ontology, one can build an ontological model of enterprise by instantiation of above objects classes with instances those can be afterwards fueled by data coming from IoT platforms, users or any other systems or services.

Basic ontology extended to the problem domain of enterprise and ontological model of enterprise forms a knowledge base of enterprise constituting an ontology-driven DT (ODDT) to be filled in with the real data. In this concept, the ODDT represent past, present and future of enterprise including schedules for all orders and resources – as a mirror of real enterprise. In case of new unpredictable event, the system will adaptively change not only current states of objects, but also their plans for future and communicate these new plans with all relevant users. New updated plans could be provided to users via mobile devices for managing their activities and also for getting their feedback (drivers, workers, engineers, etc.). The conceptual framework of autonomous CP MAS for ARM is illustrated in Fig. 1.

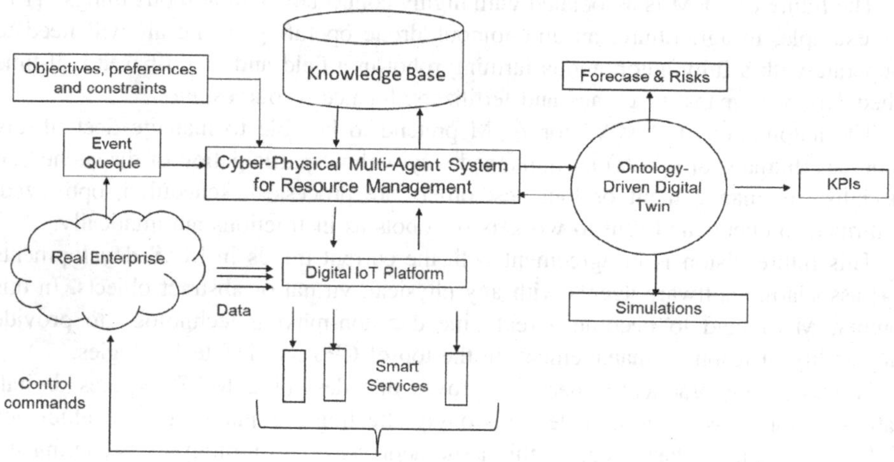

Fig. 1. Conceptual framework of autonomous CP MAS for adaptive resource management (ARM)

Using ODDT, agents can react to events, analyze situations and make decisions, as well as coordinate decisions on resource management with other agents and humans with the view of their objectives, preferences and constraints.

Users can not only set objectives for the system, change preferences and constraints, but also add new and remove out-of-date knowledge.

The ODDT resources management can be exemplified by smart farming where humans, machines, plants and other resources are managed semi-automatically. Not only agents of humans or machines can have plans here, but also agents of plants can access to knowledge base and see phases of their growth for ongoing analysis of how real plants are evolving on the real fields versus virtual plants growing on virtual fields. The detected gap (difference) between physical and virtual plants may cause CP MAS to adapt plans and form new control actions for agronomists or to initiate changes in the knowledge base because of climate changes and weather conditions.

The proposed ODDT can be used not only for operational resource management in real time, but also for real time simulations and what-if games, forecasting and risk analysis and comparing key performance indicators (KPIs) for different options of enterprise resource configurations.

In this context, the event life cycle becomes one of the most important characteristics of new CP MAS minimizing "Time-To-Go" delays as a time interval from the recognition an event in real world – to producing decision in virtual world – and to implement this decision back in real world.

The proposed framework of CP MAS for ARM will make these systems more autonomous and be able to manage real situations by analyzing events, adaptively forming plans of heterogeneous resource usage, monitoring and controlling execution of plans and running simulation-based predictions in parallel with operational management of enterprises.

The main advantage of the proposed approach is the possibility to change the DT model without re-programming of the CP MAS for ARM that can save a lot of time and money for customers.

4 Functionality and Architecture of Autonomous CP MAS for ARM

The functionality of designed autonomous CP MAS for ARM is aimed to support full cycle of autonomous resource management (Fig. 2).

The developed cycle could be considered as an extension of the well-known Deming cycle in the theory of organization management "Plan-Do-Analyze" [16]:

1. *Reaction on events* – collecting new events from real world manually or receiving information from sensors, external systems and mobile devices of users. Event queue is required for buffering events with specific policies.
2. *Allocation of resources* – matching orders to resources or resources to orders and pre-selection of the best suitable options.
3. *Planning and scheduling* – computing the best possible mode of order executions under given objectives, preferences and constraints for all parties involved.
4. *Optimization (if time resource is available)* – ongoing process of improving KPIs of developed schedule for all orders and resources.
5. *Forecasting* – process of forecasting of new events (new orders or failures), which need to be processed as a virtual events for dynamic pre-reservation of critical resources combined with recognition, assessment and analysis of risks.

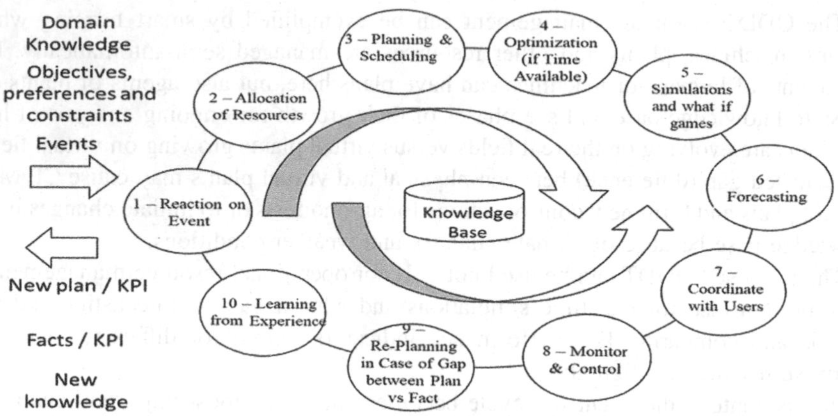

Fig. 2. Functionality of autonomous CP MAS for ARM

6. *Simulations and "What-If" games* – in parallel with the plan computation and execution, a few threads of simulations should be running in real-time mode to investigate future.
7. *On-line communication with users* – approve of decisions and recommendations, changing preferences and constraints or giving counter-proposals, initiating negotiations, fixing facts, signaling on exception issues or unexpected events.
8. *Monitoring and control of plans execution* – comparing planned and actual results and generating internal events on detected gaps with escalation of discovered problem situations to top-management.
9. *Re-scheduling in case of a growing gap between the plan and reality* – if there is growing gap between plan and fact and user is ignoring all recommendations system in some cases must be able to take decisions on its own.
10. *Learning from experience* – real time analytics of events, planned and actual time of tasks execution, for example, clustering of high-priority orders from VIP clients or efficiency of workers for future use and improve the plans.
11. *Evolutional re-design of enterprise resources* – generating proposals on "how-to" improve quality and efficiency of operations, for example, how to improve geographical position for storage or change its size, etc.

In practical applications, some of these stages could be eliminated to simplify the solution and implement it in budget and time for customers but for generic use it is "must-be" components of any CP MAS platform.

In future the developed cycle need to be supported on the level not only system as a whole but also on the level of each agent which also must be able to learn from experience, etc.

The architecture of the core part of CP MAS for ARM is illustrated in Fig. 3 and consists of the following components:

- *Ontology Editor* – aimed to formalize knowledge about the problem domain for resource management (represented as semantic network of classes of concepts and relations);
- *Knowledge Base of Enterprise* – contains instances of ontological classes for specific enterprise (ontological model of enterprise and concrete data);
- *Event Queue* – accumulates events incoming from the real world. Event queuing is regulated by policies for events processing;
- *Adaptive MAS Scheduling Engine* – consists of instances of agent classes to be executed, which are asynchronous software programs (objects) implemented and operating as state machines. Supports virtual market decision making logic and negotiation protocols with satisfaction and bonus-penalty functions [17]. Customized by knowledge base of enterprise;

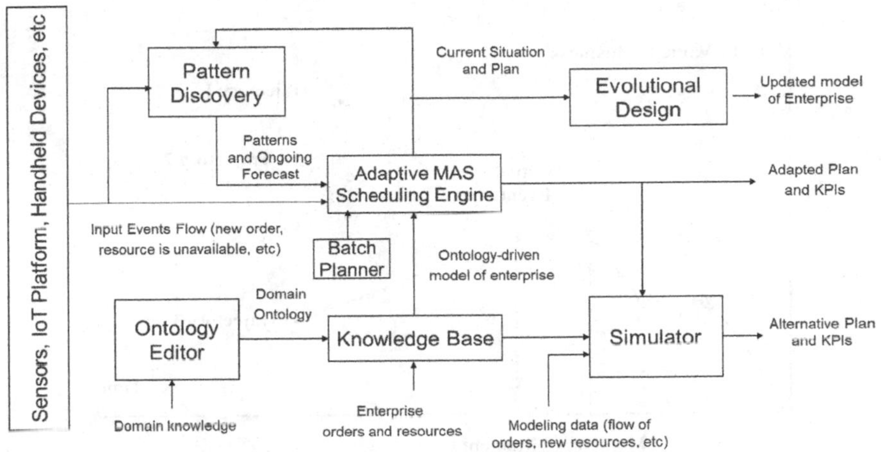

Fig. 3. Architecture of core part of autonomous CP MAS for ARM

- *Batch planner (optionally)* – represents classical planning and optimization tools for creating initial schedule (CPLEX, etc.);
- *Pattern Discovery* – software tools for pattern discovery and other data mining tools, for example, clustering tool;
- *Evolutional Design* – a tool for re-configuring enterprise resources in case of discovered bottleneck, etc.;
- *Simulator* – can copy scene from *Adaptive MAS Scheduling Engine* and run simulations in real time for forecasting.

The main output results of autonomous CP MAS is new adapted plan and new KPIs for the enterprise, but also it could be alternative plan and KPIs as well as an advise on how to re-configure the enterprise resources.

The central part of the solution is Adaptive MAS Scheduling Engine, which can be also used in Simulator. Adaptive MAS Scheduling Engine works with ODDT of enterprise, which is represented by the scene of the virtual world of agents. It consists of the past, present and future plans of all enterprise resources. In other words, the scene represents the model of situation with the current statuses of resources of the enterprise and what actions are proposed and planned. As a result, the combination of ontology-customized MAS Engine and ontology-based enterprise model constitutes ODDT not only as a data, but as a computational model which can be recomputed in real time in case of any new events or other changes in preferences, etc.

There are also IoT Platform, sensors, handheld mobile devices and other components providing data for ODDT.

The designed CP MAS is intended to work as a "co-pilot" with real business reacting on events, making plans and executing them in reality – as well as co-evolve with the business by acquiring new knowledge from users (pattern discovery) and modifying model of enterprise (evolutional design) in order to improve quality and efficiency of resource management.

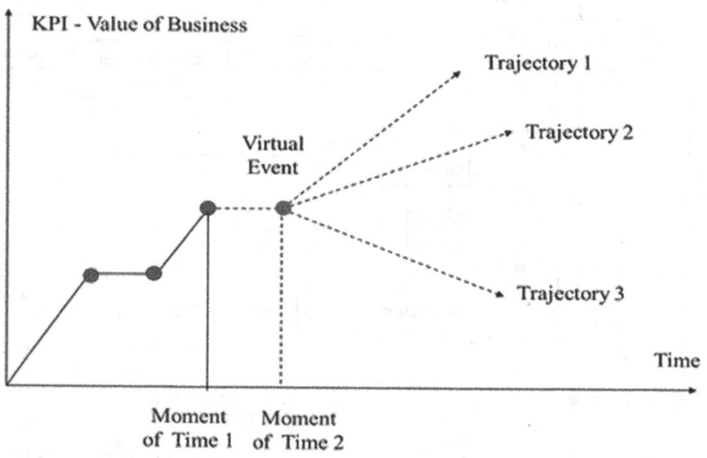

Fig. 4. Ongoing simulations in autonomous CP MAS for ARM

The proposed architecture provide possibility to run real time simulations in parallel with main trajectory of adaptive resource management (Fig. 4). For example, the weather forecast in agriculture at the Time instant 1 (right now) is saying that the heavy rain may take place in the Time instant 2 (in next 6 h). Nobody knows in advance whether it really happens or not, but CP MAS need to re-schedule agricultural operations for the fields, which could be affected by this rain and to plan other actions to mitigate risks. Such kind of "virtual event" can be introduced in the system and new trajectories will be scheduled in parallel with the main trajectory to investigate the future (how much will it cost, etc.).

5 Event Life Cycle Metrics for Autonomous CP MAS for ARM

Designed autonomous CP MAS is able to provide opportunity to measure the time-line of decision-making workflow and impact of each event or action taken by user with transparency for the enterprise on profits and losses.

The interaction between Physical and Cyber Worlds of autonomous CP MAS for ARM is shown on Fig. 5:

- new events are incoming to Physical World where they are registered and enter in the CP MAS;
- CP MAS is forming specification of current situation;
- CP MAS makes adaptive re-planning of available resources to address the event and produced adapted plan;
- the new adapted plan is negotiated by CP MAS with decision makers;
- agreed plan is communicated by CP MAS to executors (drivers, workers, etc.).

Let's define the Life Cycle of Event (LCE) in CP MAS which starts when new event takes place and completed when decision is planned and/or proposed actions are executed and value/impact of event is measured.

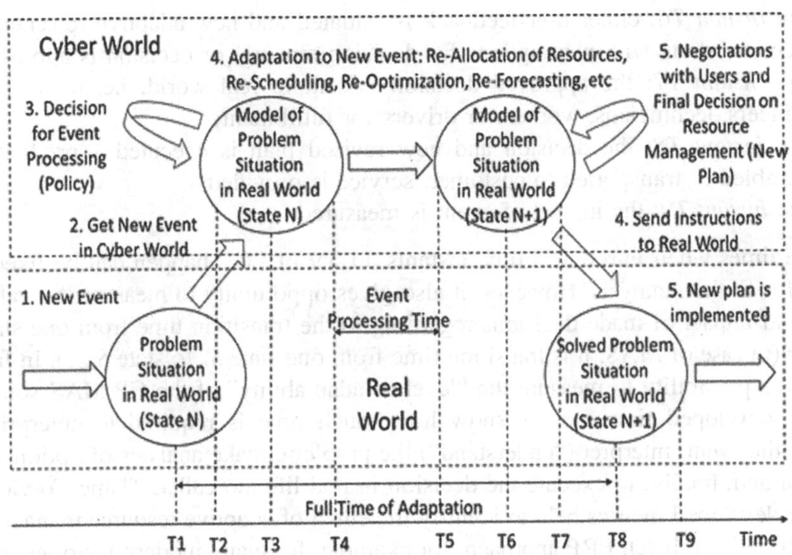

Fig. 5. Life cycle of an event in CP MAS for ARM

We consider examples of LCE for one positive event, which brings KPIs improvements and one negative event, which ruins KPIs of the system:

- for the event "new order is arriving", the LCE will start when new order is registered by users in the system and will be finished when system providing the

required product or required service delivers them to client (at that, some orders could be re-scheduled);
- for "resource unavailable" event, the LCE will start with such signal, but will finished when all affected orders (allocated for broken resource) are re-allocated to other resources.

The most important time metrics for LCE in CP MAS for ARM could be the following:

- *Time instant T1*: new event appears in real world;
- *Time instant T2*: new event is specified (attributed) by user manually or automatically;
- *Time instant T3*: based on given policy, the new event is automatically processed immediately or postponed while waiting for specific approval of authorized decision maker;
- *Time instant T4*: the event triggers resource re-allocation, re-scheduling and re-optimization in the system;
- *Time instant T5*: as a result of computations, the new decision, plan or recommendation is formed and presented to users for approval (or counter-proposal and negotiations: user also can ignore proposal, depending on policy for event processing), some decisions can go into real life automatically without approval of users;
- *Time instant T6*: either user feedback is initiated and new adaptive re-scheduling procedure starts with new options for decision making, or decision is approved;
- *Time instant T7*: the approved decision is sent to real world, i.e. to managers, engineers, technicians, workers or drivers for fulfillment;
- *Time instant T8*: the decision and new revised plan is executed – products are assembled or transported to customer, service is provided;
- *Time instant T9*: the impact of event is measured.

The times when introduced time instants T1-T9 of LCE happen can be fixed and stored for further analysis. However, it also gives opportunity to measure the value of event and impact of made decisions regarding to the transition time from one state to another (in case of MAS, it is transition time from one state S_n to state S_{n+1}). In fact, it also gives possibility to measure the "level of adaptability" of the CP MAS solution.

The developed time metrics show how much time is required to enterprise to register the event, interpret ("understand") the problem, make analysis of options, take decision and, finally, to execute the decision in real life (so called "Time-To-Go").

The developed metrics help to identify the effect of adaptive resource management versus traditional batch ERP approach, for example, for many modern factories, where plan, usually until now, has monthly granularity. Accumulated mistake of batch planning can generate big loss for enterprise because of not reacting to a new order, missing deadlines, etc.

The developed framework provides possibility to measure results and compare models, methods and tools for coordinated decision making in CP MAS for ARM.

6 Conclusions

The paper introduces CP MAS for ARM requiring growing autonomy of decision making.

The functionality and architecture of autonomous CP MAS for ARM are developed based on ontology-driven Digital Twin technology intended to supporting for operational management of resources as well as what-if simulations for forecasting.

Proposed time metrics for events life-cycle can help to measure level of adaptability of CP MAS and "Time-to-Go" for the autonomous decision making.

The described concept of autonomous CP MAS is now under implementation in a number of projects as applied to smart transport and smart manufacturing, smart farming, smart logistics and some other applications. In these applications, CP MAS is now designed to provide partial cycle of decision making, including semi-automatic reaction on events, adaptive re-planning of resources and monitoring of plans execution under full control of humans. However, already on this relatively not high level of autonomy, CP MAS is able to noticeably improve efficiency of resource usage, increase quality of the services, reduce of expenses, delivery time, risks and penalties. Combination of MAS, CPS and DT technologies will give new opportunity to move forward to "unmanned" managing of fleets of "unmanned" resources.

Full autonomy when autonomous CP MAS manages resources better than humans, will require much more time and efforts of researchers but first examples of such "uberisation" in enterprise resource management are already in place.

Developed CP MAS will allow enterprises to make step to real-time economy and Industry 5.0 based on digitalization of knowledge and automation of human's decision making.

Acknowledgments. This work is fulfilled with the financial support of the Ministry of Education and Science of the Russian Federation – contract № 14.578.21.0137, project unique ID is RFMEFI57815X013.

References

1. Lee, E.: The past, present and future of cyber-physical systems: a focus on models. Sensors **15**(3), 4837–4869 (2015)
2. Song, H., et al. (eds.): Cyber-Physical Systems: Foundations, Principles and Applications. Elsevier, Amsterdam (2016). 514 p
3. Leitão, P., Colombo, A., Karnouskos, S.: Industrial automation based on cyber-physical systems technologies: prototype implementations and challenges. Comput. Ind. **81**, 11–25 (2016)
4. Leitao, P., Karnouskos, S., Ribeiro, L., et al.: Smart agents in industrial cyber-physical systems. Proc. IEEE **104**(5), 1086–1101 (2016)
5. Rzevski, G., Skobelev, P.: Managing Complexity. WIT Press, Southampton (2014). 156 p
6. An, W., Wu, D., Ci, S., et al.: Agriculture cyber-physical systems. In: Song, H., et al. (eds.) Cyber-Physical Systems: Foundations, Principles and Applications, pp. 399–417. Elsevier, Amsterdam (2016)

7. Dumitrache, I., Caramihai, S., Sacala, I., Moisescu, M.: A cyber physical systems approach for agricultural enterprise and sustainable agriculture. In: Proceedings of the 21st International Conference, CSCS 2017, pp. 477–484. IEEE (2017)
8. Ding, K., Chan, F., Zhang, X., Zhou, G., Zhang, F.: Defining a digital twin-based cyber-physical production system for autonomous manufacturing in smart shop floors. Int. J. Prod. Res. (2019). https://doi.org/10.1080/00207543.2019.1566661
9. Leng, J., Zhang, H., Yan, D., et al.: Digital twin-driven manufacturing cyber-physical system for parallel controlling of smart workshop. J. Ambient Intell. Hum. Comput. **10**(3) (2018). https://doi.org/10.1007/s12652-018-0881-5
10. Delbrügger, T., Rossmann, J.: Representing adaptation options in experimentable digital twins of production systems. Int. J. Comput. Integr. Manuf. (2019). https://doi.org/10.1080/0951192x.2019.1599433
11. Gabor, T., Belzner, L., Kiermeier, M., Beck, M.T., Neitz, A.: A simulation-based architecture for smart cyber-physical systems. In: Kounev, S., Giese, H., Liu, J. (eds.) Proceedings of 2016 IEEE International Conference on Autonomic Computing, Wurzburg, Germany, pp. 374–379. Conference Publishing Services, Washington, July 2016. 978-1-5090-1654-9
12. Skobelev, P., Trentesaux, D.: Disruptions are the norm: cyber-physical multi-agent systems for autonomous real time resource management. In: Borangiu, T., Trentesaux, D., Thomas, A., Leitão, P., Oliveira, J. (eds.) Service Orientation in Holonic and Multi-Agent Manufacturing, vol. 694, pp. 287–294. Springer, Cham (2016). https://doi.org/10.1007/978-3-319-51100-9_25
13. Gartner Top 10 Strategic Technology Trends for 2019. Gartner. https://www.gartner.com/smarterwithgartner/gartner-top-10-strategic-technology-trends-for-2019/
14. Skobelev, P.: Towards autonomous ai systems for resource management: applications in industry and lessons learned. In: Demazeau, Y., An, B., Bajo, J., Fernández-Caballero, A. (eds.) Advances in Practical Applications of Agents, Multi-Agent Systems, and Complexity: The PAAMS Collection. PAAMS 2018. LNAI, vol. 10978, pp. 12–25. Springer, Cham (2018)
15. Rzevski, G., Skobelev, P., Zhilyaev, A., Lakhin, O., Mayorov, I., Simonova, E.: Ontology-driven multi-agent engine for real time adaptive scheduling. In: Proceedings of the International Conference on Control, Artificial Intelligence, Robotics and Optimization (ICCAIRO 2018), Prague, Czech Republic, 19–21 May 2018, pp. 14–22. IEEE (2018)
16. Deming, E.: Out of the crisis. In: The New Paradigm for Managing People, Systems and Processes, 500 p. The MIT Press (2000)
17. Skobelev, P.: Multi-agent systems for real time adaptive resource management. In: Leitão, P., Karnouskos, S. (eds.) Industrial Agents: Emerging Applications of Software Agents in Industry, pp. 207–230. Elsevier (2015)

Agent-Based Production Scheduling and Control

Plan Executor MES: Manufacturing Execution System Combined with a Planner for Industry 4.0 Production Systems

Petr Novák(✉), Jiří Vyskočil, and Petr Kadera

Czech Technical University in Prague – CIIRC, Jugoslávských partyzánů 1580/3, 16000 Prague, Czech Republic
{petr.novak,jiri.vyskocil,petr.kadera}@cvut.cz
http://ciirc.cvut.cz

Abstract. Industry 4.0 production systems have to enable flexibility in products, processes, and available production resources. Types of production resources can vary not only during maintenance process of the production systems, but also at runtime. Manufacturing recipes and assignments to production resources can no longer be hard-coded in automation and control systems, but the production has to be planned and scheduled dynamically with regards to the current status of the production systems and of customer needs. This paper proposes an architecture for a new generation of manufacturing execution systems that are tightly coupled with planners. The proposed approach is demonstrated on the Industry 4.0 Testbed use-case. An exemplary production plan deals with a robotic assembly of a construction made up from Lego bricks.

Keywords: Production system · Automation system · Planning · Control · Manufacturing execution system

1 Introduction

Current industrial production systems are becoming very complex and large-scale from their design and control perspectives. Components of production systems such as 6-axis robots, conveyor belts, work stations, or milling and 3D-printing devices have to be integrated in a flexible way to be able to react on changes in market needs. They can lead to redesigning products being manufactured on the production system, production system is frequently updated to be suitable for new types of goods, and the efficiency of the production and of the maintenance processes becomes very important for industrial stakeholders.

Operation of industrial production systems is automated by (industrial) automation systems. They have a hierarchically layered architecture, which is frequently called an automation pyramid. Many particular graphical expressions of the pyramid exist, depending on what aspects they emphasize. One of the

V. Mařík et al. (Eds.): HoloMAS 2019, LNAI 11710, pp. 67–80, 2019.
https://doi.org/10.1007/978-3-030-27878-6_6

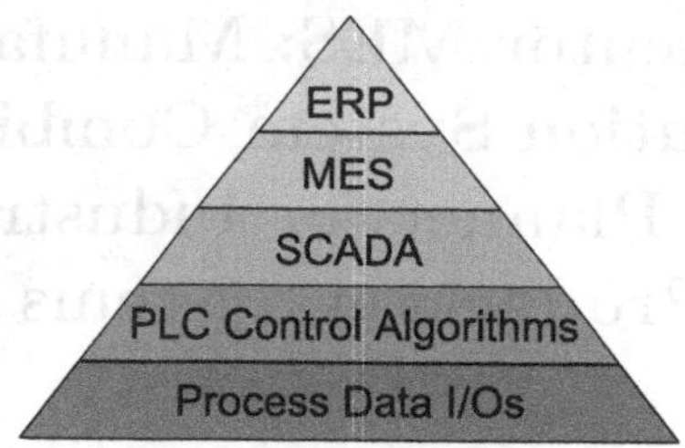

Fig. 1. Automation pyramid expressing the layered architecture of industrial automation systems. This paper contributes to the MES layer by extending it with a planner.

representations can be found in [9]. Although research effort as well as needs in industry tend to flatten the pyramid into a flexible dynamically re-configurable ecosystem as a part of the Industry 4.0 movement, the solutions being used in industry nowadays and in the near future still strongly rely on the hierarchical structuring. Due to this fact, we still consider the automation pyramid in this paper as a reference architecture for industrial automation systems.

The automation pyramid depicted in Fig. 1 represents the view on the data architecture in automation systems considered in this paper. On the very bottom layer, process data are measured by sensors in shop floor (i.e., process data outputs) and set up to control the shop floor (i.e., process data inputs). The low-level real-time control is done by programmable logic controllers (PLCs) or adequate hardware with equivalent functionality, which constitutes the second level of the automation pyramid. On the third level, a SCADA system (abbreviation standing for supervisory control and data acquisition) is a system that is intended to provide access to industrial plants, both for human operators and for upper software systems. The most visible part of SCADA systems are human machine interfaces (HMIs). They are intended to access runtime data by human operators, and to set up actions and set-points by them. They typically visualize trends, current values and their limits; they can violate alarms when any value exceeds its required limits. On the fourth level, there are manufacturing execution systems (MESs). They are responsible for executing production plans, assignment to manufacturing resources and reporting warehouse flows and product flows to the fifth level. MES systems play a role in improving manufacturing and financial performance of industrial companies [3] as many companies still rely either on manual planning and executing of production or utilize very basic MESs that are not capable even to re-order production tasks within a batch. On the fifth level of the automation pyramid, there is an enterprise resource planning (ERP) system. ERP is frequently considered as a synonym for SAP, but there exist many other ERP systems such as ABRA.

This paper is focused on improving the fourth level of the automation pyramid, i.e., on MES systems. They should no longer be simple monolithic systems, but they should consist of various sub-tools, including a planner and a digital twin for the real production system. The planning system should be generic and it should not be just a heuristics for a specific limited class of problems.

The remainder of this paper is structured as follows. Section 2 formulates the state of the art by summarizing related work in the areas of MESs and production planning. Section 3 presents the proposed improved architecture of MES systems equipped with planning, which enables not only planning of the production, but also re-planning when a problem occurs. The proposed architecture is demonstrated in Sect. 4 utilizing Industry 4.0 Testbed as use-case. The paper is concluded in Sect. 5 providing ideas for future work as well.

2 Related Work

Since the proposed approach emphasizes a tightly-coupled combination of MES and planner, the related work can be found in both domains, but with limited overlap between them in current solutions.

2.1 Manufacturing Execution Systems

Limited capabilities of commercial MESs are discussed in [1], which is mainly focused on distributed MES. The article identifies the basic common set of components of distributed MES: (1) order managers, (2) resource managers, (3) supervisors, and (4) brokers. This classification is in line with [15], dealing with strengths and threats of adopting multi-agent paradigm for industrial control especially on the MES level.

Among holonic architectures for MES, we have to remind the reference architecture PROSA [2]. The name refers to three basic types of holons: (1) product holons, (2) resource holons, and (3) order holons. Each of them is focused and responsible for a specific view on holonic MES and the operation of the system is driven by negotiation among these holons. The PROSA architecture has been extended and adapted in many ways, one of the most successful and famous is the architecture ADACOR [14]. ADACOR introduces four types of holons according to their functions and objectives: (1) product, (2) task, (3) operational, and (4) supervisor holons. The holon types (1)–(3) correspond to PROSA holon types, whereas the supervisor holon type is an extension in ADACOR that does not have an equivalent in the PROSA architecture. Although both PROSA and ADACOR are capable of solving a wide range of industrial tasks, they have not been widespread in industrial applications, excepting several pilot studies. The lessons learned from these reference architectures reflected in this paper are the focus on maximal utilization of current industrial systems used in practice and the focus on traditional way of thinking and programming rather than significant paradigm shifting as it was in strict holonic and multi-agent architectures.

Design of generic MES systems is discussed in [4]. The paper identifies the following key components of MES systems: "(1) Equipment management, (2) Production process management, (3) Quality management, (4) Order management, (5) Production scheduling management, (6) Resource management" [4].

After detailed discussion of these areas, utilization of Java 2 Platform, Enterprise Edition (J2EE) is proposed in [4], as it is platform independent and it is suitable for flexible implementation and integration of modules realizing the aforementioned needed components of MES.

Possible trends in MES development are discussed in [16]. They can be summarized as: "(1) cloud-based MES (2) IoT-based MES (3) intelligent MES (4) collaborative MES (5) supply chain linkage (6) MES mobility (7) industrial data analysis" [16]. An example of IoT-based solution for MES is discussed in [6], where IoT provides access to a broad range of sensor data.

MES functionalities can be implemented with the framework Eclipse BaSyx[1]. It is built on top of Eclipse framework. BaSyx is in progress and has not been finished yet. It should provide various communication possibilities including OPC UA and REST, a workflow engine based on BPMN 2.0, and support for various emerging industrial standards.

Integration between MES and ERP is standardized by ISA-95 [20]. This standard provides terminology and models for data integration and the approach presented in this paper is inline with ISA-95 modeling approach.

2.2 Automated Planning and Scheduling

The terms planning and scheduling are often used in different contexts with different meanings. Therefore, we have to first define these terms in the context of this paper.

Automated planning and scheduling (sometimes denoted AI planning [7,8]) is a branch of artificial intelligence that solves a problem of finding a plan (a set of tasks that need to be completed) that is represented as action sequences or action graphs (typically for execution by smart control systems, robots, or even for partial execution on various connected devices/autonomous agents) for given domains where allowed actions and related constraints are defined.

In fully specified environments with complete domain models available, planning can be done offline. Solutions/plans can be found and evaluated prior to execution. In dynamically changing environments (such as industrial production lines or shop floors), the plans frequently need to be revised online. Domains and policies have to be adapted. Finding such solutions usually tend to iterative trial and path finding/branching commonly seen in artificial intelligence. It includes machine learning, dynamic programming, and combinatorial optimization.

Planning refers to the action of establishing a plan, whereas scheduling is less concerned with what is being done and why, but more with when and where. A plan may (e.g., temporal planning) or may not (e.g., classical planning) incorporate times and dates associated to it, whereas a schedule most certainly will. Scheduling is concerned with mathematical formulations and solution methods of problems of optimal ordering and coordination in time of certain operations. Scheduling includes questions on the development of optimal schedules (Gantt charts, graphs) for performing finite (or repetitive) sets of operations.

[1] https://projects.eclipse.org/projects/technology.basyx.

The problems that scheduling deals with can be formulated as optimization problems for a process of processing a finite set of actions/jobs in a system with limited resources. In scheduling, the time of arrival for every action into the system is specified. Within the system the every action has to pass several processing stages, depending on the conditions of the problem. For every stage, feasible sets of resources are given, as well as the processing time depending on the resources used. Constraints on the processing sequence and actions are usually described by transitive anti-reflexive binary relations.

Given a description of the initial state of the world, a description of the goal conditions, and a formal specification of a set of possible actions, the planning task is to synthesize a plan that is guaranteed to generate a state (at the end) which satisfies all goal conditions.

For specification of planning tasks, several languages have been developed. *Planning Domain Definition Language* (PDDL) is supported by most state-of-art planners and we will use it also in this paper. The planning task/problem consists of two parts/files:

1. *domain description* – The problem-domain specification including every allowed *action* on state-space with its input parameters, *precondition* (condition that must hold before the action starts) and *effect* (description of changes on state-space immediately after the action is finished)
2. *problem description* – The specific planning-problem instance including its initial state and goal-state conditions.

A *solution* of some PDDL problem specified by its domain and problem description is a sequence of actions that can be sequentially applied (one by one) on the initial state of the problem and after application of all actions then the goal-state conditions of the problem are satisfied.

The latest version of the language is PDDL 3.1 [12] but there exist many variants/extensions that support various features like ontologies, probabilistic effects, numbers and goal-achieved fluents, durative actions (temporal planning), explicit problem decomposition (multi-agent planning) and others.

A selection of PDDL extensions including explanation of techniques in successful solvers is provided in [19]. A collection of simple prototypical industrial problems with their formalization in PDDL is presented in [18]. Compared to [18], the approach proposed in this paper is much more oriented to a real system of industrial scale, and we are able to utilize PDDL not only for planning but for digital twin (see Sect. 3.2) as well.

3 Proposed Architecture for MES

A large variety of current systems consist of relatively autonomous units. Such kinds of systems are frequently called systems of systems [11]. The problem of integrating autonomous units into one virtual system emerges not only in production system engineering, but also in many areas such as smart grids, water distribution networks, or logistics.

An important formal approach how to tackle these types of systems is a concept of multi-agent systems [22]. Although the multi-agent community has invested a lot of effort into a standardization of various properties and methods dealing with software aspects of distributed and multi-agent systems, the multi-agent or holonic systems still have not been widely spread in industrial applications. Due to this fact, the approach presented in this paper does not rely on any traditional multi-agent platform such as JADE, but uses a well-standardized communication protocol OPC Unified Architecture (UA), which is being widely adopted in industrial practice.

OPC UA is an industrial standard developed on a basis of the OPC classic specification and it combines data access, historical data access, and alarms & events into one unifying specification [13]. It is used for data acquisition from various distributed shop floor agents/actors such as PLCs, robot controllers, and smart sensors. Important benefit of OPC UA is that it is not limited for client-sever communication only, but it supports publish-subscribe communication as well. OPC UA is thus a privileged way for integrating the proposed MES with the two bottom-most layers of the automation pyramid.

From the top level side of the automation pyramid, we consider the traditional ERP systems to be used and we assume that manufacturing orders originate either in the ERP system, or they can be directly input via dedicated GUI, whose role is very crucial during commissioning of the system.

The overall proposed architecture of the MES accompanied with planner is depicted in Fig. 2. It includes fundamental components of the system (depicted with colored blocks) and data flows between them (depicted with numbered arrows).

In the previous text, we have already mentioned the shop floor layers of the automation pyramid (depicted in the bottom part of Fig. 2) to which the communication is solved via OPC UA (arrow numbered 8 in Fig. 2). As well, we have clarified relationships to ERP, which depicted in the upper part of Fig. 2.

The data flows are depicted in Fig. 2 by arrows and they have the following meaning, which is described in details in the subsequent paragraph:

1. Production order
2. Planning problem
3. Lisp plan without temporal information
4. Schedule as the lisp plan extended with temporal information
5. Production operation control based on OPC UA
6. Current and finished operations
7. Production status graph, statistics, and status
8. Status report about (semi-)products and warehouse flows to ERP
9. Re-plan order in case of a failure

The core part of the proposed approach is the Plan Executor (see the left-hand side part of Fig. 2). It accepts production orders from ERP or MES GUI (arrows 1a, 1b). The production order is passed (arrow 2) to the planner, which calculates the plan and if it exists, the planned production plan is provided to the scheduler (arrow 3). The plan extended with schedule information is

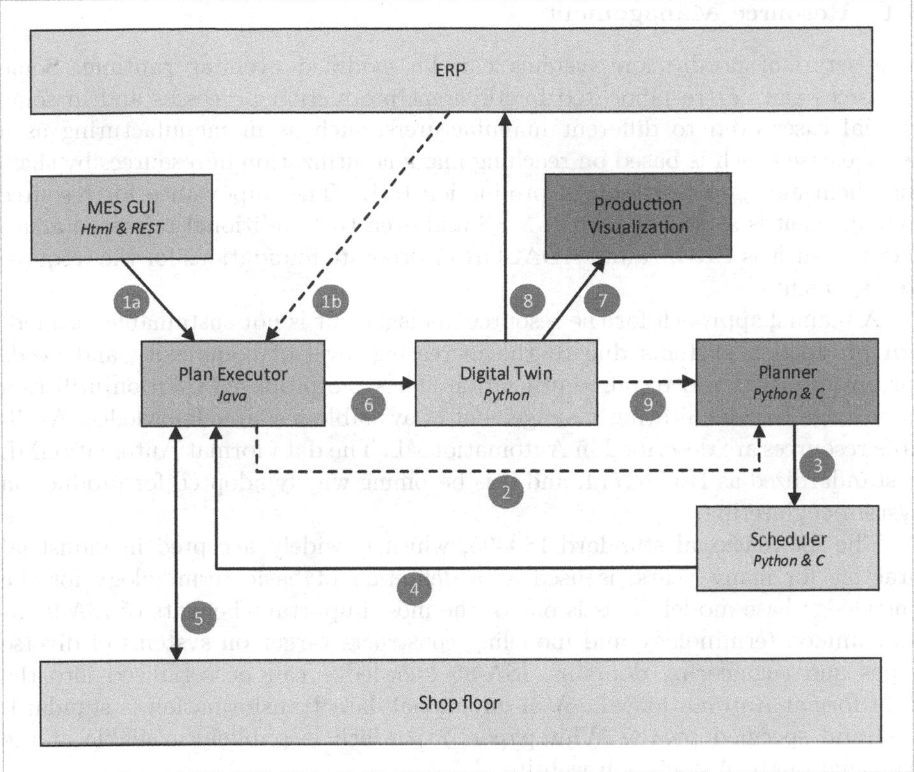

Fig. 2. Proposed architecture of the new generation of MES.

handed over back to plan executor (arrow 4). The plan executor parses this extended plan and considering OPC UA servers of production resource on the shop floor, it starts executing the plan. It starts such production operations on all resources, whose pre-conditions are satisfied. The communication related to starting operations on the shop floor and the backward notification about finished operation utilizes OPC UA (arrow 5). Checking the pre-conditions of remaining production operations and starting operations that can be started unless the production plan is finished are the main tasks of the plan executor. In addition, the plan executor updates the state of the digital twin (arrow 6) when any operation is started and finished. Hence, the digital twin has a detailed history of the production, which is important for visualizing the production for human operators (arrow 7). As well, warehouse status is updated in ERP system (arrow 8). Last but not least, if any failure happens, the digital twin detects such a problem and initiates re-planning (arrow 9). This is done in order to recover from the failure and to finish the production task.

3.1 Resource Management

The setup of production systems can be modified even at runtime. Some resources can be (re-)allocated for different production processes and in some special cases even to different manufacturers, such as in manufacturing as a service case which is based on reaching maximal utilization of resources by sharing them among a portfolio of production tasks. The importance for resource management is a crucial part of MES and even the traditional reference architectures such as PROSA and ADACOR incorporate foundations for the resource management.

A manual approach for the resource management is not sustainable for modern production systems due to the increasing level of complexity and needs for optimization and resource utilization. Thus the proposed solution utilizes a knowledge base facilitating management of available resource knowledge. Available resources are described in AutomationML. The data format AutomationML is standardized as IEC 62714, and it is becoming widely adopted for production system engineering.

The international standard ISA-95, which is widely accepted in industrial practice for many years, is used as a definition of basic terminology for the knowledge base model. This is one of the most important benefits of ISA-95 as its common terminology and modeling constructs target on systems of diverse types and engineering domains. ISA-95 knowledge can be serialized into the data format AutomationML. A bi-directional data transformation is standardized and specified by the Whitepaper [21], which is publicly available at the AutomationML Association website.

To be able to efficiently process the knowledge about the resources, we are using resource description in the AutomationML data format, with the use of ISA-95 terminology and models, and for processing purposes, we transform AutomationML to the AutomationML Ontology[2], which can be easily queried with SPARQL and new pieces of knowledge can be inferred with SWRL.

3.2 Digital Twin

A digital twin is a common term used for a digital replica of a physical system. Digital twins create living digital simulation models that update and change as their physical counterparts change. A digital twin continuously learns and updates itself from multiple sources to represent its near real-time status, working condition or position.

One of our contribution in this paper is to represent a digital twin by PDDL (see the Digital Twin module in Fig. 2). From PDDL point of view such a digital twin can be modeled and observed in the following way:

- Digital twin outer control signals need to be translated to PDDL actions that can be processes only under well specified conditions (PDDL preconditions)

[2] http://i40.semantic-interoperability.org/automationml/Documentation/index.html.

and that can have some effects to the internal digital twin state (PDDL effect on state-space).
- Interactions among digital twin components can be simulated by PDDL actions as well.
- The current PDDL state-space can access relevant output/sensor signals from digital twin sensors and returning values from digital twin components.

The major problem with creation of a digital twin, according to the previous points, is to translate outer control signals into PDDL actions. Sometimes PDDL actions need more information (as arguments) than the real outer control signals contain. In this case, the missing arguments need to be completed according to the preconditions of such actions.

Our PDDL digital twin can be used for the following different purposes:

- *Recomputation* of a new plan in case of failure or in case of any modification of production line.
- *Visualization* of the current state of the production line.
- *Global overview* that can support centralized, consistent, and formalized (computer readable) data source for further processing/analysis in related systems (e.g. ERP, predictive maintenance, etc.)

3.3 Planning and Scheduling

The task for the Planner module is to receive:

- The current status of a production line via the Digital Twin module.
- Goals of production from MES module.
- The specification of production line domain (operations/actions that are allowed on production line)

The output of Planner module is a sequence of operations/actions. The current implementation of Planner uses off-the-shelf Fast Downward Planning System [10].

The task for Scheduler module is to receive the output from Planner and creates a more detailed plan/schedule for MES module. For that purpose we developed a special format called *LispPlan*[3] that supports:

- *LISP like syntax* [5] that is human and computer readable. It can be quickly enriched by new features or we can easily encapsulate/translate this format into another more/better standardized format like XML.
- *Task and sub-task definitions* – tasks can be recursively divided into sub-tasks.
- *Locations* – description of resource location for each task.
- *Actions* – description of target actions/operations in PDDL format.
- *Requirements* – description of dependencies among tasks (tasks can be processed/executed in parallel).

[3] A short example of LispPlan is depicted in Listing 1.1.

The current implementation of Scheduler does not support scheduling tasks for concrete times and dates. Now, only accesses to resources are analyzed to produce LispPlan. In the future we would like to improve scheduling with time/duration support. For that improvement we can use algorithms based on widely studied and very successful Mixed Integer Programming [17] (as a part of combinatorial optimization techniques) or we can use temporal PDDL planners with durative actions support.

4 Industry 4.0 Testbed Use-Case

For the detailed explanation and evaluation of the proposed approach, this section describes the use-case dealing with the system Industry 4.0. The entire cyber-physical system is depicted in Fig. 3. The most apparent part of this experimental system is a monorail transportation system Montrac. It consists of rails called tracs, trac curves, trac switches, and positioning units that assure exact position of shuttles in working cells.

Three positioning units of the Montrac systems are accessed by four industrial robots. Each positioning unit is shared between two robots. This layout brings opportunity for cooperation between robots, which can be beneficial for example for final assembly.

The Industry 4.0 Testbed is equipped with industrial robots of the two types:

- 3x KUKA KR Agilus: Very fast industrial 6-axis robots programmed in the language KRL
- 1x KUKA LBR iiwa: Modern cooperative 7-axis robot programmed in the language Java

For testing purposes, assembling Lego bricks is used to evaluate designed approaches, algorithms, and tools in Industry 4.0 Testbed. The final Lego product is drawn in Lego Digital Designer[4]. This drawing is transformed to the problem file in the PDDL notation. The planner and scheduler are utilized to plan the production recipe in the form of LispPlan. The exemplary final product designed in Lego Digital Designer is depicted in Fig. 4. This assembly is uploaded via MES GUI to the Plan Executor, which hands it over to the planner. After planning the production operations, the plan is captured in the lisp plan format. An excerpt of the obtained production plan is shown in Listing 1.1. Subsequently, the production is scheduled and then executed by the Plan Executor by means of OPC UA communication to/from the shop floor.

[4] https://www.lego.com/en-us/ldd/download.

Fig. 3. Industry 4.0 Testbed at the Czech Technical University in Prague – CIIRC.

Fig. 4. Lego tower as a product to be built by the production system, exported from Lego Digital Designer 4.3.11.

Listing 1.1. Production plan example for the Lego tower

```
(define
  (task LegoProduct)
  (:location "testbed.ciirc.cvut.cz")
  (define
    (task 0)
    (:location SHUTTLE1)
    (:action (SHUTTLE_MOVE_LOCK SHUTTLE1 STATION3 STATION2))
  )
  (define
    (task 1)
    (:location SHUTTLE2)
    (:action (SHUTTLE_MOVE SHUTTLE3 STATION10 STATION100))
  )
  ... Skipping lines ...
  (define
    (task LegoAssembling)
    (:location R1)
    (define
      (task 0)
      (:action
        (PICKUP_ROTATION0 R1TABLE X-6 Y4 Z1 00 BLACK)
      )
    )
    (define
      (task 1)
      (:requirements 0)
      (:action
        (PUTDOWN_ROTATION0 SHUTTLE1 X-5 Y-2 Z1 00 BLACK)
      )
    )
    (define
      (task 2)
      (:requirements 1)
      (:action
        (PICKUP_ROTATION0 R1TABLE X6 Y4 Z1 00 BLACK)
      )
    )
    (define
      (task 3)
      (:requirements 2)
      (:action
        (PUTDOWN_ROTATION0 SHUTTLE1 X-5 Y2 Z1 00 BLACK)
      )
    )
  ... Skipping lines ...
  )
)
```

5 Conclusion and Future Work

To provide flexibility of production systems, manufacturing execution systems have to be prepared to fulfill flexibility requirements. The proposed architecture for a new generation of MES supports planning of production plans. Furthermore, when a problem in a production plan that is just being executed occurs, the continuously running digital twin provides the needed support for re-planning the remaining part of the production and continuing the manufacturing process. This is the issue that current commercial tools do not support.

The important strength of the presented approach is that the overall solution has been implemented on a prototype level and it has been deployed and tested in Industry 4.0 Testbed. It was utilized as a foundation for further testing of scientific and practical applications of methods and algorithms for Industry 4.0.

In the future work, we would like to strengthen the distributed nature of MES and to leverage it to a distributed MES. We would also like to integrate the proposed MES as a module that is able to cooperate with a commercial MES to make this approach better accessible for industrial partners without needs for significant re-implementations of current production plant setups.

Acknowledgements. The research presented within this paper has been supported by the DAMiAS project funded by the Technology Agency of the Czech Republic, by the H2020 project DIGICOR, and by the OP VVV DMS project Cluster 4.0.

References

1. Bratukhin, A., Sauter, T.: Functional analysis of manufacturing execution system distribution. IEEE Trans. Ind. Inf. **7**(4), 740–749 (2011). https://doi.org/10.1109/TII.2011.2167155
2. Brussel, H.V., Wyns, J., Valckenaers, P., Bongaerts, L., Peeters, P.: Reference architecture for holonic manufacturing systems: PROSA. Comput. Ind. **37**(3), 255–274 (1998). https://doi.org/10.1016/S0166-3615(98)00102-X
3. Chao, L., Qing, L.: Manufacturing execution systems (MES) assessment and investment decision study. In: 2006 IEEE International Conference on Systems, Man and Cybernetics, vol. 6, pp. 5285–5290, October 2006. https://doi.org/10.1109/ICSMC.2006.385148
4. Fei, L.: Manufacturing execution system design and implementation. In: 2010 2nd International Conference on Computer Engineering and Technology, vol. 6, April 2010. https://doi.org/10.1109/ICCET.2010.5486065
5. Gabriel, R., Steele, G.: The evolution of Lisp. In: Companion to the 23rd ACM SIGPLAN Conference on Object-oriented Programming Systems Languages and Applications, OOPSLA Companion 2008. ACM, New York (2008)
6. Gao, Q., Li, F., Chen, C.: Research of internet of things applied to manufacturing execution system. In: 2015 IEEE International Conference on Cyber Technology in Automation, Control, and Intelligent Systems (CYBER), pp. 661–665, June 2015. https://doi.org/10.1109/CYBER.2015.7288019
7. Ghallab, M., Nau, D.S., Traverso, P.: Automated Planning - Theory and Practice. Elsevier, Amsterdam (2004)

8. Ghallab, M., Nau, D.S., Traverso, P.: Automated Planning and Acting. Cambridge University Press, Cambridge (2016)
9. Harjunkoski, I., Nyström, R., Horch, A.: Integration of scheduling and control - theory or practice? Comput. Chem. Eng. **33**(12), 1909–1918 (2009). https://doi.org/10.1016/j.compchemeng.2009.06.016
10. Helmert, M.: The fast downward planning system. J. Artif. Intell. Res. **26**, 191–246 (2006). https://doi.org/10.1613/jair.1705
11. Jamshidi, M.: Systems of Systems Engineering - Principles and Applications. CRC Press Taylor & Francis Group, Boca Raton (2008)
12. Kovacs, D.L.: Complete BNF description of PDDL 3.1. Language specification, Department of Measurement and Information Systems, Budapest University of Technology and Economics (2011). https://helios.hud.ac.uk/scommv/IPC-14/repository/kovacs-pddl-3.1-2011.pdf
13. Lange, J., Iwanitz, F., Burke, T.J.: OPC - From Data Access to Unified Architecture. VDE Verlag, Berlin (2010)
14. Leitão, P., Restivo, F.: ADACOR: a holonic architecture for agile and adaptive manufacturing control. Comput. Ind. **57**(2), 121–130 (2006). https://doi.org/10.1016/j.compind.2005.05.005
15. Mařík, V., McFarlane, D.: Industrial adoption of agent-based technologies. IEEE Intell. Syst. **20**(1), 27–35 (2005). https://doi.org/10.1109/MIS.2005.11
16. Pan, F., Shi, H., Duan, B.: Manufacturing execution system present situation and development trend analysis. In: 2015 IEEE International Conference on Information and Automation, pp. 535–540 (2015). https://doi.org/10.1109/ICInfA.2015.7279345
17. Pochet, Y., Wolsey, L.A.: Production Planning by Mixed Integer Programming. Springer, New York (2006). https://doi.org/10.1007/0-387-33477-7
18. Rogalla, A., Fay, A., Niggemann, O.: Improved domain modeling for realistic automated planning and scheduling in discrete manufacturing. In: Proceedings of the 23rd IEEE International Conference on Emerging Technologies and Factory Automation (ETFA), pp. 464–471 (2018). https://doi.org/10.1109/ETFA.2018.8502631
19. Sousa, A.R., Tavares, J.J.P.Z.S.: Toward automated planning algorithms applied to production and logistics. IFAC Proc. Vol. **46**(24), 165–170 (2013)
20. Unver, H.O.: An ISA-95-based manufacturing intelligence system in support of lean initiatives. Int. J. Adv. Manuf. Technol. **65**, 853–866 (2012). https://doi.org/10.1007/s00170-012-4223-z
21. Wally, B.: Application recommendation provisioning for MES and ERP - support for IEC 62264 and B2MML. AutomationML e.V. c/o IAF, 7 November 2018. https://www.automationml.org/o.red/uploads/dateien/1542365399-AR_MES_ERP-1.1.0.zip
22. Weiss, G. (ed.): Multiagent Systems, 2nd edn. Massachusetts Institute of Technology, Cambridge (2013)

Multi-agent Supply Planning Methods Allowing the Real-Time Performance of the Supply Network Management Systems

Alexander Tsarev(✉)

ICCS RAS, Samara, Russia
a@tsarev.info

Abstract. The paper deals with the questions of how to develop the automated planning systems that are fast enough to be used in real-time management of supply networks, considering the manual plan corrections by the users. Several practical situations and planning system use cases are considered. The paper proposes several methods that allow the increase of the data processing speed in practical cases. The methods include parallel data processing, dynamic control of the solutions space depth search, self-regulation of the system behavior based of the specifics of the data processed.

Keywords: Distributed planning · Self-regulation · Parallel processing · Coordination · Performance · Real-time scheduling · Real-time management · Multi-agent planning · Supply network · Supply chain

1 Introduction

Effective management always required a permanent re-evaluation of the available options, planning, modelling and making in-time decisions based on this analytical work. Finally, the success depends on how good the analysis is, and how fast it is.

Just making a good optimization is not enough anymore. Growing complexity and dynamics of modern business demand new paradigms in resource management [1, 4]. New approach to increase efficiency of business is associated today with the real-time economy, which requires adaptive reaction to events, ongoing decision making on resource planning, optimization and communication results with decision makers. This is especially important in supply network management, as it is a highly competitive environment with many participants trying to be fast and efficient all the time.

The main feature of real-time scheduling and optimization methods is the ability to produce a result fast enough to cope with the changes in the input data (events). It means that the model or the plan should be re-evaluated, re-built before the next significant change comes (new order, order cancellation, resource availability, etc.).

Multi-agent technology is considered to be a design methodology and framework to support distributed problem solving methods in real-time scheduling and optimization of resources [5, 6].

Figure 1 illustrates the difference in actuality of scheduling results (how well they reflect reality) in the changing environment. Having frequent data updates, it becomes

V. Mařík et al. (Eds.): HoloMAS 2019, LNAI 11710, pp. 81–95, 2019.
https://doi.org/10.1007/978-3-030-27878-6_7

more important to process them faster to get a valid result (green line). Otherwise, one can use a lengthy processing to get an optimal result (yellow/red line), but this result does not consider the last changes. Then, we are forced to always base your decisions on an optimal, but outdated picture.

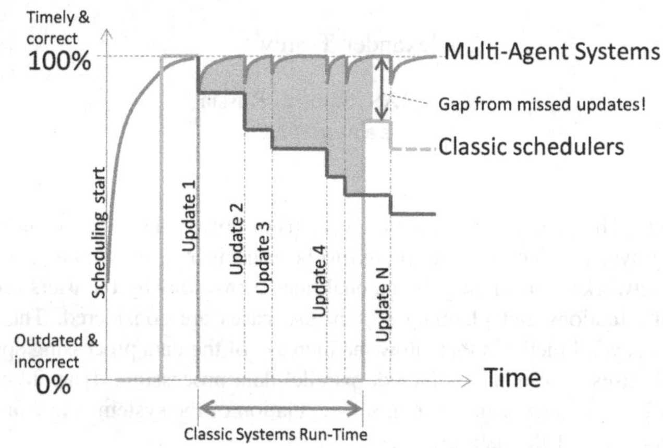

Fig. 1. Real-time adaptive scheduling effects. (Color figure online)

The quality and efficiency of decision making in resource scheduling and optimization process can be influenced by the number of factors: the intensity of events flow, the number and current state of resources, individual specifics of orders and resources, time interval between the events and processing time for events, productivity of resources and many others.

A big challenge is to ensure that certain quality of scheduling results is achieved in a short time after the event to make it possible to finish the processing before the next event and to always have a valid schedule needed for decision-making.

Although the multi-agent approach allows fast reaction to events, it still requires methods to ensure the processing time is short enough to produce results before the next event.

2 Task Definition and Practical Cases

In order to effectively manage supply networks, you need, first of all, to build a plan for the operation of the entire network and keep it up to date in a constantly changing environment. Efficiency at the same time depends on two main parameters: the quality of the plan (how high indicators are achieved when it is executed) and the speed of its re-building in response to events. These two parameters are in conflict, so the planning method should ensure the best quality of the plan, achievable in a characteristic time between successive events entering the system.

The quality of a plan when managing supply chains is usually determined by how much demand closes (which is directly related to income) and how much money is required to spend on executing this plan (expense). In practice, the expenditure part may include not only real costs, but also conditional, associated with administration, reputational risks, etc. But it is proposed to use a linear combination of revenue and all consumable parts with coefficients that regulate the importance of each component as the basic overall objective function of the network.

$$Q = k^R R - C$$

R - total satisfaction of needs $R = \sum k_i^r r_i$, r_i - satisfaction of an individual demand (ratio of the satisfied quantity to the need), k_i^r - need importance factor (assigned automatically, the more urgent the need, the higher the coefficient).

The cost (cost of the plan) may be different for each case of the supply network. For example, for the task of material support, taking into account several projects in the supply network:

$$C = k^{Co} C^o + k^{Cf} C^f + k^{Cp} C^p + k^{Ca} C^a + k^{Ct} C^t$$

C^o - conditional administrative costs of transfer between owners.
C^f - conditional administrative costs of transfer from free stocks.
C^p - conditional administrative costs for transfer between projects.
C^a - the cost of using analog.
C^t - the cost of transportation in the logistics network.
$k^R, k^{Co}, k^{Cf}, k^{Cp}, k^{Ca}, k^{Ct}$ are weight coefficients.

The analysis showed that for most tasks it is convenient to apply a linear function of dependence of satisfaction coefficients on their remoteness in time:

$$k_s^{d\,default}(\Delta t) = \begin{cases} k_s^{d\,max}, \Delta t \leq t_s^{min} \\ k_s^{dmax} - \frac{\left(k_s^{d\,max} - k_s^{d\,min}\right)\left(\Delta t - t_s^{min}\right)}{t_s^{max} - t_s^{min}}, t_s^{min} < \Delta t < t_s^{max} \\ k_s^{d\,min}, \Delta t \geq t_s^{max} \end{cases}$$

where t_s^{min} is the end of the "red" zone (the rest of the time, in which, as a rule, nothing can be fixed), t_s^{max} is the beginning of the "green" zone, where plans can change more than once and there is not much point in planning so far, $k_s^{d\,min}$ - the coefficient of importance of orders at the node s in the "green" zone, $k_s^{d\,max}$ - the coefficient of importance of orders at the node s in the "red" zone.

The method itself should not impose significant restrictions on the form of the objective function.

The solution in the system should be achieved through distributed agent negotiations, which are guided by individual objective functions. In order to better match the solution achieved as a balance of interests of individual agents, the overall objective function of the supply network, the network agent (headquarters agent) should be able to provide targeted feedback to the agents' needs and resources.

In various situations, in the process of the agents, and for the weighted evaluation of the planning results, other performance indicators may be used.

We used the described model to build the systems for mass production and distribution (LEGO, Coca-Cola), energy production and distribution, railway cars supply, construction supply.

For LEGO the main focus was to dynamically reschedule the replenishment of the products in the network of the brand retail stores in USA based on the sales forecast, current stocks and supply network limitations. The supply network included 50 retail stores, 3 distribution centers, about 1000 products.

For Coca-Cola in Germany we built the system to automatically schedule the order execution in real time as the orders are placed by the customers. The goal was to improve the order fulfillment and reduce the transport costs, especially in the peak seasons. The task included production and transportation scheduling in the distributed supply network of 300 DCs and 8 factories.

Energy production and distribution model included up to 100 energy production points including big coal plants as well as small solar and wind production and energy accumulation. It allowed dynamical rescheduling of the production at different plants and redistribution of flows in response to the changes in consumption forecasts, production power limitations and price.

Railway cars supply case was about redistribution of about 30000 cars of different types in the railway network of about 1000 production sites, ports, customers to ensure that they have enough cars to deliver their products.

Construction supply case deals with several interconnected networks related to big construction sites in oil industry. It focuses on in-time delivery of all components needed for construction in difficult weather conditions with many unpredicted transportation limitations, multi-modal delivery using trucks, railways, ships and helicopters. The supply scheduling includes the planning of transportation resources as well as loading-unloading equipment and personnel.

3 Proposed Methods

3.1 Distributed Parallel Processing

First of all, the most obvious approach we used to improve the performance is to do things in parallel. We see that for practical application of the planning software in open market involving several independent companies, it is important to let the companies have different policies, isolated data processing, and standardized API for interaction between different planning systems.

At the same time, it is crucial for planning scalability to perform the planning in a distributed, but coordinated way, to reduce processing time, but keep the plans synchronized.

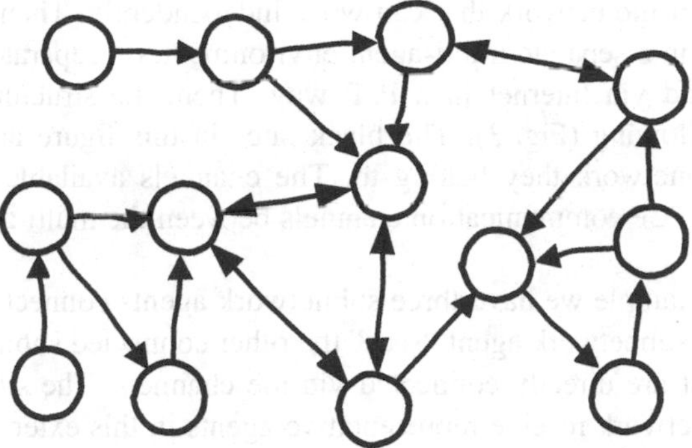

Fig. 2. Abstract example of the supply network.

Based on the multi-agent approach, it is possible to solve the problem in a distributed way, running software agents on the company-related hardware instead of the central server. This approach is very suitable for solving tasks in open environments. However, it is important to consider that the structure of the energy grid can change dynamically (customers and suppliers can connect and leave the network).

To illustrate the proposed approach to the distributed coordinated planning, let's consider the abstract network example shown in Fig. 2. Each node (site) in the network may supply or consume, and the channels are used to deliver the energy to other sites. Currently, the developed software prototype uses a separate agent for each site, and thc agents communicate and negotiate in the single environment.

The internal constraints of each site in the network are hidden from external actors and affect the result via the restrictions and costs calculated and presented to neighbor sites in the network during negotiations.

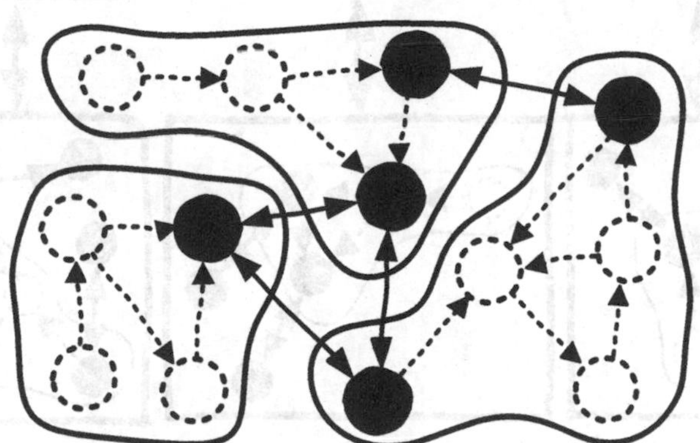

Fig. 3. Example of the network segmentation.

The further development of the planning software is seen in the establishment of subnetwork agents or company agents (depending on the situation) that are responsible for separate parts of the network that can work independently. Then, each subnetwork may be processed in a separate multi-agent environment, on separate remote hardware units interconnected via Internet in a P2P way. Then, the structure of the example changes to the following (Fig. 3). The black sites in this figure are the only visible outside of the subnetwork they belong to. The channels available between the sub-networks form the P2P communication channels between the multi-agent environments (swarms).

Thus, in this example we have three subnetwork agents connected via P2P service bus (Fig. 4). Each subnetwork agent "sees" the other connected subnetwork agents and the site agents that are directly connected via the channels. The sites that are visible from another subnetwork receive representative agents in this external network. These representative agents have limited functionality and only accept requests from other agents in the subnetwork to deliver them later to the real agent in another swarm. They also receive results (including planned limitations and costs) from the real agent and may respond fast to local requests inside the subnetwork swarms they are delegated to considering the previously detected limitations.

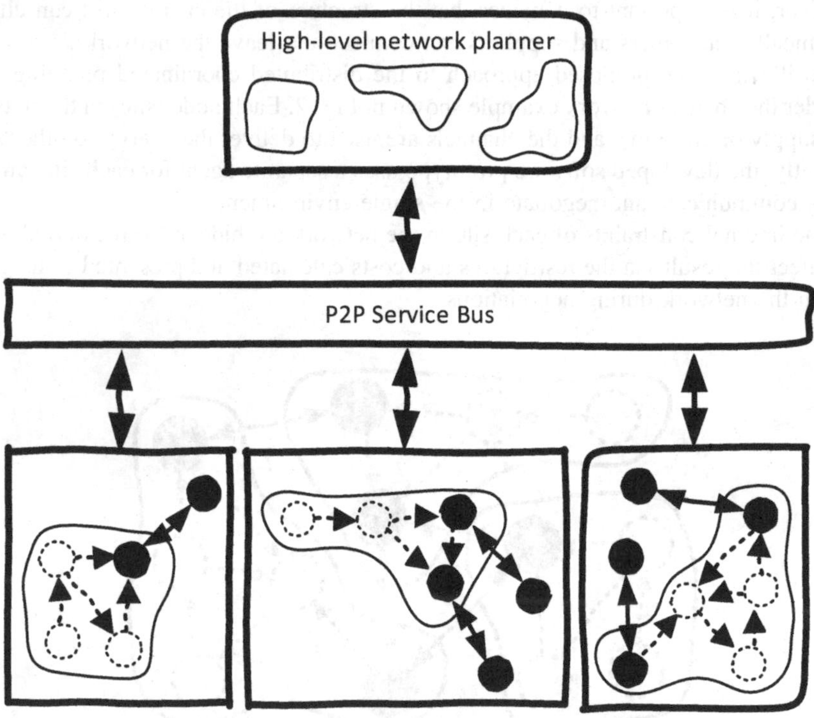

Fig. 4. Distributed architecture.

The planning principle is that any event is processed first inside the directly influenced multi-agent environment (planning application). If the result of this processing includes new supply requests to external sites or new supply limitations and costs affecting the existing contracts, the subnetwork agent negotiates changes with other subnetwork agents in the network.

The subnetwork agent is also responsible for the intensity and reasonability of the communication between the subnetworks (or companies). It may introduce additional virtual costs on the external requests, and thus motivate the local agents to solve the problems locally. It also decides when to coordinate with other subnetworks depending on how many changes (events to be sent) are accumulated and how fast the other agents respond.

It is important to note that the distributed coordinated planning system may include not only automatic multi-agent software planners, but also legacy planning software and even manual planning software depending purely on users. In this case, these software components are also connected to the same service bus using the same protocols and API. Users can see the incoming events, requests and limitations from other subnetworks, and can propose decisions based on the current plans, available options and target KPIs.

3.2 Asynchronous Processing

We compared two different approaches to the organization of multi-agent interaction in relation to the supply scheduling. One approach is based on request and reply and follows the rejection presumption principle, which means that if no reply is given it is an equivalent of rejection (sender must wait for an answer). This approach is referred to as rejection assumed interaction in the paper. Another approach is based on the acceptance presumption principle, which means that without explicit rejection from the counterpart of communication the acceptance of request is assumed. This approach is referred to as acceptance assumed interaction in the paper. Of course, this relates to the requests that do not require an informational feedback, but only ask another site to do something, while the feedback is optional.

Following the rejection presumption principle, the sites cannot process next request until they get a response from other sites regarding the previous request. Thus, in our case the Storage A becomes a bottleneck because both shops ask it first (as potentially cheaper source), and it cannot answer them both until Storage B answers the request. For example, the request processing is blocked at the Storage A on the steps ‘c’, ‘d’, and ‘e’ on the following diagram (Fig. 5), which leads to the delay of the processing of the request from the Shop Y on step ‘g’.

Specifically, when Storage A gets a request from Shop Z at step ‘c’, it sends a request for this product to Storage B (as it does not have it in the stock). When the request from Shop Y comes (almost the same time as from Shop Z), it cannot be processed until the request to Storage B is accepted.

We consider only one product in the network in the paper, so the orders compete for the same stock. If you get requests for different products, they theoretically may be processed immediately one after another, but this is an abstract situation. In practical tasks there are much more interdependencies between resources and demands other than just product type. For example, the channel capacity between Storage A and

Storage B, or the dispatch capacity at Storage B can be limited, or the transportation cost may depend nonlinearly on the volume transported. This prevents Storage A from answering the second request even if it is for a different product, until the acceptance of the first delivery is received (or assumed).

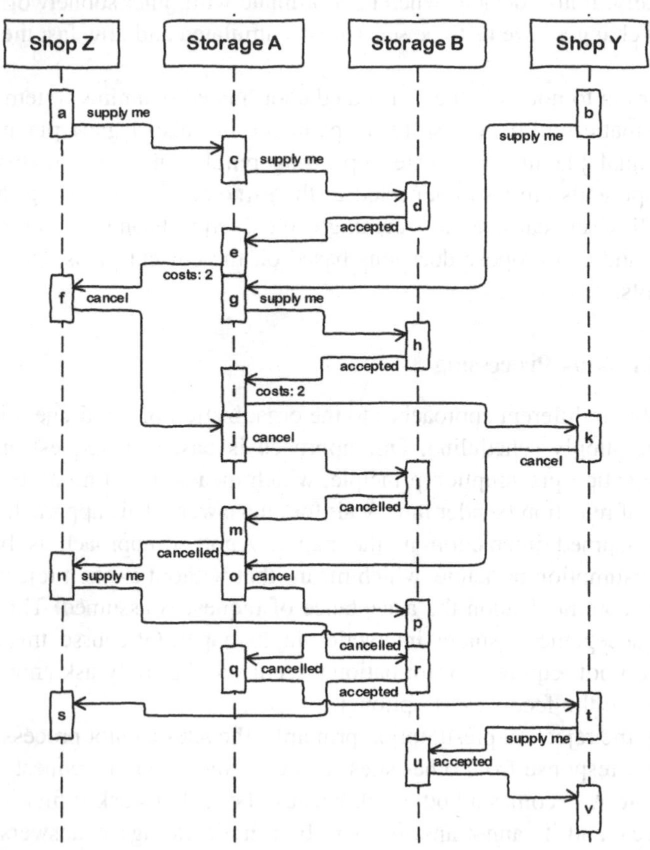

Fig. 5. Competitive interactions with rejection presumption.

The complete processing of the two orders with this approach takes 22 steps. Considering that some of them are done in parallel and some of them are very quick, this exact sequence takes 12.4 tu (time units).

Actually, we do not consider here the fully synchronous interaction that requires all events to be processed separately. It means that the order from the Shop Z is completely processed first, and only then the processing of the order from the Shop Y starts. This forces the whole sequence to go in one thread and take 16.6 tu.

The next diagram (Fig. 6) shows the interactions using acceptance presumption protocols.

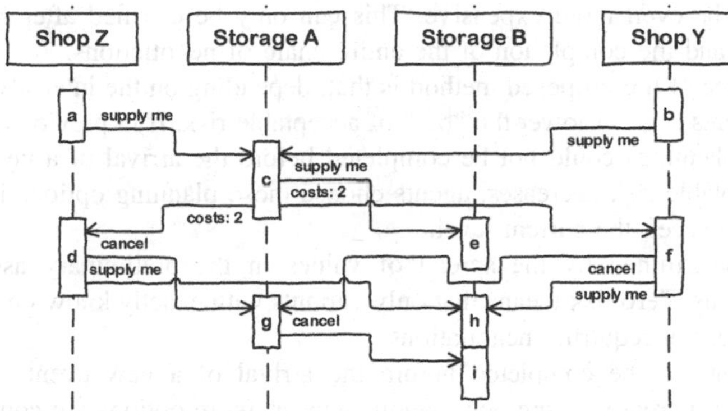

Fig. 6. Competitive interactions with acceptance presumption.

We can see that, in this example, the structure of the interactions is the same as in the case where we have only one order. The significant difference from the rejection presumption case is that at some steps several requests are processed by the site simultaneously. From one point of view, such steps should take more time, but from the other point of view, the processing of several requests at once never takes more time than separate processing of the same requests. What is more important, having several requests at once allows avoiding blind decisions that should be re-considered when the next request comes.

3.3 Self-regulation of the Processing Time

To ensure high speed of event processing, a method has been proposed that allows automatic adjustment of the duration of event processing by agents.

When choosing a planning option, each agent considers several possibilities and assesses them in terms of potential benefits. Normally, the agent, when he decides with whom to try to reach an agreement, chooses the most promising. But usually at this stage (before, in fact, negotiations) it is impossible to determine exactly what the negotiations will lead to. Therefore, there is always a chance that time will be spent, and the result will not improve.

In a situation where events are rare, you can consider more risky options, if they can potentially give a better result. If there is not enough time for processing, it is more reasonable to choose the option with the least risk (as a rule, with less negotiations) in order to get the result quickly.

For example, an agent may need a choice of how to deliver a product: request that it be added to a half-empty delivery or offer another need (later) to make room in a delivery that is full.

In the first case, a preliminary assessment will give more shipping cost, because half-empty delivery is less effective and more expensive. But at the same time there are almost no risks that it will not be possible to agree with the delivery agent.

In the second case, the cost of delivery is potentially lower (that is, more profitable), but there is a risk that a later need will not be able to find a resource for itself or the resource will be even more expensive. This can only be clarified after a request for another need and the completion of the entire chain of negotiations.

The essence of the proposed method is that, depending on the intensity of the flow of events, agents raise or lower the "bar" of acceptable risk. If in previous iterations of planning it (planning) could not be completed before the arrival of a new event, the level of acceptable risk decreases, agents choose those planning options in which the risk does not exceed the current level.

Risk is determined by the spread of values in the preliminary assessment of planning options. Zero risk means that only variants with exactly known results will be considered, i.e. not requiring negotiations.

If planning can be completed before the arrival of a new event, the level of acceptable risk increases, more negotiations appear, more options are considered.

3.4 The Method of "Negative Experience"

To improve the quality of planning without increasing its duration, it is proposed to introduce into the planning method an element of self-study, which consists in the following.

After reaching equilibrium and completing the planning iteration, the network agent (headquarters agent) evaluates the received plan for the overall network objective function. If the plan is improved, the staff agent initiates the iteration of the improvement in accordance with the "weak link" method. If the plan has worsened, the changes are not only canceled, but each agent in the chain of negotiations that led to deterioration, associates the magnitude of the deterioration with those agents with whom he entered into negotiations.

The next time when an agent considers a planning option, it not only assesses how much this option will improve its objective function, but also reduces this estimate if this option requires negotiations with those agents with whom there were previously negative results.

Thus, first of all, variants without "negative experience" are considered, which increases the probability of finding a better solution sooner.

4 Analysis of the Results

To determine the features of the developed methods, studies were conducted on the nature of the dependence of the processing results on various parameters of input data, incl. on their quantity. In a series of experiments, a model supply network with 30 suppliers, 100 distribution nodes and 1000 consumption points was used.

The dependence of the planning time on the number of orders was checked. At the same time, it is necessary to distinguish the number of orders and the volume of demand, because, unlike the volume of demand, each order can have its own preferences, purchase cost, delivery time and other parameters. In the series, the number of orders varied from 5 to 100 per node in the network, and for each value 8 separate experiments were carried out to eliminate the influence of random factors on the processing time. The measurement results show that the dependence of the planning time on the number of orders is close to linear (Figs. 7 and 8).

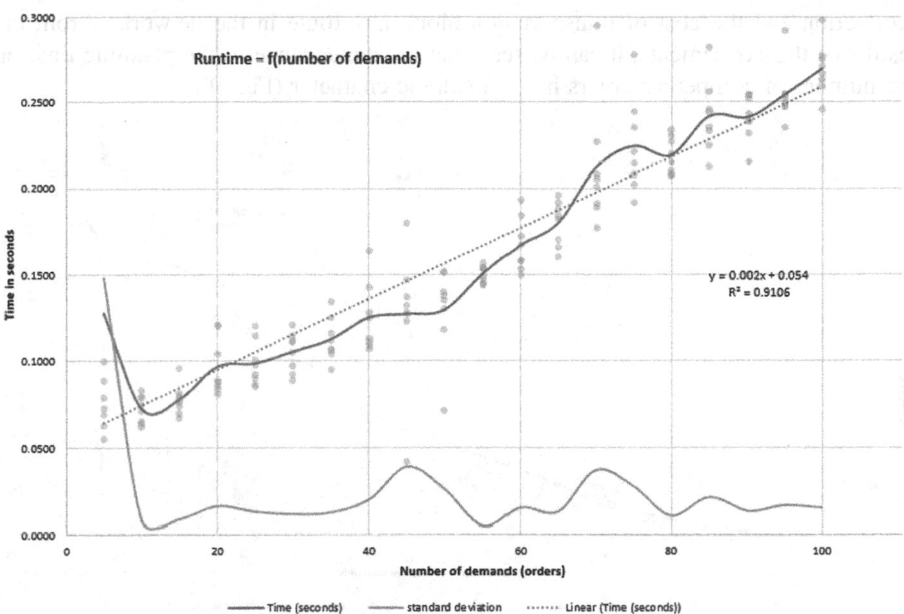

Fig. 7. The dependence of the duration of planning on the number of orders

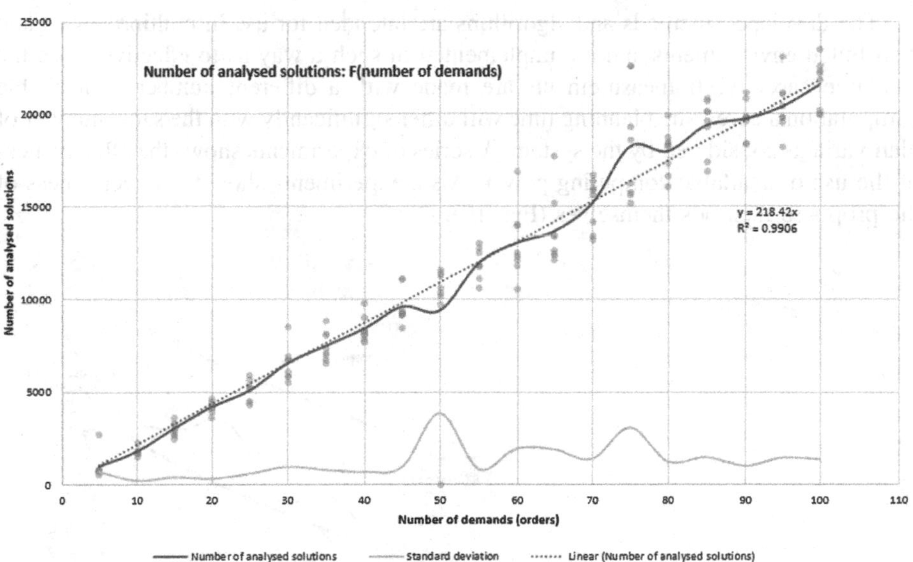

Fig. 8. Dependence of the number of analyzed solutions on the number of orders

In another series of experiments, the dependence of the planning time on the number of competitive orders is considered. At the same time, all orders are given the same price, high enough for any of them to be profitable (taking into account the cost of production and the cost of transportation along any route in the network). From the results of the experiments, it can be seen that the dependence of the planning time on the number of competing orders has a quadratic character (Fig. 9).

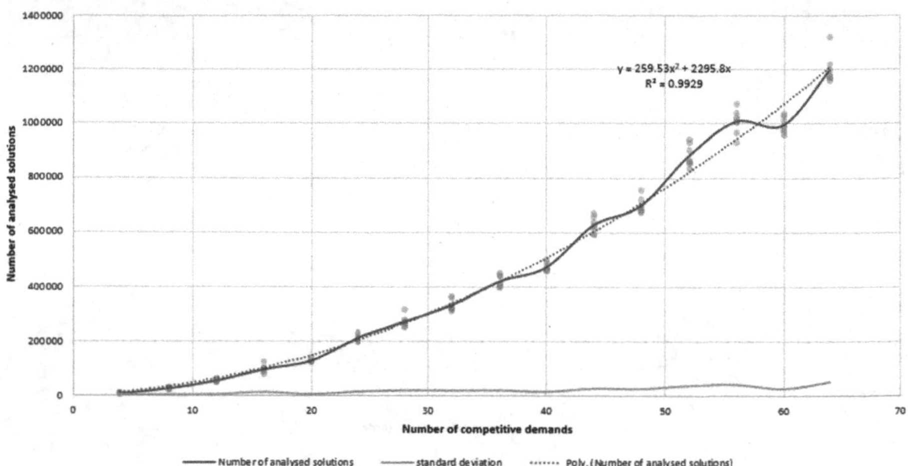

Fig. 9. Dependence of the number of analyzed solutions on the number of competitive orders

The developed methods and algorithms are intended for use in multiprocessor and distributed environments and are implemented in such a way as to effectively use the available capacity. If measurements are made with a different number of available computational cores, the planning time will differ significantly with the same number of plan variants considered by the system. A series of experiments shows the effectiveness of the use of available computing power. Also, experiments show the effectiveness of the proposed methods themselves (Fig. 10).

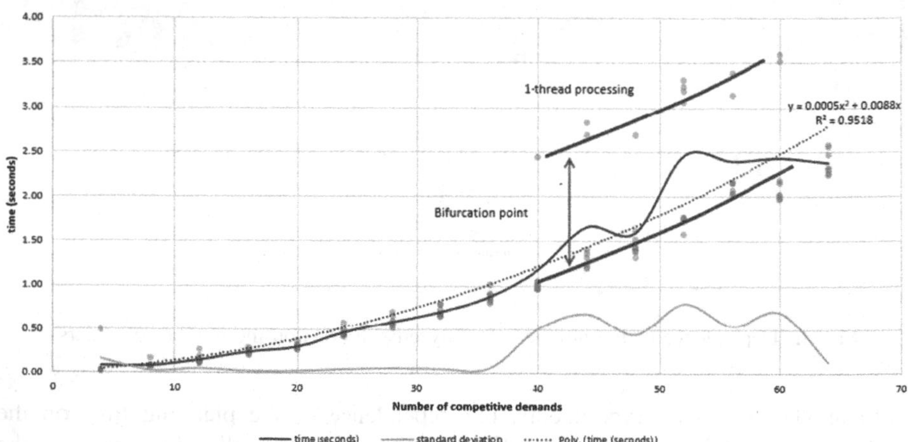

Fig. 10. Effect of parallel async processing

The choice of the approaches described in 3.2 depends very much on the specific practical case characterized by structure of the network and competitiveness of the demands. In general, more distributed networks are better processed using acceptance presumption approach. We used a real case data including more than 300 sites in the network (part of which is fully interconnected) and about 10 000 orders to model different interaction protocols. The network to be scheduled includes several factories, their storages that can interexchange materials and final products, and customer distribution centers that should be supplied. The model also includes production scheduling and some other features that affect the processing time in different situations. The modelling has been done using 16-core processor. The table below shows the results of the comparison (Fig. 11).

	Processing time (ms)	Messages between sites	Achieved quality ($)
Fully synchronous processing	737236	3200	1813499
Rejection presumption	191334	3140	1813359
Acceptance presumption	50275	2333	1812240

Fig. 11. Agent negotiation approaches comparison

The slight difference in quality between the synchronous processing and the rejection presumption most probably happens because of asynchronous stock competition between different orders.

Comparing the last two rows we can see that the use of acceptance presumption approach gives us 3.8 times faster processing and decreases the quality by about 0.1%, which seems to be a fair price in most cases.

A series of experiments was conducted in which the methods developed were compared with the simplex method. The number of consumers in the series increased from 50 to 300. Every consumer could receive products from any supplier. In this case, the total size of the network (the complexity of the problem) is determined by the number of possible delivery methods from the supplier to the consumer (the number of delivery channels). The total production capacity, its distribution over the network, the cost of production and transportation were set randomly for each individual experiment in the series.

According to the experiments, the processing time of an individual event remains approximately the same for any network size. It averages 14 ms, which is about 10 times faster than full rescheduling for a network with more than 250 customers.

The paper is prepared based on the results of the state financed research of ICCS RAS AAAA-A19-119030190053-2 “Development and analysis of the methods of analytical construction, digital knowledge representation, computing algorithms and multi-agent technologies used for optimisation of the control processes of complex systems”.

5 Conclusion

Based on the practical applications of the developed methods and the analysis we did it can be said that they allow achieving better results in terms of scheduling speed. Thus, they are especially useful in the tasks where real-time processing is needed.

Distributed parallel processing methods improve equipment utilization and can be applied efficiently in almost any practical case. Asynchronous processing also provides improvement in processing speed in multi-thread and distributed environment, but the specific approach should be chosen based on the specific practical case. Self-regulation and "negative experience" methods improve the real-time performance of the supply network scheduling systems by adapting the agent negotiations to the specific demand patterns and network structure, and make the dependence of the processing time on the number of demands more linear.

The future research will include the extension of the self-regulation methods with more parameters taken into consideration and automatically switching negotiation approaches based on the scheduling results evaluation.

References

1. Matsune, T., Fujita, K.: Designing a flexible supply chain network with autonomous agents. In: ICAART 2019, vol. 1, pp. 194–201 (2019)
2. Toader, F.A.: Production scheduling in flexible manufacturing systems: a state of the art survey. J. Electr. Eng. Electron. Control Comput. Sci. **1**, 1–6 (2017)
3. Rzevski, G., Skobelev, P.: Managing Complexity. WIT Press, Boston (2014)
4. Park, A., Nayyar, G., Low, P.: Supply Chain Perspectives and Issues: A Literature Review. Fung Global Institute and World Trade Organization, Geneva (2014)
5. Mohammadi, A., Akl, S.: Scheduling algorithms for real-time systems. Technical report, no. 2005–499, School of Computing Queen's University, Kingston (2005)
6. Joseph, M.: Real-Time Systems: Specification. Prentice Hall, Verification and Analysis (2001)
7. Pinedo, M.: Scheduling: Theory, Algorithms, and Systems. Springer, Heidelberg (2008)
8. Leung, J.: Handbook of Scheduling: Algorithms, Models and Performance Analysis. CRC Computer and Information Science Series. Chapman & Hall, London (2004)
9. Binitha, S., Sathya, S.: A survey of bio inspired optimization algorithms. Int. J. Soft Comput. Eng. **2**(2), 2231–2307 (2012)
10. Sun, S., Li, J.: A two-swarm cooperative particle swarms optimization. Swarm Evol. Comput. **15**, 1–18 (2014)
11. Tasgetiren, M., Sevkli, M., Liang, Y., Yenisey, M.: Particle swarm optimization and differential evolution algorithms for job shop scheduling problem. Int. J. Oper. Res. **3**(2), 120–135 (2008)
12. Vittikh, V., Skobelev, P.: Multiagent interaction models for constructing the demand-resource networks in open systems. Autom. Remote Control **64**(1), 162–169 (2003)
13. Chevaleyre, Y., et al.: Issues in multiagent resource allocation. https://staff.science.uva.nl/u.endriss/MARA/mara-survey.pdf. Accessed March 2015

14. Barbuceanu, M., Fox, M.S.: Coordinating multiple agents in the supply chain. In: Proceedings of the fifth Workshops on Enabling Technology for Collaborative Enterprises, WET ICE 1996, pp. 134–141. IEEE Computer Society Press (1996)
15. Stockheim, T., Schwind, M., Wendt, O., Grolik, S.: Coordination of supply webs based on dispositive protocols. In: 10th European Conference on Information Systems (ECIS), Gdańsk, 6–8 June 2002
16. Oliinyk, A.: The multiagent optimization method with adaptive parameters. Artif. Intell. J. **1**, 83–90 (2011)

Operationalization of a Machine Learning and Fuzzy Inference-Based Defect Prediction Case Study in a Holonic Manufacturing System

Phillip M. LaCasse[1(✉)], Wilkistar Otieno[1], and Francisco P. Maturana[2]

[1] University of Wisconsin – Milwaukee, Milwaukee, WI 53211, USA
placasse@uwm.edu
[2] Rockwell Automation, Milwaukee, WI 53201, USA

Abstract. Industry 4.0 capabilities have enabled manufacturers to collect and analyze smart manufacturing data across a broad array of diverse domains including but not limited to scheduling, production, maintenance, process, and quality. This development necessarily proceeds in a logical sequence by which first the organization develops the capability to capture and store this data and, at best concurrently but frequently lagging, develops and refines the competencies to analyze and effectively utilize it. This research presents an applied case study in surface mount technology (SMT) manufacture of printed circuit board (PCB) assemblies. Parametric data captured at the solder paste inspection (SPI) station is analyzed with machine learning models to identify patterns and relationships that can be harnessed to preempt electrical defects at downline inspection stations. This project is enabled by the recent conclusion of an Industrial Internet of Things (IIoT) capability enhancement at the manufacturing facility from which the data is drawn and is the logical next step in achieving value from the newly-available smart manufacturing data. The operationalization of this analysis is contextualized within the *product-resource-order-staff architecture* (PROSA) of a Holonic Manufacturing Systems (HMS). A Trigger Holon is nested between the Resource Holarchy and Product Holarchy that, at scheduling, distributes implementation instructions for the defect-prediction model. The Defect Prediction Holon is containerized within the Product Holarchy and provides instructions for corrective action when the model flags a record as exhibiting increased probability of a downline electrical defect.

Keywords: Ball grid array · Solder paste inspection · Surface mount technology · Printed circuit board · Defect prediction · Machine learning · Holonic manufacturing system

1 Introduction

A holonic systems approach is one in which complex systems are divided into autonomous and cooperating functional entities called holons, a term proposed by Arthur Koestler in his book, The Ghost in the Machine [1]. The word “holon” is an amalgamation of the Greek word for “whole” and the Greek word for “entity” or “part”.

V. Mařík et al. (Eds.): HoloMAS 2019, LNAI 11710, pp. 96–104, 2019.
https://doi.org/10.1007/978-3-030-27878-6_8

A holon, therefore, is an independent entity but is also a subset or piece of a larger whole, subject to control from a central supervisory entity [2].

A Holonic Manufacturing System (HMS) applies the concepts of a holonic system to the manufacturing context in such a way as to combine the best features of hierarchical systems[1] and heterarchical systems[2]. As a check and balance against the rigid structure of a hierarchical system, individual holons have autonomy to act and make decisions. To guard against the low predictability of the flatter heterarchical control architecture, holons work together in a loose hierarchy, where a single holon can be a member of multiple hierarchies but those hierarchies are not necessarily permanent [3].

The product-resource-order-staff architecture (PROSA) reference architecture for the HMS was introduced by Van Brussel et al. as a framework for HMS containing four basic types of holons: process, resource, order, and staff holons [4]. The PROSA reference architecture maps coherently to manufacturing functions of logistics, task/order instances, and task/order types.

This research conceptualizes the operationalization of a smart manufacturing case study in defect prediction within the PROSA reference architecture for an HMS. The case study employs machine learning models to predict defects in printed circuit board (PCB) assemblies employing ball grid array (BGA) package types during assembly. The pilot stage of the case study, detailed in a manuscript currently submitted for review in International Journal of Data Science and Analytics, has produced sufficiently encouraging results on pilot datasets that the project has transitioned to development of a conceptual and data architecture framework supporting real-time defect prediction for the in-progress PCB assemblies.

2 Background

2.1 PCB Manufacturing Process

In PCB manufacture on a surface mount technology (SMT) line, a BGA package type is a means to affix components such as microprocessors to the PCB. Solder spheres are deposited on the component in a grid that contains, for each solder sphere, a corresponding pad on the PCB. The component is temporarily affixed to the PCB using a wet solder paste, and the assembly then passes through a reflow oven to activate the fluxes, melt the solder spheres, and form a mechanical and electrical connection between the component and PCB. Figure 1 contains a cross-section of a PCB and affixed BGA package, prior to the reflow stage.

[1] In a hierarchical control architecture, levels of control have specific functionality with strict relationships constraining control decisions from one level to the next.

[2] In a heterarchical control architecture, distributed locally autonomous entities cooperate with each other directly but without higher-echelon oversight or control.

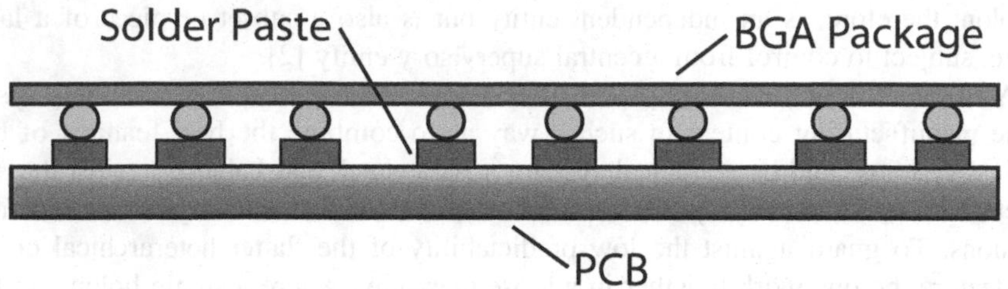

Fig. 1. PCB with BGA package, prior to reflow

BGA package types are of interest because, after the mechanical and electrical connection has been formed, defective components are costly to rework and require a higher-level skill set in the operator. The earlier in the SMT process that a BGA defect can be preempted, the better, since the cost of rework exponentially increases down stream.

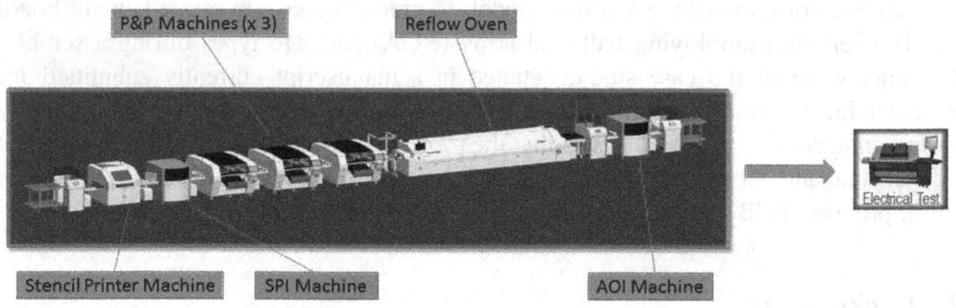

Fig. 2. SMT line

Figure 2 contains a typical SMT line. The first station is a stencil printer machine, which applies solder paste to a clean PCB. A prefabricated stencil is employed to ensure that the correct amount of solder paste is placed in the correct places. Immediately following stencil printing, a solder paste inspection (SPI) machine inspects the individual solder deposits for compliance with specifications and takes measurements for five parametric quantities: offset (x-direction), offset (y-direction), height, volume as a percentage of specification, and area as a percentage of specification. Figure 3 contains a cross-section of the application of solder paste to a PCB with the overlaid stencil, and

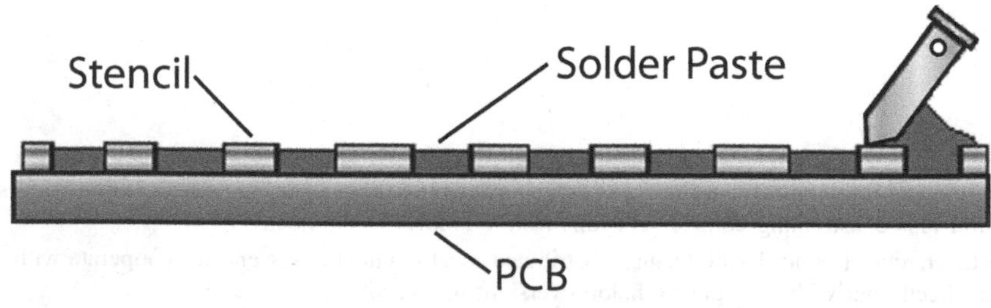

Fig. 3. Solder paste application

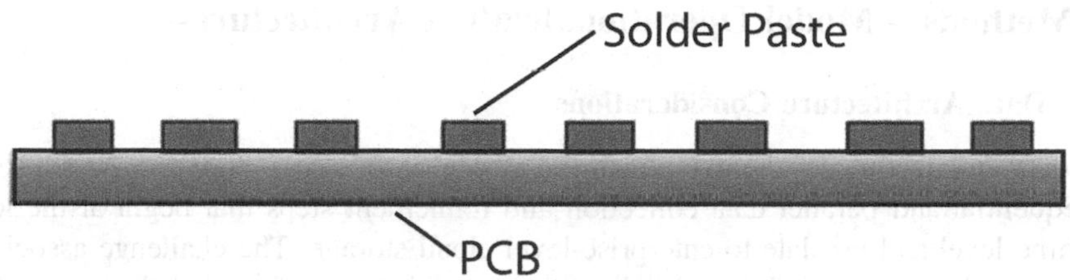

Fig. 4. PCB and solder paste deposits at SPI measurement

Fig. 4 shows the PCB at the point of SPI measurements, after the stencil is removed but before placement of any components.

After SPI, the board moves to a pick-and-place (P&P) machine which affixes components to the wet solder paste. There may be several P&P machines in series, and the last P&P machine typically affixes the BGA packages. After P&P, the board moves through the reflow oven and enters a queue for automated optical inspection (AOI). The AOI machine checks quality of assembly and identifies visible defects such as missing parts, solder volume, solder bridge, insufficient solder, or misaligned parts. Electrical testing is performed at an in-circuit testing (ICT) station, and boards passing ICT are moved to final assembly (FA) and functional testing.

2.2 Case Study Background and Pilot Dataset Results

The case study that undergirds this research utilizes an applied machine learning model to link SPI parametric data with downline ICT defects. This case study is innovative in the landscape of surface mount technology literature, as the bulk of current research into BGA defects focuses on optical means to locate them [5–12], metallurgical properties of the solder [13–16], or rework [17–19]. Employing parametric data measured on the individual solder paste deposits is an approach that is only possible in the Connected Enterprise Environment and is enabled by a circa-2017 Industrial Internet of Things (IIOT) capability enhancement project at the manufacturing facility from which the data is obtained.

Solder paste deposits for a single BGA package were analyzed holistically by organizing the measurements into arrays and sorting those arrays according to some rule. Feature extraction software was applied to the data arrays, with feature relevance being determined by a sequential application of statistical strength of association and a fuzzy inference approach introduced in [20] and previously used on a different application in [21]. Decision tree models using the reduced feature sets were scored for each of two different datasets, with metrics for classification accuracy exceeding 96.16%, precision exceeding 82.35%, recall exceeding 50%, and F1 score exceeding 62.22%.

3 Methods – Model Operationalization Architectures

3.1 Data Architecture Considerations

The data architecture for the manufacturing system in this case study employs a series of sequential and parallel data collection and refinement steps that begin at the local machine level and escalate to enterprise-level cloud storage. The challenge associated with operationalization of the models utilized in this research is that there is a short window of time before which the benefits of the defect prediction algorithm become moot. Specifically, intervention of a PCB flagged as defective must occur prior to the board passing through reflow.

These time constraints necessitate edge level computing because, by the time the data migrates to the cloud level and predictions are routed back, the window of opportunity to intervene will almost certainly have passed. Figure 5 contains a simplified data architecture in the Industry 4.0 connected factory context.

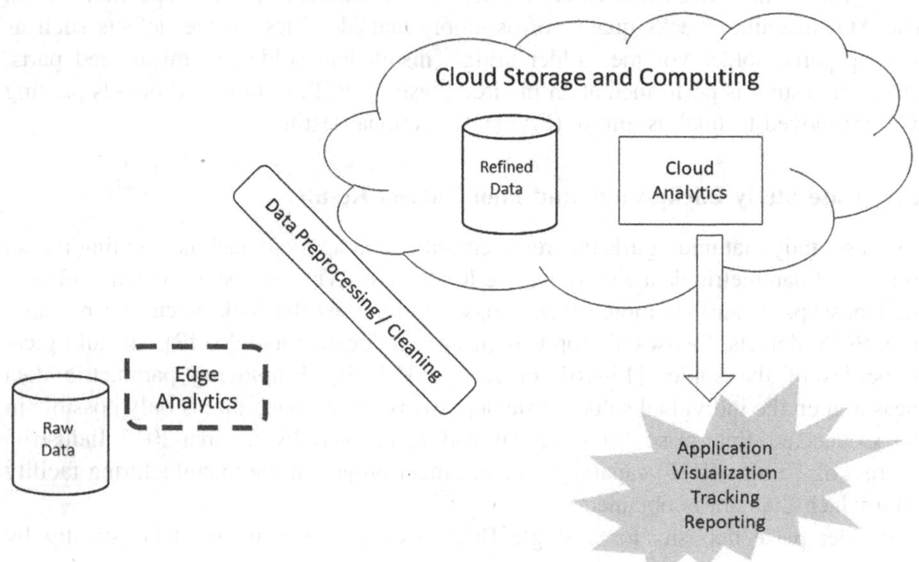

Fig. 5. Data architecture example

In Fig. 5, raw data is collected on any number of different items of interest such as production data, machine diagnostic data, sensor readings, scheduling, or other relevant information. Cloud storage and computing is necessarily preceded by some layer of preprocessing or cleaning of the data. "Clean" data is uploaded to Cloud Storage as per predefined parameters and is available for incorporation into Cloud Analytics capabilities. The dashed-line surrounding the "Edge Analytics" cell indicate the variation that might exists in placing the proposed computing capabilities to produce time-sensitive output before the cleaning and preprocessing steps. The only stipulation is that model output should be produced quickly enough for it to be actionable.

In the current case study, the ideal intervention window is after SPI and before the first P&P machine, which is a time frame of approximately 30 s to five minutes, depending on the PCB batch in the process. The next best scenario is for intervention to take place prior to the final P&P machine, at which point the BGA component is placed. This adds approximately five minutes per P&P machine. The latest acceptable point of intervention is after the final P&P machine but before the reflow oven, giving approximately five more minutes for the model to output its results, instructions to be passed and understood, and action to be taken.

3.2 Holonic Manufacturing System Architecture

In conceptualizing this case study as an HMS, it is proposed that the entire model can be incorporated into a holarchy[3] consisting of a Trigger Holon and a Defect Prediction Holon. The Trigger Holon could be viewed as the functional equivalent a Staff Holon that is nested between the larger Resource and Product holarchies. Figure 6 illustrates the Trigger Holon with its internal capabilities.

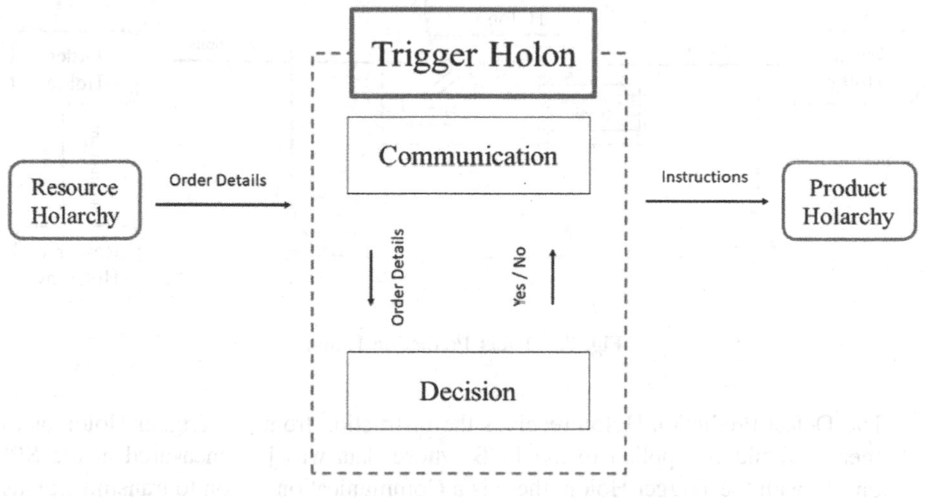

Fig. 6. Trigger Holon

As indicated in Fig. 6, the Trigger Holon contains two internal holons. The Communication Holon sends and receives signals to and from the internal and external holons. In this case, the Communication Holon receives detailed order information from the Resource Holarchy and passes it to the Decision Holon. The function of the Decision Holon is to compare the PCB assembly parameters for the specific product against a list of PCB assemblies that are appropriate for the defect prediction model. The model in its current state is intended to be applied to PCB assemblies employing

[3] A holarchy is a system of holons that cooperate to achieve a goal or objective.

BGA package types. Additional information that the Decision Holon will consider is the specific PCB assembly type because different PCB assembly types may require different models. Pilot datasets were created specifically for PCB assemblies whose frequency of production and frequency of defects were suitable to build a model. As the capability matures, a repository of data from other PCB assemblies will be built and a family of models trained.

The decision returned to the Communication Holon prompts instructions to be sent from the Trigger Holon to the Product Holarchy for whether or not to initiate the Defect Prediction Holon. These instructions would be received by an Order Holon (not depicted) nested within the Product Holarchy.

The Defect Prediction Holon, inserted into the Product Holarchy, is shown in Fig. 7.

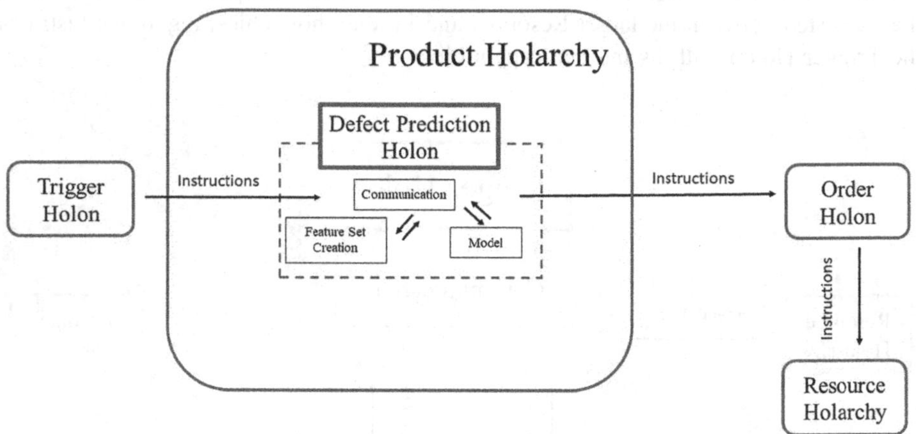

Fig. 7. Defect Prediction Holon

The Defect Prediction Holon receives the instruction from the Trigger Holon as to whether it should be applied to the PCB whose data was just measured at the SPI station. As with the Trigger Holon, there is a Communication Holon to transmit signals to internal and external holons. A feature set creation holon builds a feature set from the SPI parametric data and then refines it by selecting the features best suited for defect prediction based on the approach in [20]. The features for model inclusion are transmitted back to the Communication Holon, which forwards them to the Model Holon. The Model Holon implements the machine learning algorithm, obtains a prediction, and forwards that information back to the Communication Holon. The Communication Holon then transfers the appropriate instructions to an Order Holon which then passes them back to the Resource Holarchy.

It should be noted that model training does not take place at the Defect Prediction Holon. Models have already been trained at the Cloud level due to the quantity of data and the time required. The Defect Prediction Holon is applied in the run-time environment to individual PCB assemblies exiting the SPI machine.

4 Conclusion

Models for defect prediction in a complex manufacturing system take on an entirely different tenor when transitioning them from self-contained pilot models on the data scientist's local machine to an operationalized system for real-time corrective action. While it is clearly necessary for models to perform adequately and output trustworthy results, these are not sufficient conditions for a successful transition to a practical, usable product. Additionally, the model must be placed at the appropriate juncture in the data architecture and be configured in such a way as to be adaptive to the unpredictable nature of the complex manufacturing environment.

The smart factory as a holonic manufacturing system is an appropriate framework to conceptualize the transition of the featured defect prediction case study from ad hoc analysis to a steady-state, real-time quality assurance tool. The proposed two-holon framework, with a Trigger Holon nested between the Resource and Product Holarchies, combined with a Defect Prediction Holon nested within the Product Holarchy, is a viable architecture in the Industry 4.0 environment. This ongoing effort will continue to be developed for industrial applications and analyzed for lessons learned in future academic research.

References

1. Koestler, A.: The Ghost in the Machine. Macmillan, New York (1968)
2. Valckenaers, P., Van Brussel, H.: Laws of the artificial. In: Design for the Unexpected, pp. 27–40. Elsevier (2016)
3. Valckenaers, P., Van Brussel, H.: Holonic manufacturing systems. In: Design for the Unexpected, pp. 41–76. Elsevier (2016)
4. Van Brussel, H., Wyns, J., Valckenaers, P., Bongaerts, L., Peeters, P.: Reference architecture for holonic manufacturing systems: PROSA. Comput. Ind. **37**(3), 255–274 (1998)
5. Bernard, D., Krastev, E.: Modern 2D X-ray tackles BGA defects. SMT Surf. Mt. Technol. Mag. **22**(7), 22–24 (2008)
6. Do Peng, S., Nam, H.: Void defect detection in ball grid array X-ray images using a new blob filter. J. Zhejiang Univ. Sci. C **13**(11), 840–849 (2012)
7. Wang, Y., Wang, M., Zhang, Z.: Optik microfocus X-ray printed circuit board inspection system. Opt. - Int. J. Light Electron Opt. **125**(17), 4929–4931 (2014)
8. Castellanos, A., Feng, Z., Geiger, D., Kurwa, M.: Head-in-pillow X-ray inspection. SMT Surf. Mt. Technol. Mag. **29**(5), 16–29 (2014)
9. Sumimoto, T., et al.: Detection of defects of BGA by tomography imaging. J. Syst. Cybern. Inform. **3**(4), 10–14 (2005)
10. Hui, T.W., Pang, G.K.H.: Solder paste inspection using region-based defect detection. Int. J. Adv. Manuf. Technol. **42**(7–8), 725–734 (2009)
11. Kuo, C.H., Yang, F.C., Wing, J.J., Yang, C.K.: Construction of 3D solder paste surfaces using multi-projection images. Int. J. Adv. Manuf. Technol. **31**(5–6), 509–519 (2006)
12. Chu, M.H., Pang, G.K.H.: Solder paste inspection by special led lighting for SMT manufacturing of printed circuit boards. In: IFAC, vol. 8, no. Part 1 (2007)
13. Li, X.P., Xia, J.M., Zhou, M.B., Ma, X., Zhang, X.P.: Solder volume effects on the microstructure evolution and shear fracture behavior of ball grid array structure Sn-3.0 Ag-0.5 Cu solder interconnects. J. Electron. Mater. **40**(12), 2425–2435 (2011)

14. Yang, D., Cai, J., Wang, Q., Li, J., Hu, Y., Li, L.: IMC growth and shear strength of Sn–Ag–Cu/Co–P ball grid array solder joints under thermal cycling. J. Mater. Sci.: Mater. Electron. **26**(2), 962–969 (2014)
15. Pandher, R., Jodhan, N., Raut, R., Liberatore, M.: Head-in-pillow defect - Role of the solder ball alloy. In: 2010 12th Electronics Packaging Technology Conference, EPTC 2010, pp. 151–156 (2010)
16. Scalzo, M.: Addressing the Challenge of Head-In-Pillow Defects in Electronics Assembly. In: APEX EXPO Technical Conference (2009)
17. Zhao, Z.: Effects of package warpage on head-in-pillow defect. Mater. Trans. **56**(7), 1037–1042 (2015)
18. Chen, C., et al.: Characterization of after-reflow misalignment on Head-in-Pillow defect in BGA assembly. In: 2014 15th International Conference on Electronic Packaging Technology, pp. 1177–1180 (2014)
19. Wettermann, B.: Top 5 BGA challenges to overcome. SMT Surf. Mt. Technol. Mag. **32**(9), 25–29 (2017)
20. LaCasse, P.M., Otieno, W., Maturana, F.P.: A hierarchical, fuzzy inference approach to data filtration and feature prioritization in the connected manufacturing enterprise. J. Big Data **5**(1), 45 (2018)
21. Omwando, T.A., Otieno, W.A., Farahani, S., Ross, A.D.: A bi-level fuzzy analytical decision support tool for assessing product remanufacturability. J. Clean. Prod. **174**, 1534–1549 (2018)

Cloud-Based Digital Twin for Industrial Robotics

Timon Hoebert, Wilfried Lepuschitz, Erhard List, and Munir Merdan(✉)

Practical Robotics Institute Austria, Wexstrasse 19-23, 1200 Vienna, Austria
{hoebert,lepuschitz,list,merdan}@pria.at

Abstract. Production systems are becoming more flexible and agile to realize the need for more individualized products. Robotics technology can accomplish these demands, but programming and re-configuration of robots are associated with high costs, especially for small- and medium-sized enterprises. The use of digital twins can significantly reduce these costs by providing monitoring and simulation capabilities for the robot and its environment using real-time data. The integration with an ontology as a knowledge base to describe the robot and its 3d-environment enables an automatic configuration of the digital twin and the particular robot. In this paper, this concept is coupled with cloud-computing to enable an effortless integration as service in existing cloud architectures and easy access using the common web-technology-stack for the end-users. A novel architecture is presented and implemented to incorporate the real system with its digital twin, the ontology and a planner to infer the actual operations from the knowledge base. Finally, the implementation is applied to the industrial manufacturing domain to assemble different THT-Devices on a PCB to evaluate the concept.

Keywords: Digital twin · Industrial robotic · Autonomous system · Ontology

1 Introduction

In order to handle the ever-increasing number of individualized products with short delivery times, the production system has to become much more flexible and agile. Particularly in the field of assembly systems the growing variety of products adds new complexities to the planning process and increases the costs, because (re-)planning efforts tend to grow exponentially to the number of variants [16]. Robotics technology, which is able to prove high efficiency, precision and repeatability, seems like a viable solution to cope with these challenges. However, robot systems still often do not meet the demands of small- and medium-sized enterprises (SMEs); with a high number of small lot sizes and product variants, frequent re-configuration and re-programming, but also little or no in-house robot expertise. Also, the setup and operation of a robot in an SME environment are not that easy, since it is typically less structured and involves more uncertainties than large-scale or mass production industries [5].

In order to be able to dynamically adapt to new products and unpredicted production changes, robotic systems need to work autonomously. Autonomous systems, in

V. Mařík et al. (Eds.): HoloMAS 2019, LNAI 11710, pp. 105–116, 2019.
https://doi.org/10.1007/978-3-030-27878-6_9

this context, means that robots systems are able to perform high-level task specifications without explicitly being programmed [3]. In order to reach specific goals, such systems employ automated reasoning and choose their actions knowing their own capabilities and their current state. To perform an aimed action successfully, the autonomous systems have to have a realistic representation of their own capabilities and environment as well as of the current state of the production process. Nonetheless, the complexity of the issues involved in systems, a large number of subsystems and factors that directly or indirectly affect the productivity, efficiency, and synchronization of a production or assembly process, requires searching and verification of the possible solutions in the processes of designing and modeling these systems [17]. Besides, to guarantee safety, new control methods and architectures have to be fully tested and proven before practical usage. According to the International Federation of Robotics (IFR), the challenges of adopting new technologies as well as the lack in advanced safety systems for the supervision of human-robot workspace sharing and cooperation represent some of the main reasons that companies do not use robots yet [13].

However, performing tests in a running production process can generate additional costs and put the personal and production equipment in danger. Simulation can be a very effective way of testing different control architectures and improving the quality of the designed solutions and can enable to some extent the reliability and effectiveness of the entire system. The application of simulation solutions for designing, testing, and verification of control programs and algorithms in the industry but also in service robotics is well established and there are a lot of solutions currently available (e.g. RobotStudio, KUKA SimPro, Robotics Suite, Gazebo, etc.). An overview of current robot offline programming tools can be found in [4, 6, 8]. Nevertheless, most of these tools do not support semi-automatic program generation on the abstraction level of process steps [10]. Furthermore, most of them are focused on processes where they are used to specify basic robot movements and are mostly not suitable for all use cases within specific domains. Besides, there is usually a strict separation between the virtual runtime environment provided by robotic simulation frameworks, and the motion and grasp planning components, imposing severe limitations on the interaction possibilities between planning and runtime components when it comes to robotic simulations [1]. Data models used by engineering and simulation tools are mostly not compatible or insufficient to fulfill all parameters of others, restricting the interoperability in an increasingly multi-vendor tool environment [20]. In this context, software that aims to mimic robotic work cells needs to represent exactly all components and display them accurately while facilitating poses, paths and trajectories testing [18]. Besides, to evaluate the impact of external and internal changes and to react in a timely manner to critical influences on production management, changes within a physical environment have also to be mirrored within the virtual model [20].

From a simulation point of view, the Digital Twin approach is seen as the next big step in modeling, simulation and optimization technology [15]. The idea of the digital twin is to create a digital counterpart to mimic the characteristics and behaviors of its corresponding twin, realizing in an effective way the communication and interaction between the physical and digital world [23]. It is essential to represent the characteristics, behavior, and relations of the system components like products, resources, sensors as well as the kinematics of a robot properly within the digital twin [9]. Digital twin technology establishes feedback loops between real-world objects and their virtual substitutes. In this article, our goal is, on the one hand, to reduce the required manual steps for the modeling of digital twin environments with sensors, actuators, and devices. The digital twin generation should also support the communication and interaction between the physical and digital environment. On the other hand, the established digital twin should enablc easier tests and development of autonomous robotic systems including their automated configuration and programming in realistic environments under specific conditions and constraints. The entire framework provides also monitoring means of involved devices represented through their digital twins. A further aim was to present data through the digital twin framework and to visualize the information in a user-friendly graphical interface as well as to perform proof of concept tests on laboratory equipment.

This paper is structured as follows. Section 2 discusses the framework architecture. Section 3 shows the digital twin integration and configuration. In Sect. 4, we present in detail the implemented framework. Section 5 describes the digital twin, when applied in specific use case. Finally, the paper is concluded in the sixth section.

2 Framework Architecture

The main goal of this research is to create a digital twin of an autonomous robotic system. The twin should be automatically created from the semantical description of the system, and furthermore, it should able to supervise the real system's current actions based on the data that the digital twin receives from it. The digital system analyzes the current situation in the real system, tests some alternative scenarios and gives relevant feedback to the real system when these scenarios result in improved action. The digital twin collects all relevant knowledge about the product, production equipment, and the production process and uses this knowledge to suggest suitable actions to the real system. It enables the correct and efficient modeling of the environment but takes a vital role in the prediction of the possible autonomous system behaviors. In this setting, the digital twin is a vital enabler of autonomy and an important factor for achieving a new level of flexibility in automation systems. There are basically four major components contained in the digital twin framework, including the semantic description of the robot system environment, a decision-making mechanism (planner), the digital environment model and the real system (Fig. 1).

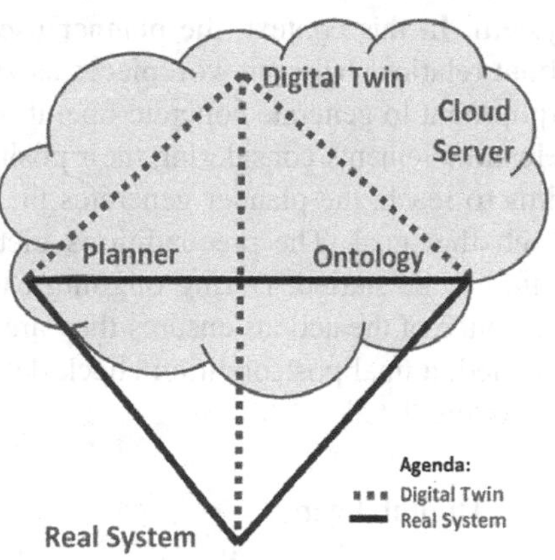

Fig. 1. Digital twin concept

2.1 Ontology

In order to realize the digital twin, a vital part is the development of a digital model of the environment, which must be as precise and detailed as its real twin in order to execute accurate simulations and evaluations [9]. Lately, the attention has been also oriented on the application of ontologies to meet the goals of modeling, meta-modeling, and interoperability between the digital tools in the Virtual Factory context in order to guarantee an accurate digital link. The key benefits of using an ontology-based approach include (i) the exploitation of semantic web technologies in terms of interoperability, data distribution, extensibility of the data model, querying, and reasoning; and (ii) the re-use of general purpose software implementations for data storage, consistency checking and knowledge inference [19]. In this context, it is crucial to accurately model and represent the relevant elements of the system such as products, robots, actuators, users, tools, sensors, etc., considering their properties, behavior, and relations to each other as well as corresponding locations. For instance, the kinematics of a robot must be properly represented as well as sensor and actuator specifications (e.g., their accuracy and frequency). Based on the exact virtual representation of the physical environment, the model can provide information about the concrete position of the specific element. The ontology also specifies technical details, which are required for automated device registration and enabling access to the devices.

2.2 Planner

The reasoning functions of the robotic system are realized in the planner, the second important part is the digital framework. The responsibility of the planner is to link the semantic description of the framework and the skills of the acting resources in the system. In this context, the planner uses an ontology-based product model to reason about relations between workpieces as well as to connect abstract processes and needed equipment to generate concrete operations. Based on the initial state of the system (its relevant elements considering their positions and orientations) and goal that the system aims to reach, the planner generates the list of high-level actions, which are needed to reach that goal. The preconditions dictate items that must be initially valid for the action to be started. During ongoing execution, the continuous evaluation of the performance of the actions ensures they are executed as expected. When the execution has finished, a final postcondition check determines if the effects of the undertaken actions are as predicted.

2.3 Digital Twin

Autonomous systems are aware of their own capabilities (skills) as well as about their current state. Nevertheless, in order to be able to undertake appropriate actions, they need to have a meaningful representation of the surrounding environment. Moreover, considering the fact that they act autonomously and that their actions are sometimes not predictable, it is of crucial importance to test or supervise their behaviors. Their control programs and related behaviors can be developed and tested using real control systems in combination with a digital representation of the later real application environment, including all relevant models of resources, tools, sensors, etc. The test planning and testing environment can be used to validate robotic tasks and actions. Creating a digital production environment including all relevant elements gives a possibility to compare the actual path of a workpiece with an optimal one. It can be also used to validate robot actions for specific initial states and adjust particular parameters of the control strategy until one or more optimal cases are resolved. Also, the integration of collision detection in the digital twin enables a virtual sensing domain which is not possible with current industrial robots, where a collision is fatal during application.

2.4 Cloud

Cloud technologies provide a shared environment of manufacturing capability, computing power, knowledge, and resource, offering an environment to connect the computing and service resources in the digital world to the machines and robots in the physical world [22]. The integration of digital twins into cloud manufacturing systems imposes strong demands such as reducing overhead and saving resources [7]. We have created a cloud-based digital twin framework that exploits modern Web technologies and offers modeling, simulation, and supervision environment to the end-users' needs. The digital twin layout is generated automatically online and can be accessed via a web browser, even via a mobile device. In our approach, we have every physical component in the system represented by its digital twin hosted in the cloud. Every time the real world state changes, an update of the current component status is sent to its digital representation in the cloud. Additionally, the use of cloud-based technology enables easy use of the digital twin as service without a user interface, for example, directly connected to the path planning component for collision detection of a proposed path.

3 Framework Integration

The components, as presented above, are integrated into the digital twin framework as visualized in Fig. 2. In our previous work, we described the function and implementation of the ontology-driven industrial robotics system as well as its automated configuration [12]. As a basis for this system and presented digital twin framework, the Rosetta ontology [24], which is concentrating on robotic devices and particular skills. We also integrated the BREP ontology [21], which represents geometric entities in a semantic way. Within the digital twin framework, we particularly focused on representations of industrial robots and their features: manufacturer, type, axes, segments, weight, tools, etc. The ontology describes also concepts which are required for an automated configuration and access to the devices.

The Planner automatically determines a set of suitable actions that lead to the final goal state. Nevertheless, the selected plan is strongly related to the current state of the entire robotics system. The action schemas of a planning domain include parameters, preconditions, and effects. The preconditions dictate items that must be initially valid for the action to be legal. The effect equation dictates the changes in the world that will occur due to the execution of the action.

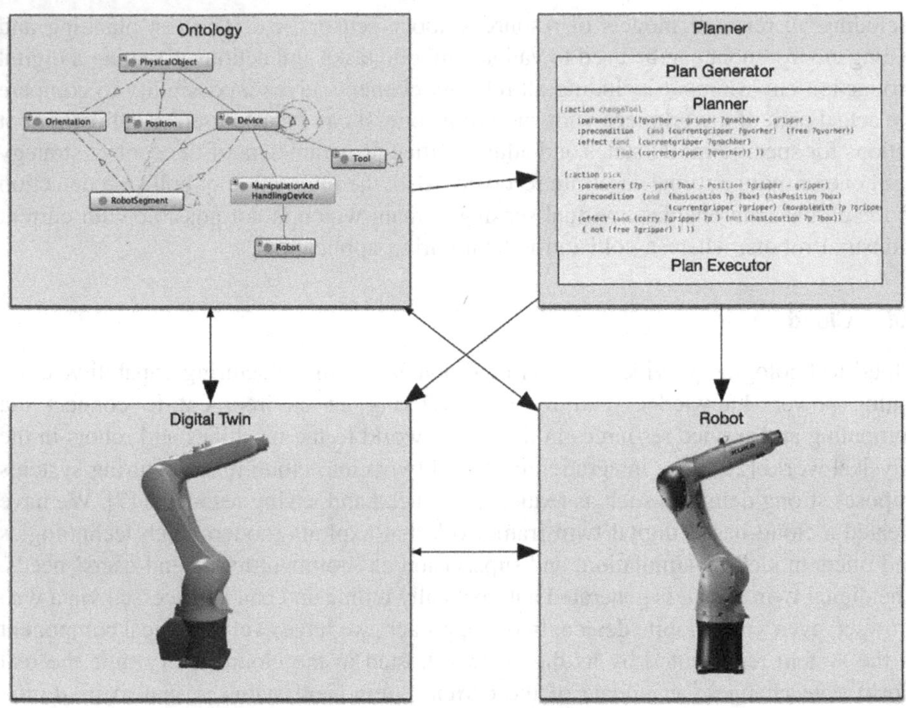

Fig. 2. The implemented framework of the digital twin

The digital twin is automatically configured based on the information of the ontology and the real system. The ontology provides spatial information, which is interconnected with other semantic data-structures, for example, skills. Especially the spatial information about the geometry and positioning of the workpieces, the robot itself and its environment are relevant to automatically adapt the digital twin. Therefore the abstract representation of the joints of the robots and its actual triangulated geometry are transferred to the digital twin for the initial configuration. The segments of the robot are represented using their length and the link to the next connected segments. The orientation and position of the next connection point is defined in a local coordinate space, based on the current segment. This process enables the fast configuration of new robots based on similar or slightly changed geometry. In a similar way, the tools are represented. Each tool has an operation reference point, for example, the center of the vacuum gripper. Similarly, the environment of the robot is also mapped into the digital-twin, to determine the working area of the robot. Using the collision detection of the digital twin, changes in this mapped environment can lead to adapted robot paths to avoid collisions with the surroundings. In the ontology, the workpiece and its sub-parts are defined by the geometry and the handling information. The handling-information contains information about the local picking position of the part and the possible tool which can carry out the operation. This information adapts the used tool of the robot and path-planning.

As stated before, the digital twin also configures based on spatial information of the robot and its sensor data. In this context, the current angles of the axes and the sensor values of the tool are transmitted to the digital twin. This information helps to monitor the robot and to gain insight into the robot's autonomous movements.

4 Implementation

The digital twin framework consists of 5 components, as shown in Fig. 3. The main component is the cloud-based Service Hoster, which connects the different components transparently.

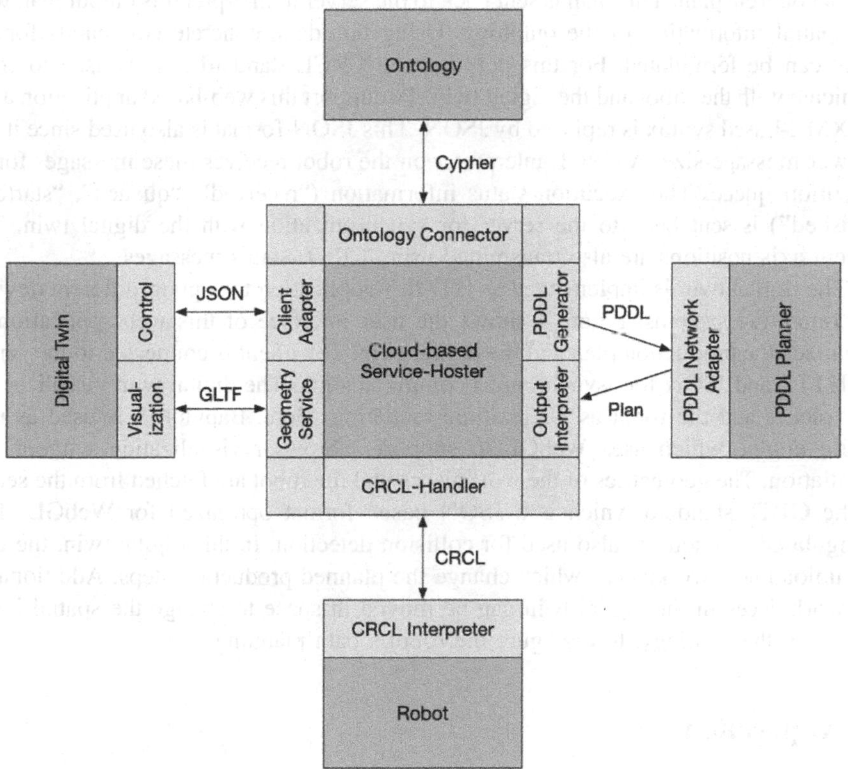

Fig. 3. The implemented framework of the digital twin

It is implemented using Node.JS for maximal interoperability with the other components because of existing included frameworks. It has a dedicated Ontology-Connector service to interact with the ontology. The ontology is implemented using the open-source named property graph database Neo4j to handle the performance demands of geometry data processing and storing. The Sci-Graph project is used to migrate

OWL-Ontologies into the database[1]. This implementation choice led to the use of the Cypher query language, which is used to query the ontology data.

As mentioned before, the ontology stores all information about the workpieces, their geometry, and the production process. The geometry is associated with production information, for example, the possible handling tools. Also, the capabilities and geometry of the robot are stored and linked here via relations. Additionally, the saved information of the composition of the final workpiece is relevant for planning. Hereby, a planner is used to generate a possible production plan based on a minimal cost function, e.g. minimal production time. The PDDL-standard [11] is used for this purpose. A generic network adapter is implemented to connect the planner with the service. The PDDL problem and domain files are generated based on the information of the ontology. The generated files are sent to the planner, which solves the problem instance with a concrete plan. This plan is sent back to the server to interpret this output plan with the spatial information of the ontology. Using this data, concrete commands for the robot can be formulated. For this purpose, the CRCL-standard [14] is used to communicate with the robot and the digital twin. To support this web-based application area, the XML-based syntax is replaced by JSON. This JSON-format is also used since it has a lower message-size. A CRCL-interpreter on the robot receives these messages for its execution queue. The execution status information ("received", "queued", "started", "finished") is sent back to the server for synchronization with the digital twin. The current axis positions are also transmitted using CRCL-status messages.

The digital twin is implemented as HTML5-application to support different devices and operating systems. Figure 4 shows the user interface of this web-application. It visualizes the production plan and the digital twin. The client is connected to the server via HTTP and JSON for asynchronous communication. The digital twin visualizes the workpieces and the robot as 3D-realtime rendering. Here, BabylonJS is used as rendering engine which uses WebGL to support a browser visualization without any installation. The geometries of the workpieces and the robot are fetched from the server in the GLTF standard which is a JSON based format optimized for WebGL. This triangulated geometry is also used for collision detection. In this digital twin, the user can upload new workpieces which change the planned production steps. Additionally, the workpieces in the digital twin can be moved in space to change the spatial information in the ontology, to configure the robot's path planning.

5 Application

The assembly process is one of the most important production phases since the quality, life, performance, reliability, and maintainability of a product mostly depend on assembly results [25]. Assembly operations are considered being among the most intensive and costly processes in production lines, due to the variability of the assembled parts and the complexity of the executed tasks [2]. The assembly process can become especially extensive when coordination of several different actions need to

[1] https://github.com/SciGraph/SciGraph.

be integrated and performed by an autonomous robotics system. Especially considering that this system also requires an exact representation of the current state of the production process and of its actions.

These difficulties make the assembly domain relevant to the use of the digital twin concept. As mentioned before, the digital twin can collect all this vitally important information on the production process and make it available to the autonomous system. This information can be simulated with the digital twin model to anticipate the consequences of actions by the autonomous system in a given situation and possibly modify the course of action [15]. Due to these reasons, we apply the digital twin for the test case that focuses on the assembling of different THT-Devices (relay, capacitor, screw terminal, and potentiometer) on a PCB. In this scenario, THT-Devices for an assembly line are placed in boxes at the workstation. Each box contains different parts, which have an exact position in the box. In the automated pilot case, the KUKA robot KR 6 R900 sixx performs a series of pick-and-place operations in assembling the PCB board, as presented in Fig. 4.

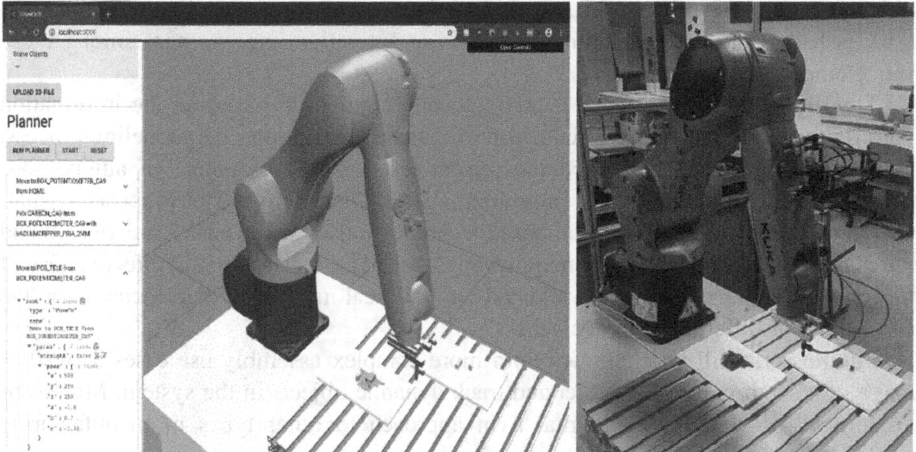

Fig. 4. Digital twin applied in the assembly domain

In the digital twin, the end product is specified by the user through the GUI as the final goal, being defined as the assembled PCB board with the geometric information containing the characteristics (weight, position, and orientation) of the individual parts). These data are forwarded in combination with the semantic description to the planner. Once the user starts the process, the digital twin provides the information about the current state of the system and the planner starts with the specification of the single assembly activities autonomously. Each activity consists of a series of operation that can be executed with different tools or by one or more resources. The PDDL planner extracts the corresponding production/assembly operations and links the particular action with the required tool, which has to be used to perform the specific operation (e.g. handling, assembly, fixing). These tools and relevant skills, as well as resources, are represented in the ontology. Based on these specific operations the robot can reason about the required tool (e.g. a gripper for handling). This activate sequence is then mapped accordingly into a robot program, which is then executed. The activities are then reviewed by the user who could then approve them or change specific parameters in order to improve the efficiency of the operations.

6 Conclusion

The application of the digital twin technology to support the development of an autonomous robotics system is proven as a promising approach. In this paper, we use the digital twin framework for modeling, simulation, supervision, and optimization of the autonomous robotics system. The developed framework is composed of four major components: semantic description of the robot system (ontology), decision-making mechanism (planner), digital environment model and the real system. The use of an ontology provides a unified structure for the representation of the system environment. The reasoning functions of the robotic system are realized in the planner and connected with the ontology-based world model. The function of the entire digital twin framework is based on the continuous interaction and iterative improvement among those four elements.

The digital twin framework is automatically configured based on the information from the ontology and enables reduction of manual steps during the modeling process. The developed digital twin facilitates easier tests and development of autonomous robotic systems including their programming and monitoring. The proposed visualization technique and use of cloud-based technology also enable easier supervision and better understanding of the autonomous approach. The feasibility and effectiveness of the proposed framework are validated on the real use case that focuses on the assembling of different THT-Devices.

Future work will be continued with more complex assembly use cases as well as usage of a depth-camera to detect and track dynamic objects in the system. Moreover, we aim also to extend the digital twin approach to other types of manufacturing machines (cutting and grinding machines, etc.).

Acknowledgment. The authors acknowledge the financial support from the "Production of the Future" program of the Austrian Ministry for Transport, Innovation and Technology under contract FFG 858707.

References

1. Aichele, F., Schenke, B., Eckstein, B., Groz, A.: A framework for robot control software development and debugging using a real-time capable physics simulation. In: Proceedings of ISR 2016: 47st International Symposium on Robotics, Munich, Germany (2016)
2. Argyrou, A., Giannoulis, C., Papakostas, N., Chryssolouris, G.: A uniform data model for representing symbiotic assembly stations. Proc. CIRP **44**, 85–90 (2016). 6th CIRP Conference on Assembly Technologies and Systems CATS, 2016
3. Beckey, G.A.: Autonomous Robots. MIT Press, Cambridge (2005)

4. Gan, Y., Dai, X., Li, D.: Off-line programming techniques for multirobot cooperation system. Int. J. Adv. Robot. Syst. **10**, 282 (2013)
5. Haage, M., Profanter, S., Kessler, I., Perzylo, A., Somani, N., Sörnmo, O.: On cognitive robot woodworking in SMErobotics. In: Proceedings of ISR 2016: 47st International Symposium on Robotics, pp. 1–7 (2016)
6. Harris, A., Conrad, J.: Survey of popular robotics simulators, frameworks, and toolkits. In: Proceedings of IEEE Southeastcon (2011)
7. Hu, L., et al.: Modeling of cloud-based digital twins for smart manufacturing with MT connect. Proc. Manuf. **26**, 1193–1203 (2018)
8. Kumar, K., Reel, P.: Analysis of contemporary robotics simulators. In:2011 International Conference on Emerging Trends in Electrical and Computer Technology (ICETECT) (2011)
9. Kuts, V., Modoni, G.E., Terkaj, W., Tähemaa, T., Sacco, M., Otto, T.: Exploiting factory telemetry to support virtual reality simulation in robotics cell. In: De Paolis, L., Bourdot, P., Mongelli, A. (eds.) Augmented Reality, Virtual Reality, and Computer Graphics, AVR 2017. LNCS, vol. 10324, pp. 212–222. Springer, Cham (2017). https://doi.org/10.1007/978-3-319-60922-5_16
10. Macho, M., Naegele, L., Hoffmann, A., Angerer, A., Reif, W.: A flexible architecture for automatically generating robot applications based on expert knowledge. In: Proceedings of ISR 2016: 47st International Symposium on Robotics, pp. 1–8 (2016)
11. Mcdermott, D., et al.: PDDL - the planning domain denition language (Technical report). CVC TR-98- 003/DCS TR-1165, Yale Center for Computational Vision and Control (1998)
12. Merdan, M., Hoebert, T., List, E., Lepuschitz, W.: Knowledge-based cyber-physical systems for assembly automation. Prod. Manuf. Res. **7**, 223–254 (2019)
13. Michalos, G., Makris, S., Spiliotopoulos, J., Misios, I., Tsarouchi, P., Chryssolouris, G.: ROBO-PARTNER: seamless human-robot cooperation for intelligent, flexible and safe operations in the assembly factories of the future. In: 5th CIPR Conference on Assembly Technologies and Systems, (CATS 2014), Dresden, Germany, November 2014
14. Proctor, F., Balakirsky, S., Kootbally, Z., Kramer, T., Schleno, C., Shackleford, W.P.: The canonical robot command language (CRCL). Ind. Robot: Int. J. **43**, 495–502 (2016)
15. Rosen, R., von Wichert, G., Lo, G., Bettenhausen, K.D.: About the importance of autonomy and digital twins for the future of manufacturing. In: 15th IFAC Symposium on Information Control Problems in Manufacturing (INCOM), vol. 48, no. 3, pp. 567–572 (2015)
16. Schlick, C.M., Faber, M., Kuz, S., Bützler, J.: A symbolic approach to self-optimisation in production system analysis and control. In: Brecher, C. (ed.) Advances in Production Technology. LNCS, pp. 147–160. Springer, Cham (2015). https://doi.org/10.1007/978-3-319-12304-2_11
17. Sekala, A., Gwiazda, A., Kost, G., Banaś, W.: Modelling and simulation of a robotic work cell. In: IOP Conference Series: Materials Science and Engineering, vol. 227, p. 012116 (2017)
18. Tavares, P., Silva, A., Costa, P., Veiga, G., Moreira, P.: Flexible work cell simulator using digital twin methodology for highly complex systems in industry 4.0. In: Iberian Robotics conference, pp. 541–552 (2017)
19. Terkaj, W., Tolio, T., Urgo, M.: A virtual factory approach for in situ simulation to support production and maintenance planning. CIRP Ann.- Manuf. Technol. **64**(1), 451–454 (2015)
20. Um, J., Weyer, S., Quint, F.: Plug-and-simulate within modular assembly line enabled by digital twins and the use of AutomationML. IFAC-PapersOnLine **50**(1), 15904–15909 (2017)
21. Perzylo, A., Somani, N., Rickert, M., Knoll, A.: An ontology for CAD data and geometric constraints as a link between product models and semantic robot task descriptions. In: International Conference on Intelligent Robots and Systems (IROS), pp. 4197–4203 (2015)

22. Wang, X.V., Wang, L., Mohammed, A., Givehchi, M.: Ubiquitous manufacturing system based on cloud: a robotics application. Robot. Comput. Integr. Manuf. **45**, 116–125 (2017)
23. Yan, K., Xu, W., Yao, B., Zhou, Z., Pham, D.: Digital twin-based energy modeling of industrial robots. In: the 18th Asia Simulation Conference (AsiaSim 2018), Kyoto, Japan, 27–29 October 2018
24. Patel, R., Hedelind, M., Lozan-Villegas, P.: Enabling robots in small-part assembly lines: the "rosetta approach"—an industrial perspective. In: The 7th German Conference on Robotics, Proceedings of ROBOTIK, pp. 1–5 (2012)
25. Zhuang, C., Liu, J., Xiong, H.: Digital twin-based smart production management and control framework for the complex product assembly shop-floor. Int. J. Adv. Manuf. Technol. **96**, 1149–1163 (2018)

Data and Knowledge

Semi-automatic Tool for Ontology Learning Tasks

Ondřej Šebek[1(✉)], Václav Jirkovský[1], Nestor Rychtyckyj[2], and Petr Kadera[1]

[1] Czech Institute of Robotics, Informatics, and Cybernetics, Czech Technical University in Prague, Prague, Czech Republic
{ondrej.sebek,vaclav.jirkovsky,petr.kadera}@cvut.cz
[2] Ford Motor Company, Dearborn, MI, USA
nrychtyc@ford.com

Abstract. The (semi-)automated integration of new information into a data model is a functionality which is required in cases when input documents are extensive and therefore a manual integration difficult or even impossible. We proposed an ontology learning procedure combining information acquisition from structured resources, such as WordNet or DBpedia, and unstructured resources using text mining techniques based on an evaluation of lexico-syntactic patterns. This approach offers a robust way, how to integrate even previously unknown information disregarding target application or domain. The proposed solution was implemented in the form of semi-automatic ontology learning tool used for integration of Excel document containing spare part records and Ford Supply Chain Ontology.

Keywords: Ontology · Ontology learning · Web mining · Text mining · Automotive

1 Introduction

This paper is motivated by a requirement for facilitating interoperability in supply chain management together with a formation of a new suitable data model (or improvement of existing one) represented in an ontology. This problem may be defined as deriving an ontology (or its part) from given data, also known as an ontology learning task [9].

The integration of new information into an existing data model is a problem which may be observed in many systems. The integration is necessary for example when a company replaces a supplier (information about spare parts has to be imported in a company system) or the company changes a production plan and needs to adapt the data model of the information system adequately. In all cases, we have to face a heterogeneity, which is caused by different designers of given concepts or by different target applications. Thus, the heterogeneity has to be resolved for ensuring proper information integration.

V. Mařík et al. (Eds.): HoloMAS 2019, LNAI 11710, pp. 119–129, 2019.
https://doi.org/10.1007/978-3-030-27878-6_10

We proposed the solution which includes information acquisition from the Web (web mining) in the ontology learning process. This approach offers a robust way, how to integrate even previously unknown information disregarding target application or domain. The solution deals with facilitating identification of input data among existing concepts or with the definition of a new concept. The proposed solution was experimentally verified on the integration of Excel document containing spare parts and Ford Supply Chain Ontology.

The paper is organized as follows: Next section introduces the problem of ontology learning and some of the developed ontology learning methods. Section 3 describes our proposed approach to ontology learning. Application of the proposed method on the case of integration of spare part records into the Ford ontology is presented in Sect. 4. The paper concludes with a summary in Sect. 5.

2 State of the Art

The (semi-)automatic methods for ontology construction are typically referred to as the ontology learning altogether [8]. In other words, ontology learning deals with the construction of a domain model from available data.

Ontology learning can be often considered as a reverse engineering process. Implicit domain models that were created by a single or multiple authors represent given input data. The ontology learning procedure reconstructs the universal world model from these existing implicit models. The task is complex especially because only a small part of the authors' domain knowledge is involved in the data model creation process and furthermore a conceptualization (which is used by the author) is rarely mentioned explicitly.

The ontology learning process can be divided into several separated tasks:

1. Acquisition of appropriate vocabulary.
2. Identification of synonym terms and linguistic variants (possibly across languages).
3. Formation of concepts.
4. Hierarchical organization of the concepts.
5. Learning relations, properties or attributes, together with the appropriate domain and range.
6. Hierarchical organization of the relations.
7. Instantiation of axiom schemata.
8. Definition of arbitrary axioms.

These tasks with their exactly fixed order are typically referred to as the ontology learning layer cake. Various methods have been proposed to deal with particular steps of the ontology learning problem. However, the applicability of a particular method strongly depends on the target domain and the ontology learning is thus a very challenging task.

One of the approaches to the problem of semi-automated ontology learning is to employ structured datasets such as WordNet [10] or DBpedia[1]. WordNet is

[1] http://wiki.dbpedia.org.

a large lexical database of English, where nouns, verbs, and adverbs are grouped into sets of cognitive synonyms (named synsets). Every synset corresponds to a distinct concept. These synsets are interlinked by means of conceptual-semantic relations. DBpedia is a crowd-sourced community effort to extract structured content from the information created in various Wikimedia projects, i.e., DBpedia contains not only definitions of concepts but also relations between these concepts represented in some standard form (e.g., by using Dublin Core[2]). The existence of the relations between individual concepts in such datasets can be easily employed for the fourth and fifth layer of the ontology learning process outlined above.

Zhou et al. [13] proposed ontology learning method where the initial human-designed core ontology is expanded using semantic relations in WordNet. This process may be repeated until the resulting ontology is sufficiently rich. Luong et al. [7] developed a method for enriching concepts using WordNet. In their approach, correct sense of given WordNet term is evaluated on the basis of comparing hypernymy trees inferred from WordNet. Booshehri and Luksch [1,2] proposed the use of Linked Data as an additional tool (besides standard ontology generating from a text) to find new relations and thus obtain more expressive ontology.

Another approach to derive relations between concepts is based on the search of lexico-syntactic patterns in unstructured text. Such an approach was pioneered by Hearst in 1992 [4] for hyponymy/hypernymy relation. The idea behind this approach is to identify patterns which usually indicate specific semantic relation. Throughout the years this approach was also extended to other semantic relations (e.g., [3,11]). Example of ontology learning based on lexico-syntactic patterns may be found in [6].

3 Proposed Solution

Each of the ontology learning methods has its advantages and suitable domain of application. For example, the structured datasets (such as WordNet or DBpedia) already contain much valuable information, e.g., relations to concepts with broader or narrower sense, relations to meronyms and holonyms. On the other hand, these resources contain rather general concepts, and more specialized concepts may not be covered in these resources. Unstructured text resources provide much larger space for search but extraction of the required information is complicated, and the accuracy of obtained results is uncertain.

For these reasons, we proposed a hybrid ontology learning procedure which combines the acquisition of information from structured datasets as well as from unstructured text using text mining methods [5,12]. In the first step, the required information is extracted from the structured dataset. This requires to identify the concept in the dataset. However, querying the whole dataset only on the basis of the concept name may produce ambiguous results. For example, even when limiting to the words of type *artifact*, a search of word *Seal* in WordNet

[2] http://dublincore.org

produces four different results. Some additional method would have to be then employed to identify the correct concept related to the domain in interest as discussed in the previous section. In our solution we propose to use an inverse approach where the amount of concepts in the structured dataset is constrained to the domain of interest and the required term is searched only on this subset of the dataset. In this approach, the search space is limited even more, but it is ensured that if an equivalent concept is found in the dataset, it is really related to the domain in interest.

When the concept is not found in the structured dataset, text/web mining may be used for information extraction as the next step. In our approach, the hierarchy of concepts derived from the structured dataset forms base of the resulting ontology and text/web mining techniques are used to find relations between these base concepts and the more specialized concepts not covered in the structured dataset. The relations are formed by searching lexico-syntactic patterns between relevant concepts in text/web documents. The overview of the proposed solution's workflow is shown in Fig. 1.

The procedure outlined above represents the basic set of steps to follow in our proposed solution. However, the application of particular resources (WordNet, DBpedia, Web mining) may be combined arbitrarily within each step to obtain better outcomes. Naturally, this must be tailored for specific application to ensure the required results. For instance, some form of web mining may be required in a preprocessing phase in order to define suitable concept labels for the subsequent ontology learning process. Furthermore, even if some semantically equivalent concept was found in the structured dataset, it may be suitable to apply the text/web mining methods to extend the knowledge about the concept, to find paths to other concepts in the ontology, etc. Furthermore, it is good to notice the proposed solution is not aimed to be fully automatic and a certain user effort is still required during the integration.

4 Semi-automatic Tool for Ontology Learning Tasks

In this paper we implemented the proposed solution on the case of integration of spare part records into the Ford Supply Chain ontology. The input data for this case is extensive and detailed Excel document where records for various spare parts are saved. Every record of spare parts has a unique (or in other words is identified by) part-number and is characterized by a brief part label. The part-number is considered as an attribute which is difficult to utilize for subsequent semantic processing (mining) and is only used to identify whether given spare part already exists in the ontology. The part label is taken into consideration for subsequent semantic processing. An example of the spare part number is *AT4E_6701_AA* and example of the part label is *crankshaft rear oil seal*.

We evaluated the suitability of various resources and methods for this case of application in an automotive domain. We considered WordNet and DBpedia as potential structured datasets to derive the hierarchy of general concepts. As described in the previous section, we don't attempt to query the whole dataset

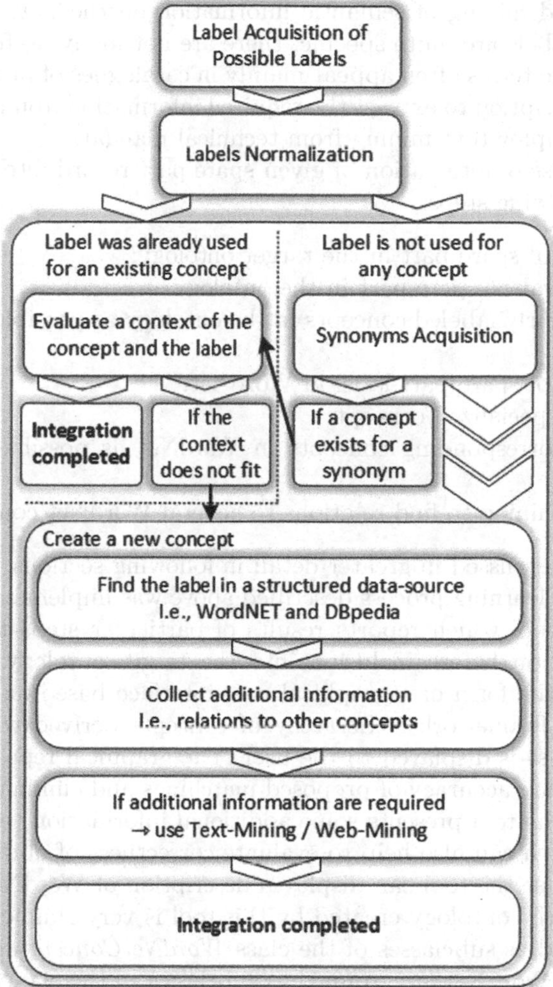

Fig. 1. Workflow of proposed solution

but only a predefined subset corresponding semantically to the target domain. To constrain the WordNet database, we consider hierarchy of concepts that are related to super-concepts *Automotive vehicle* or *Automobile* through various semantic relations (hypernymy, meronymy). Similarly, we constrain the query in DBpedia by condition that the concepts must be related to super-concept *Vehicle technology* through relations "skos:broader"[3] and "dc:subject"[4]. WordNet database was evaluated to be more suitable for this application mainly due to the existence of the meronymy relation.

[3] https://www.w3.org/TR/skos-reference/#broader.
[4] http://dublincore.org/documents/dces/.

We considered mining of semantic information on the web. However, since the spare part labels are quite specific, there are not many useful results found on the web. These terms often appear mainly in catalogues of producers without any detailed description to extract the required information from. For this reason we decided to employ text mining from technical manuals.

Overall process of integration of given spare part record into the ontology is divided into following steps:

1. Identification of spare part in the target ontology:
   (a) Find equivalent spare part in the ontology.
   (b) Find similarly labeled concepts in the ontology as possible candidates for matching.
2. Identification of spare part label in WordNet.
3. Definition of specialized concept:
   (a) Identify corresponding concepts in WordNet as possible canditates for matching.
   (b) Use text mining to find relations to general WordNet concepts.

These steps are discussed in greater detail in following sections.

The ontology learning process described above was implemented in a form of semi-automatic tool which reports results of particular steps to the user and requires verification before inclusion into the target ontology. Verification is implemented in the form of a graphical user interface based on Java Universal Network/Graph Framework[5]. Hierarchy of concepts derived within particular step of the process is displayed to the user. The graphical representation helps the user to evaluate accuracy of proposed matchings and eliminate the incorrect ones. Moreover the tool presents some additional information to the user about the concepts which can also help to evaluate correctness of obtained results. In this particular case the tool can display a description of WordNet concepts.

Structure of the ontology created by this tool is very simple. WordNet concepts are grouped as subclasses of the class *WordNetConcept* and the concepts not found in the WordNet are grouped as subclasses of the class *SpecializedConcept*. There are several object properties relating these concept classes, these properties are namely *hasPart* and its inverse *isPartOf*, *hasBroader* and its inverse *hasNarrower*, and general property between classes *isRelatedTo*. The property *hasBroader* is equivalent to the property rdfs:subClassOf. All spare parts are included as instances of class *SparePart* and given spare part is also added as an instance of corresponding concept class. Spare parts are labeled in the ontology by their part number.

In following paragraphs we describe particular steps of the above outlined procedure in greater detail and we present examples of integration for some specific cases.

[5] http://jung.sourceforge.net/.

4.1 Step 1: Identification in Target Ontology

In the first step the tool explores existing target ontology for matchings between processed spare part and spare parts and concepts already included in the ontology. First, labels of all spare part instances (i.e., part numbers) in the ontology are extracted and compared with the part number of processed spare part. If the tool finds exact agreement, this spare part was already included in the ontology and the procedure ends.

Next, labels of all concepts in the ontology are extracted and compared against part label of the processed spare part. This comparison is performed also for permutations and subsets of the spare part label. If some matching is found, it is reported to the user. The user then decides whether some of the matchings is correct and can specify a type of relation between the processed spare part and found corresponding concepts.

For example, let us assume the processed spare part has label *crankshaft rear oil seal* and the ontology already contains concept with label *rear crankshaft oil seal.* The user can decide that this concept represents the same type of spare part and order the tool to include new relation in the ontology: *exampleSparePart – isInstanceOf – rear crankshaft oil seal.* Similarly, if the ontology contained concept with label *crankshaft oil seal*, the user could order the tool to include relation *exampleSparePart – isInstanceOf – crankshaft rear oil seal – hasBroader – crankshaft oil seal.* Finally, if the ontology contained only the concept *crankshaft*, the user could order the relation *exampleSparePart – isInstanceOf – crankshaft rear oil seal isPartOf – crankshaft.*

4.2 Step 2: Identification in WordNet

In our application each WordNet concept represents single WordNet synset. The synset is a set of synonyms, i.e., terms representing approximately the same thing. For example terms *cylinder* and *piston chamber* form one synset in WordNet and both are represented by single WordNet concept in our tool. Within this step the tool compares full part label with the set of WordNet concept labels. Multiple matches can be found in the WordNet in case that more WordNet synsets contain the same term. Within the constrained WordNet hierarchy used in our application this holds for example for the part label *cap* which matches two WordNet synsets, one with description "a top (as for a bottle)" and the other with description "something serving as a cover or protection".

When a match is found, full path from the mapped concept to the super concept is displayed. Figure 2 shows the concept hierarchy produced for search of the part label *cap.* The square represents the spare part instance and the circles represent WordNet concepts (three dashes in the concept labels split different synonyms of given WordNet synset). Dotted lines represent the relation *isInstanceOf*, dashed lines represent the relation *hasBroader*, and solid lines represent the relation *isPartOf.* The figure indicates that there are three different paths to the super concept *motor vehicle.* By clicking particular nodes in the graph, the user can select which concepts (and relations) should be added into the ontology. Selected concepts are marked by green color in this example.

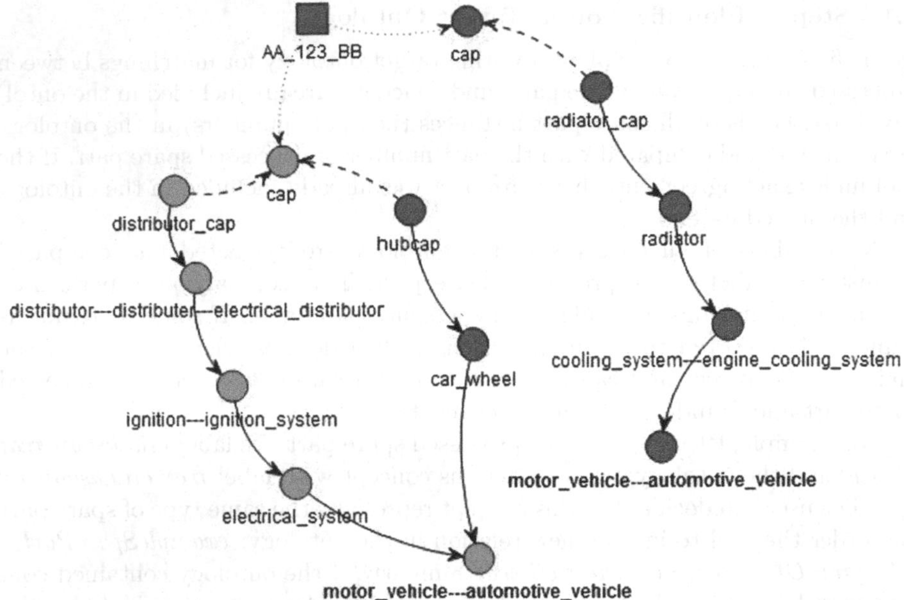

Fig. 2. Displayed concept hierarchy for search of spare part label cap. (Color figure online)

4.3 Step 3: Definition of Specialized Concept

Since the WordNet database contains rather general concepts, exact match of the full spare part label and some WordNet concepts is found only for limited number of spare parts. For the others the procedure continues by defining specialized concept and looking for semantic relations with other concepts. This task is divided in two substeps. First, possible candidates for matchings are searched in the WordNet database. This step is basically identical to the previous step but in this case permutations and subsets of the spare part label are taken into consideration. When a match is found, graphical representation of the concept hierarchy is displayed again. In this case relations between the specialized concept and corresponding WordNet concepts are shown and user can define type of relation between them by selecting one (or more). This is demonstrated in Fig. 3 on the example search of part label *piston pin retainer*. There are five relations between the specialized concept and corresponding WordNet concepts *piston—plunger* and *pivot—pin*, relation *isPartOf* in both directions (solid), *hasBroader* in both directions (dashed) and general relation *isRelatedTo* (dotted).

When all attempts to integrate the spare part performed in the previous steps of the procedure fail, the tool looks for semantic relations in unstructured text using text mining methods. Extraction of semantic relations is based on searching lexico-syntactic patterns. These pattern have form *first phrase – key phrase – second phrase*, where one of the phrases contains label of given

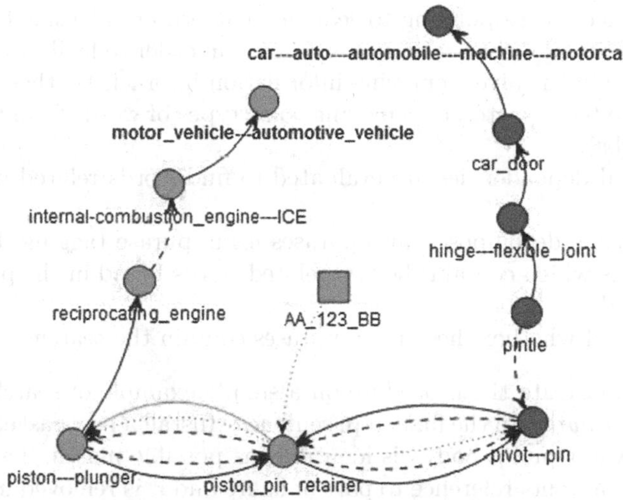

Fig. 3. Displayed concept hierarchy for search of spare part label piston pin retainer.

spare part (or permutation or subset of the label), the other contains name of some concept from the derived WordNet hierarchy, and the key phrase specifies semantic relation. These key phrases may be divided into four categories according to semantic relationship—hypernymy (e.g., "is a", "is defined as a", etc.), hyponymy (e.g., "called", "like", etc.), meronymy (e.g., "is part of", "in"), holonymy (e.g., "consists of", "having", "made of", etc.).

Found lexico-syntactic patterns may be processed in various ways. If the searched concepts are well covered by available resources, occurrence of particular patterns could be processed statistically to find the most frequent patterns as candidates for semantic relations. However, as discussed above, this domain is quite specific so that such an approach was not considered to be suitable. One also needs to decide whether to search the pattern explicitly or allow some unspecified words within the pattern. In the case of explicit search the procedure fails on inserted words, e.g., search of pattern *crankshaft–is part of–engine* fails on sentence "crankshaft is part of reciprocating engine". On the other hand, when the pattern is not strictly specified, the search may catch incorrect dependencies, e.g., pattern *crankshaft–in–automobile* is found in sentence "crankshaft is part of reciprocating engine in automobile", so that false relation pairs are found. In order to increase precision of obtained relation pairs, natural language processing methods are involved within analysis of found patterns, such as part-of-speech tagging, phrase tagging, and derivation of grammatical dependencies. For these tasks we use libraries developed at the Stanford Natural Language Processing Group[6].

The procedure of extracting semantic relation used in this application can be described as follows:

[6] https://nlp.stanford.edu/.

1. First, sentences corresponding to searched pattern are identified in the text.
2. The complexity of a given sentence is reduced in order to facilitate subsequent processing. This involves removing information in brackets (these are usually references to figures, etc.) or removing some types of words from the sentence (e.g., adverbs).
3. Grammatical dependencies are evaluated to find words related by given key phrase.
4. The sentence is decomposed into phrases using phrase tagging. Lowest level noun phrases which contain the two related words found in the previous step are identified.
5. It is evaluated whether these noun phrases contain the searched labels.

Let us demonstrate the procedure on a simple example of search of pattern *gasket–of–water pump*. In the first step, sentence "Install a new gasket (13) on the flange of the water pump body" is identified as possible match. The bracket in the sentence represents reference to part of figure and it is removed in the second step. Evaluation of grammatical dependencies shows that words *flange* and *body* are related by the phrase *of*. The lowest level noun phrases corresponding to these two words are *flange* and *the water pump body*. In this case the search fails because the searched term *gasket* is not contained in the first noun phrase. The procedure would succeed in this case for the search of pattern *flange–of–water pump*. In this case the tool reports the result to the user together with suggested semantic relation (meronymy). The user can then decide to add the relation *flange – isPartOf – water pump* to the ontology.

5 Summary

In this paper, we deal with a problem of integration of new information into existing knowledge model, i.e., ontology learning problem. Automated extension of existing ontology is a very demanding task and is strongly dependent on the given application as well as on available resources of additional information.

Our proposed solution to the ontology learning problem combines extraction of required knowledge in structured resources, e.g., DBpedia or WordNet, and acquisition of additional knowledge by means of text/web mining techniques. This approach aims to overcome problems when a given domain or given resources are very specific so that the existing structured data-sources are not convenient.

We presented the application of the proposed approach for integration of spare part records into Ford ontology. Proposed approach was implemented in a semi-automatic ontology learning tool which reports results of the ontology learning process to the user and allows him to verify the information to be added to the ontology. The proposed solution for seems to be promising for the facilitation ontology learning process based on the presented application in automotive domain.

Acknowledgment. This work is supported through the Ford Motor Company University Research Proposal (URP) program and by institutional resources for research by the Czech Technical University in Prague, Czech Republic.

References

1. Booshehri, M., Luksch, P.: Towards adding linked data to ontology learning layers. In: Proceedings of the 16th International Conference on Information Integration and Web-Based Applications, pp. 401–409 (2014)
2. Booshehri, M., Luksch, P.: An ontology enrichment approach by using DBpedia. In: Proceedings of the 5th International Conference on Web Intelligence, Mining and Semantics (2015)
3. van Hage, W.R., Kolb, H., Schreiber, G.: A method for learning part-whole relations. In: Cruz, I., et al. (eds.) ISWC 2006. LNCS, vol. 4273, pp. 723–735. Springer, Heidelberg (2006). https://doi.org/10.1007/11926078_52
4. Hearst, M.: Automatic acquisition of hyponyms from large text corpora. In: Proceedings of the Fourteenth International Conference on Computational Linguistics, pp. 539–545 (1992)
5. Jirkovský, V., Šebek, O., Kadera, P., Rychtyckyj, N.: Heterogeneity reduction for data refining within ontology learning process. In: IECON 2018–44th Annual Conference of the IEEE Industrial Electronics Society, pp. 3108–3113 (2018)
6. Klaussner, C., Zhekova, D.: Lexico-syntactic patterns for automatic ontology building. In: Proceedings of the Second Student Research Workshop Associated with RANLP 2011, pp. 109–114. Association for Computational Linguistics, Hissar, September 2011. https://www.aclweb.org/anthology/R11-2017
7. Luong, H.P., Gauch, S., Speretta, M.: Enriching concept descriptions in an amphibian ontology with vocabulary extracted from WordNet. In: 2009 22nd IEEE International Symposium on Computer-Based Medical Systems, pp. 1–6 (2009)
8. Maedche, A., Staab, S.: Ontology learning for the semantic web. IEEE Intell. Syst. **16**(2), 72–79 (2001)
9. Maedche, A., Staab, S.: Ontology learning. In: Staab, S., Studer, R. (eds.) Handbook on Ontologies. INFOSYS, pp. 173–190. Springer, Heidelberg (2004). https://doi.org/10.1007/978-3-540-24750-0_9
10. Miller, G.A.: WordNet: a lexical database for English. Commun. ACM **38**(11), 39–41 (1995)
11. Tesfaye, D., Zock, M., Teferra, S.: Combining syntactic patterns and Wikipedia's hierarchy of hyperlinks to extract meronym relations. In: Proceedings of the NAACL Student Research Workshop, pp. 29–36. Association for Computational Linguistics, San Diego, June 2016. https://doi.org/10.18653/v1/N16-2005. https://www.aclweb.org/anthology/N16-2005
12. Šebek, O., Jirkovský, V., Rychtyckyj, N.: Concepts and relations acquisition within ontology learning process for automotive. In: Data a znalosti & WIKT, pp. 115–119 (2018)
13. Zhou, W., et al.: A semi-automatic ontology learning based on WordNet and event-based natural language processing. In: Information and Automation (2006)

Agent-Based Approach for Decentralized Data Analysis in Industrial Cyber-Physical Systems

Jonas Queiroz[1(✉)], Paulo Leitão[2], José Barbosa[2], and Eugénio Oliveira[1]

[1] Faculty of Engineering - LIACC, University of Porto, Porto, Portugal
{jonas.queiroz,eco}@fe.up.pt

[2] Research Center in Digitalization and Intelligent Robotics (CeDRI), Instituto Politécnico de Bragança, Campus de Santa Apolónia, 5300-253 Bragança, Portugal
{pleitao,jbarbosa}@ipb.pt

Abstract. The 4th industrial revolution is marked by the use of Cyber-Physical Systems (CPSs) to achieve higher levels of flexibility and adaptation in production systems that need to cope with a demanding and ever-changing market, driven by mass customization and high quality products. In this context, data analysis is a key technology enabler in the development of intelligent machines and products. However, in addition to Cloud-based data analysis services, the realization of such CPS requires technologies and approaches capable to effectively support distributed and embedded data analysis capabilities. The advances in Edge Computing have promoted the data processing near or at the devices that produce data, which combined with Multi-Agent Systems, allow to develop solutions based on distributed and interacting autonomous entities in open and dynamic environments. In this sense, this paper presents a modular agent-based architecture to design and embed cyber-physical components with data analysis capabilities. The proposed approach defines a set of data processing modules that can be combined to build cyber-physical agents to be deployed at different computational layers. The proposed approach was applied in a smart inspection station for electric motors, where agents embedding data analysis algorithms were distributed among Edge, Fog and Cloud layers. The experimental results illustrated the benefits of distributing the data analysis by different computational layers.

Keywords: Cyber-physical systems · Data analysis · Multi-agent systems · Edge computing

1 Introduction

The 4th industrial revolution (4IR) is marked by the use of Cyber-Physical Systems (CPSs) to achieve higher levels of flexibility and adaptation in production systems that need to cope with a demanding and ever-changing market, driven

V. Mařík et al. (Eds.): HoloMAS 2019, LNAI 11710, pp. 130–144, 2019.
https://doi.org/10.1007/978-3-030-27878-6_11

by mass customization and high quality products. CPSs are systems of systems that comprise a set of networked autonomous entities, combining cyber and physical counterparts that can cooperate to reach the systems' goals [9]. CPSs are suitable to solve problems in complex and large-scale systems that can be found in smart manufacturing, smart cities and smart electrical grids [9].

In this context, CPSs are supported by several disruptive ICT technologies, namely Internet of Things (IoT), Edge and Cloud Computing, and Big Data analysis [5,11]. Particularly, Artificial Intelligence (AI) is a key enabler that can provide powerful solutions for the realization of the envisioned CPS and its features, like autonomy, self-awareness and reconfigurability. In industrial environments, the use of AI can contribute to develop smart machines and products, consequently leading to the creation of intelligent production systems and factories [7]. AI can address the CPS's requirements by providing data analysis solutions, such those based on Machine-Learning (ML) [7,14], as well as distributed problem solving approaches, like Multi-Agent Systems (MASs) [8,15].

The first provides data analysis algorithms capable of learning patterns and extract actionable information from the produced data, devising data models for prediction and data-driven decisions [6,14]. Lately, the increasing availability of data, mainly powered by the use of IoT technologies, and computational resources have contributed to several advancements in this field. The second provides a framework to support the development of solutions based on interacting autonomous software agents that are capable of distributing intelligence in open and dynamic environments. In such approach, the system's behavior emerges from the interaction among autonomous agents, where the decisions are taken in a decentralized manner, in opposition to traditional centralized and rigid structures that are not able to address flexibility, robustness, and on-the-fly reconfigurability. In this sense, MASs completely enable the development of CPSs with distributed and embedded data analysis capabilities [8].

On the other hand, CPSs go beyond the traditional IoT applications, where smart sensors send all data to Cloud systems, which provide a well-established platform for on demand storage and processing capabilities. Besides software components, the CPSs envision intelligent hardware equipment with embedded processing capabilities that should be able to analyze and reason over their data, as well as interact and collaborate with other components. In this context, the increasing popularity and development of Fog and Edge Computing [2] have allowed to deploy several processing capabilities, including data analysis, close to the places where data is generated. Such approaches promote the decentralization of Cloud data analysis along the Edge and Fog layers, that besides attending important industrial requirements, such as, data-sensitive, responsiveness and constrained network bandwidth [3], is aligned with the CPS concepts.

In this context, this paper presents a modular agent-based architecture to develop cyber-physical components with embedded data analysis capabilities to be deployed in different computing layers, from Cloud to Edge, supporting the decentralization of data analysis. The proposed approach defines a set of modules that can be combined to build cyber-physical agents with different data analysis capabilities. Such capabilities should be defined based on the application requirements, and considering where the agent will be deployed, e.g., Cloud or Edge. Besides that, this approach considers the use of IoT and Edge technologies to be compliant and interoperable with related technologies and applications. The proposed approach was applied in a smart inspection station for electric motors, where agents embedding data analysis algorithms were distributed among Edge, Fog and Cloud layers. The experimental results illustrate the benefits of distributing the data analysis by different computational layers.

The remaining of this paper is organized as follows. Section 2 discusses the decentralization of data analysis from Cloud to Edge, and Sect. 3 presents the proposed agent-based industrial CPS that distributes intelligence horizontally and vertically. Section 4 illustrates the implementation of the proposed approach in a case study, discussing some preliminary experimental results. Finally, Sect. 5 rounds up the paper with the conclusions.

2 Decentralization of Intelligence in Industrial CPS

A CPS encompasses cyber-physical components capable of performing some data processing, instead of only collect data and send to the Cloud, as in traditional IoT approaches. Thus, besides Cloud computing, CPSs also explore the Edge and Fog Computing approaches, which provide a layered infrastructure that spans from virtual to physical world defining what, where and how computational resources are deployed and made available. In this sense, they play an important role in the decentralization of the computational resources from Cloud to the equipment at the edge of the network, as well as to the end-devices.

Although the terms Fog and Edge Computing have been used interchangeably [4], this work considers that Fog comprises the intermediary computing layer between Cloud and IoT devices, while the Edge is used for embedding processing capabilities in IoT-based end-devices, covering the physical systems, as illustrated in Fig. 1 (left). Fog aims to provide direct support to Edge, mainly regarding time constrained tasks, while contributing to offloading and providing more meaningful information to Cloud systems. On the other hand, having a complete view of the system, Cloud applications are responsible for providing a high-level support for the systems at lower layers.

Regarding the intelligence distribution, Fig. 1 (right) illustrates how industrial tasks that can be supported by AI may be distributed from Cloud to Edge. A more detailed discussion of a wide range of AI algorithms, including Deep Learning, and their applications in industry, specially manufacturing is provided in the surveys [6,14]. In general, at the Edge or Fog (when considered resource constrained equipment), the intelligence is governed by rule-based and simple data analysis tasks. Since these entities comprise execution instead of development environments, i.e., they are not designed to train ML models, which should be performed at the Cloud. For instance, classification and prediction models can be easily deployed at these devices, since after the model creation its execution comprises a set of rules or equations (e.g., decision tree or even Neural Network algorithms). Moreover, some algorithms can have different parts performed in

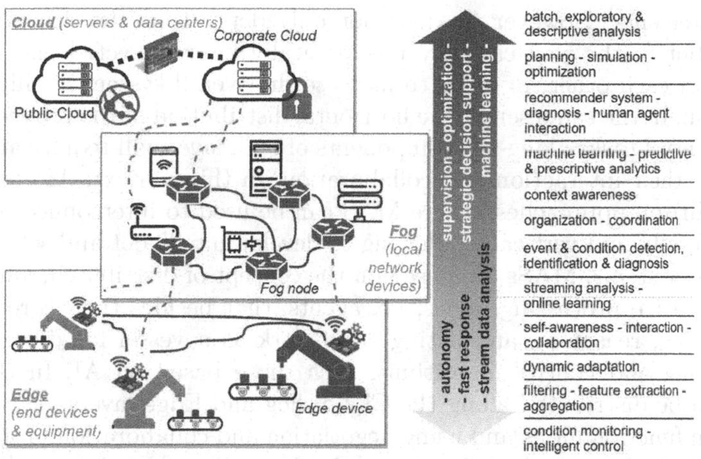

Fig. 1. CPS along Cloud, Fog and Edge layers

different layers. For example, some neural network models can distribute the layers, along Cloud to Edge, which besides offload the computation in central servers can also provide a local, faster and partial response [10,13]. At these levels, the components can also support a set of on-line learning approaches, or even the update of data models, in order to cope with the environment dynamics.

Additionally, when considering Edge devices with their limited resources and very local and incomplete view of the system, data processing can only provide a very simple and highly uncertain notion of the environment conditions. This can be addressed at the Fog, which encompasses a diverse number of devices (from routers to high end computers) that enable to host almost any kind of AI-based applications. They can perform a variety of data intensive tasks, processing and integrating multiple real-time data streams that can be sent to Cloud or local applications. Considering all these aspects, at the Edge and Fog levels, examples of applications of AI in industrial automation include real-time monitoring, early detection of abnormality, local diagnoses, as well as obstacle identification and avoidance, by mobile robots [1,16].

In this sense, Edge and Fog are highly suitable for the operational levels, aiming to provide autonomy to the system's components and fast response for monitoring and control. On the other hand, Cloud fits better the needs of enterprise and business levels, oriented for supervisory and decision support tasks, since it can face connectivity issues (like latency, limited bandwidth and security). In this sense, in an industrial environment, most of the operational tasks will require the support of applications running in a private corporate Cloud or Fog-based infrastructure. Thus, at operational level the use of public Cloud-based applications usually is very limited and will demand extra security concerns.

There is no doubt that the decentralization of data processing and consequently the intelligence from Cloud to Edge layers are essential to attend the

4IR requirements. However, it does not only depend on the decentralization of tasks, but in the way each layer is vertically interconnected and how they can support each other, in order to increase the overall system intelligence and automation. In the same sense, the horizontal distribution of the related processing and control tasks along the components of each layer will require approaches to manage their interaction and collaboration. In this context, AI goes beyond ML data-driven approaches, where MAS can be used to interconnect these layers horizontally and vertically, allowing to develop intelligent and self-organized distributed systems. MASs are based on the concept of distributed, autonomous and cooperative processing nodes, i.e. agents, that besides their core functionality (sensing, reasoning and acting) also work as a vessel for different kinds of processing and control algorithms, such those based on AI. In this sense, agents can be distributed along the Cloud, Fog and Edge layers, encapsulating the system functionalities and using negotiation and collaboration protocols and strategies to interact with each other and achieve the system's goals [8,15].

3 Proposed Agent-Based CPS Approach

Based on the facts that data analysis is the key technology enabler of the 4IR and MAS is a suitable approach to distribute intelligence, this paper proposes a modular agent-based approach for the development of industrial CPSs.

In this sense, instead of defining a set of agents with specific roles to develop a CPS, this approach defines a set of modules that can be properly combined to build data analysis agents. This way, this approach mainly focuses on the data processing and analysis aspects, covering the different data analysis scopes of a CPS (stream and batch), where other application-dependent capabilities can be added to the agents according to their role in the CPS.

3.1 Modular Architecture of a Cyber-Physical Agent

An agent belonging to the proposed approach follows an architecture based on a set of plug-in modules, as illustrated in Fig. 2 (left side), where each module can be seen as an agent behaviour, which may have its own control thread. In this sense, the idea of this modular internal agent architecture is to enable the design of different agent configurations by combining a set of modules according to the application requirements and the constraints of their execution platforms, e.g., Edge devices or Cloud servers. This enables the development of lightweight agents to be embedded in Edge devices, as well as complex agents to be deployed at the Cloud. While the first aims to provide fast adaptation to condition change, the second aims to provide actionable information for optimization and knowledge generation.

In the *Stream Analysis scope*, the modules aim to process raw data streams continuously and in (near) real-time, thus representing common elements of agents deployed in the Edge that aim to attend fast response requirements.

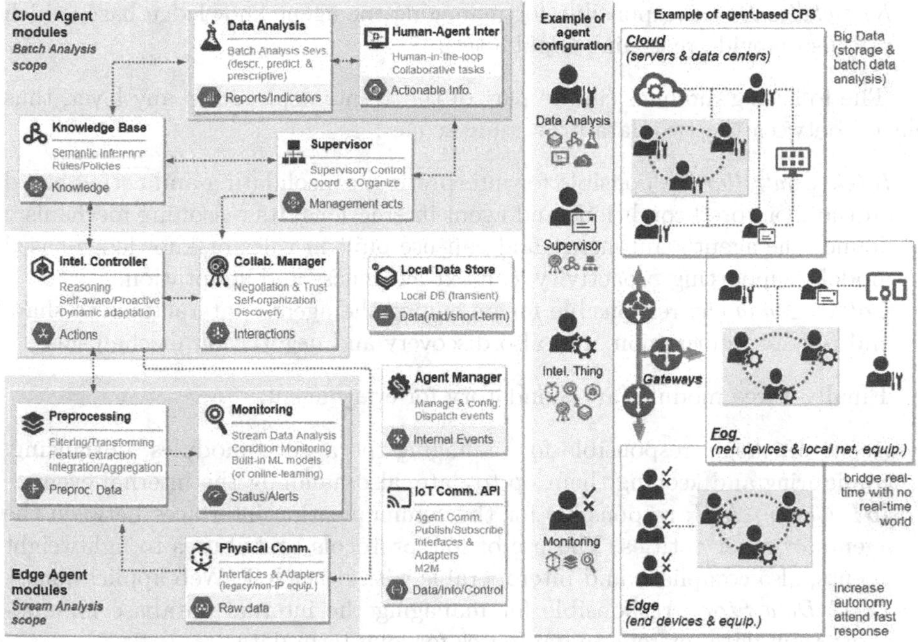

Fig. 2. Modular approach to build agent-based cyber-physical components. Left: modules with main capabilities and outputs. Right: examples of agent configurations and their organization and interactions in a CPS

- *Physical Comm.*: responsible for managing the communication interfaces between the embedded software system and the physical equipment.
- *Preprocessing*: responsible for the raw data preprocessing, namely data filtering, transforming, feature extraction, aggregation and integration.
- *Monitoring*: responsible for the continuous analysis of parameters, performing simple rule-based or complex data analysis algorithms, which may include context-awareness and on-line adaptation capabilities.

On the other hand, modules in the *Batch Analysis scope* aim to perform supervisory and complex data analysis, considering data integrated from different sources, being more suitable for agents to be deployed at Cloud or Fog layers.

- *Supervisor*: responsible for supervising, coordinating and supporting the other agents. Its global scope enables high level decision-making based on the integration and processing of information from different agents.
- *Data Analysis*: responsible for providing data analysis services for other modules or components, using ML algorithms to integrate and analyze data from different sources (historical or real-time).
- *Human-Agent Inter*: responsible for providing mechanisms and interfaces for the access and interaction with humans for supervisory and control tasks.

- *Knowledge Base*: responsible for managing the agent knowledge base, which can also provide reasoning capabilities.

The following modules can be part of the agents deployed in any layer, thus placed between the two data processing scopes:

- *Intel. Controller*: responsible for interpreting, consolidating and acting based on the monitored conditions and agent interactions. Its reasoning mechanism defines the agent's autonomy and can use built-in rules or knowledge-based models, supporting proactivity, context-awareness and adaptation.
- *Collab. Manager*: responsible for managing the agents' interactions to share and request information, and also discovery and negotiation mechanisms.

Finally, three modules are mandatory for every agent:

- *Agent Manager*: responsible for managing the agent's modules, initializing, configuring and keeping them up to date, also handling the internal events.
- *IoT Comm. API*: responsible for the communication interfaces between the agents or other entities. The use of IoT protocols contributes to lightweight agents, also compliant and interoperable with other IoT/Web applications.
- *Local Data Store*: responsible for managing the internal database for mid-short term data, or remote databases for long-term data.

Figure 2 (right) illustrates some examples of agent configurations that can be deployed in a Cloud-Fog-Edge environment. As example, the *Monitoring* agent configuration can be embedded in an Edge device, retrieving, preprocessing and monitoring the measured data and publishing the outputs to other components (e.g., preprocessed data, operation status, and alerts). On the other hand, the *Data Analysis* agent configuration can be seen as the back-end of a supervisory system, performing data analysis and providing reports to users.

3.2 Behaviors of the Modules

The proposed approach considers the use of an event-driven architecture, where the agent's modules (or behaviours), consume and produce events, instead of being directly linked with each other. Moreover, the modules were designed to perform independent tasks, thus facilitating the development of agents with different configurations. The expected relations among modules were represented by dashed arrows in the Fig. 2 (left).

Following an event-driven architecture, the modules can be designed using UML activity diagrams, as illustrated in Fig. 3, for the *Monitoring* and *Supervisor* modules. Both modules consider an event queue that is fed with events produced by other modules. The incoming events are processed according to their types, and may produce new event(s). In the *Monitoring* module (Fig. 3 left), the *process* task comprises the application of conditional rules or data analysis models. The outputs can be events about status and alerts that will be consumed and handled by other modules, such as the *Intel. Controller* and *Supervisor*.

The *Supervisor* module (Fig. 3 right) presents a more complex task structure, where the income events may need to be integrated (and synchronized), e.g., if the module handles data from multiples modules or agents. Then, some reasoning or inference process should be performed that may yield to a set of actions. These actions may be information to feed and update other modules or agents. This module also considers the handling of requests from other components and periodic tasks that may follow the same reasoning process.

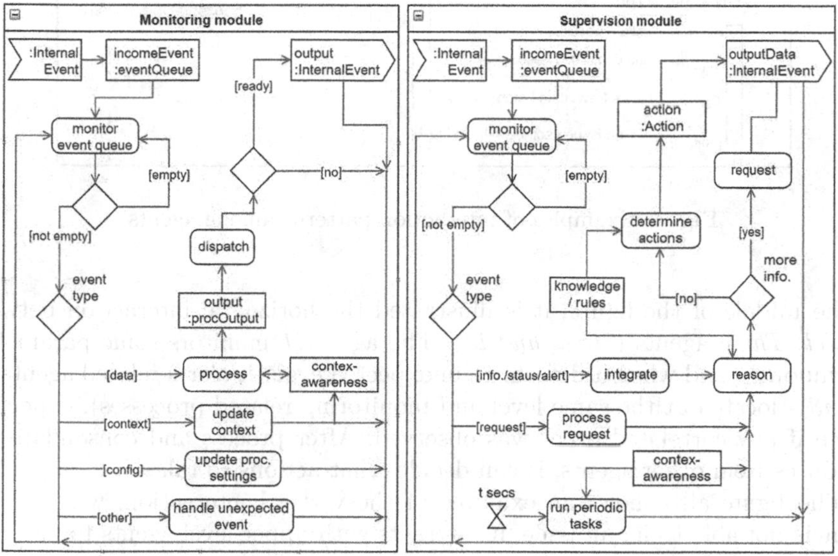

Fig. 3. Example of the modules' internal tasks based on an event-driven approach

3.3 Interactions Among Agents

The global system behavior emerges from the interaction among the agents, each one embedding data analysis capabilities according to the application requirements, as previously described. Figure 2 (right) illustrates different kinds of interaction among the agents placed along the Cloud-Fog-Edge layers, which follow basic interaction protocols, like request, inform and subscribe defined by FIPA specifications. Moreover, IoT technologies, such as MQTT and CoAP, are also considered to address the interoperability of components and other systems, through the use of request-response and publish-subscribe mechanisms.

Besides responsive behaviors, the agents can also present a proactive behavior, where they inform others about certain events, regarding monitored conditions and other analysis outputs. In this sense, as illustrated in the top-left of Fig. 4, the agents can subscribe to receive data and events from each other.

Given the multi-level agent organization, the agents can perform horizontal and vertical interaction, with agents at the same or different levels, respectively.

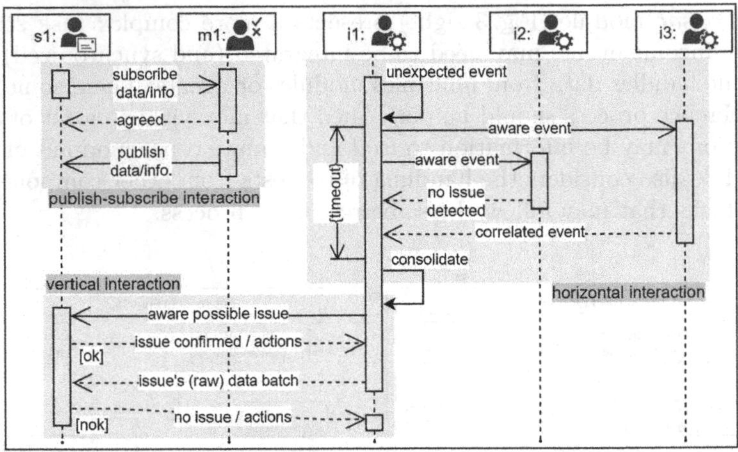

Fig. 4. Examples of interaction patterns among agents

In the middle of the figure, it is illustrated the horizontal interaction between 3 *Intel. Thing* agents (*i1, i2 and i3*). The agent *i1* monitors some parameters continuously, and when it detects an unexpected event it alerts related agents (*i2 and i3* - located at the same level and monitoring related processes), expecting to see if any correlated event was observed. After process and consolidate the responses from other agents, it can decide what actions to take.

The figure also shows an example of the vertical interaction, where if the agent is not able to fix an issue, it interacts with upper level agents to alert the possible issue. In this example, a *Supervisor* agent (*s1*) processes the alert and replies with confirmation and possible control actions.

4 Experimental Results

The proposed agent-based CPS approach was implemented and tested under several scenarios, aiming to analyze the applicability and performance of distributing the data analysis algorithms.

4.1 Description of the Case Study

The case study is a smart inspection station [12], where the performance of electric motors is tested according to several operating scenarios. The monitored data corresponds to electric voltage/current, vibration, temperature and rotation speed, and is acquired by Edge agents, deployed in an Edge Computing board (UDOO QUAD). These agents are able to extract and communicate data streams, and have computational capabilities (data processing and storage) to enable local data analysis and interaction with upper level components.

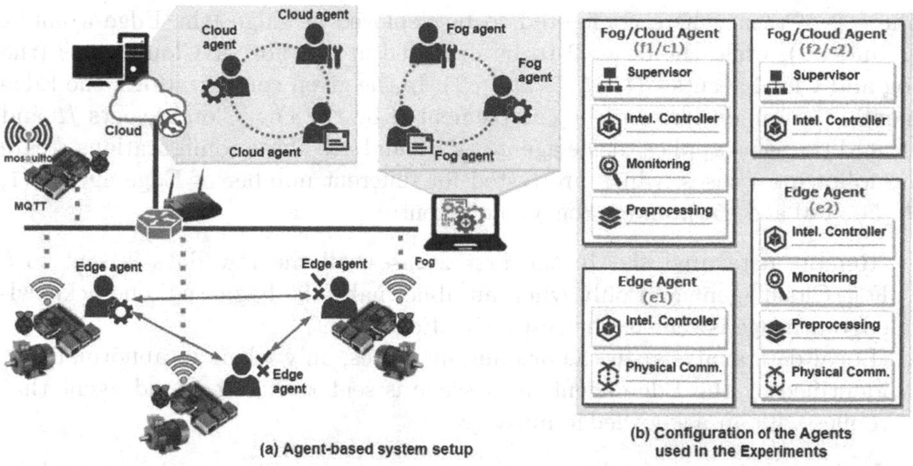

Fig. 5. Experimental agent-based CPS for the inspection station. (a) distribution of agents among Cloud, Fog and Edge layers, (b) configuration of the agents

Figure 5 illustrates the deployed experimental agent-based CPS, showing how the several agents were distributed along the Cloud, Fog and Edge layers, as well as the configuration of each agent using the modules previously described.

Since the idea of the testbed is to create and test a CPS environment with a large number of entities producing and processing data streams, the physical inspection station was replicated through simulation (particularly to simulate the execution of a large number of Edge components). The simulation consisted of collecting and saving the raw data from the available physical electric motor. Then, the dataset was loaded in 10 Raspberry Pis, where Edge agents were deployed to simulate other instances of the electric motor. In other to achieve an even greater number of Edge agents, another PC connected to the local network was used to run other instances of these agents. It is important to notice that the Edge agents running in the PC were not used for the experiment evaluation, since the idea was to assess the performance in Edge platforms. Thus, the role of these agents was just to provide a more challenging environment, i.e., high network traffic and computational load for the Fog and Cloud components. Another Raspberry Pi was used as a MQTT broker to support the agent communication.

4.2 Implementation of the Agent-Based CPS

The agent-based system was implemented in JAVA following the approach described in Sect. 3, and implementing the modules illustrated in Fig. 5b, as well as the common modules. The experiments focused on the analysis of the CPS behavior when the data analysis is performed by Fog or Cloud agents, or locally by the Edge agents, as well as considering different number of agents in the system. The designed scenario considers 4 configurations of agents (Fig. 5b), where 2 of them where configured to be deployed at Edge (the Edge agents - *e1* and *e2*), while the other 2 to be deployed at the Fog or Cloud levels (the Fog and Cloud agents - *f1*, *c1*, *f2* and *c2*). In the given configurations, the Edge agents *e1* were designed to be complemented by the Fog/Cloud agents *f1* and *c1*, and the same applies to the agents *e2*, *f2* and *c2*. These configurations create the following 4 cases, which are tested for different number of Edge agents (1, 10, 50, 100 and 150), and 1 Fog/Cloud agent:

- (Remote data analysis) In the first 2 cases, all the raw data is sent to a Fog/Cloud agent and only when an abnormality is diagnosed, one acknowledge message is sent to the respective Edge agent.
- (Local data analysis) In the 3rd and 4th cases, only when an abnormality is identified by the Edge agent, a message is sent to a Fog/Cloud agent that replies with an acknowledge message.

In the experiments the data processing starts at the *Physical Comm.* module, which retrieves the raw data. This data is aggregated and normalized by the *Preprocessing* module (in a Fog/Cloud agent - *f1/c1* or in the same Edge agent - *e2*). Then, the *Monitoring* module applies a ML pre-trained model and the *Intel. Controller* performs the abnormality diagnosis, checking if the data analysis output is above a given threshold. Finally, the *Supervisor* module, for the sake of simplicity, just confirms the diagnostics and sends an acknowledge of the abnormality to the Edge agents.

The data analysis was conducted following a common industrial scenario, where streams of unlabeled time-series data need to be analyzed continuously and in (near) real-time for abnormality detection. In this context, aiming to illustrate the potentials of ML in industrial applications, artificial neural network techniques were deployed in the agents, particularly Autoencoder and LSTM (Long-Short Term Memory) [14], which were implemented using the DeepLearning4J Java library (deeplearning4j.org). In this kind of neural networks, the model is trained in an unsupervised manner, learning to reconstruct the patterns of the input signal. Thus, when an abnormal signal is presented to the trained model, it will not be able to reconstruct it, leading to a high reconstruction loss score (see Fig. 6). For the experiments, the Autoencoder model was built based on LSTM layers, comprising $400 \times 50 \times 10 \times 50 \times 400$ LSTM nodes/neurons per layer.

4.3 Analysis of the Experimental Results

The dataset used in the experiments consists in 120.904 data samples (5 ms as the sample rate) collected from the inspection station when performing an operation where a load is applied to the motor in a regular interval. In this operation, some abnormalities are injected, namely the load is not applied as expected. The experiments reported in this paper only consider the data analysis of the electric current values. Figure 6 (top) illustrates an interval of the measured values, exemplifying 2 periods where the load is applied, followed by one that it is not applied, i.e., an abnormality in the operation.

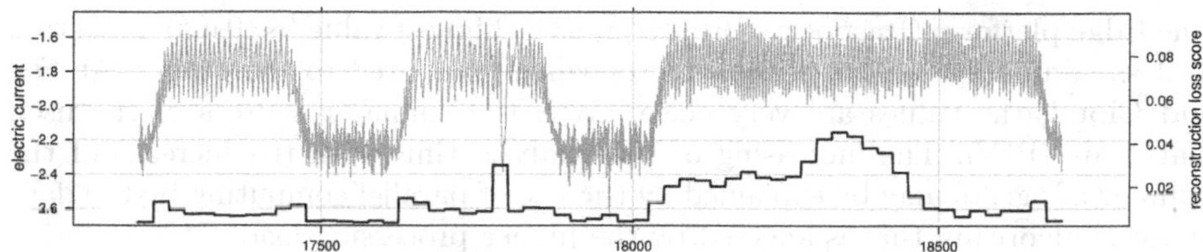

Fig. 6. Motor raw electric current data, showing the load pattern with an abnormality (top). Autoencoder reconstruction loss score, indicating the abnormality (bottom)

The first half of the dataset containing no abnormalities, was used to train the Autoencoder model, while the other half, containing 12 abnormalities, was used for the tests. The trained model was serialized and loaded to be used by the agents. Instead of compute the Autoencoder every time step, a window of 25 time steps is accumulated. Figure 6 (bottom) illustrates the reconstruction loss score of the trained model in a sampling interval.

Figure 7 illustrates 3 charts with the results of these experiments. The first evaluates the data analysis time, i.e., the time to execute the Autoencoder model by the *Monitoring* module in the agents placed at Cloud, Fog and Edge layers.

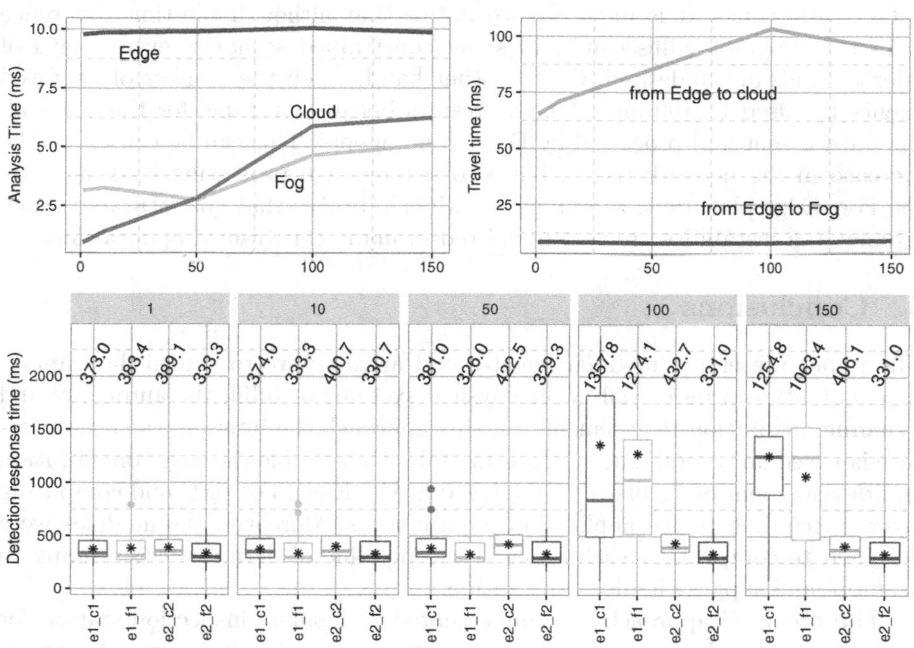

Fig. 7. Experimental results. Top-left: data analysis time at Edge, Fog and Cloud platforms. Top-right: travel time from Edge to Fog and Cloud. Bottom: diagnosis time in different scenarios

The Edge platform (Raspberry Pi) presents the highest value (~10 ms), reflecting its less computational processing power when compared to the others. At Fog and Cloud, the values are very close, given the similar resources of the used platforms (PCs). The increasing of the analysis time with the increase of the number of agents may be explained by the use of parallel computing by the data analysis algorithm that is affected by the higher processing load.

The second chart illustrates the messages' round-trip time, from Edge to Fog and Edge to Cloud. Since the Fog is a PC in the local network (only 2 hops), it presents a much lower time (~22 ms) than Cloud, which is in a remote network (11 hops). In this context, another aspect regards the bandwidth consumption, which in the experiments showed that performing local data analysis (i.e., in the Edge agents), resulted in 4.1 KB sent and 5.9 KB received per agent, for the whole test. On the other scenario, i.e., send raw data to be analyzed by Fog/Cloud agents, resulted in 14 MB sent and 5.9 KB received, per agent for the whole test. This showed the importance to perform some data analysis locally, which in this case can significantly reduce the bandwidth consumption and associated costs.

The third chart analyses the time to detect an abnormality and acknowledge it to the Edge agent. When 1, 10 or 50 Edge agents are deployed, the average values (the stars in the chart, with the values printed in the top) are practically the same. This illustrates that in this scenario in spite of the higher processing power of the Fog/Cloud platforms, the processing at the Edge presented slight better total times. It is important to notice that although the time difference is in the order of milliseconds, in some constrained scenarios even delays of microseconds are undesired. On the other hand, when the number of deployed agents is raised to 100 and 150, the results became unstable for the cases all the data is sent and processed by Fog/Cloud agents. This can be caused by the increase in the network traffic, but also by the high processing load faced by the Fog/Edge platforms, as well as the MQTT broker that got saturated. Such latency and instability are very undesired in many constrained applications.

5 Conclusions

The paper presents a modular agent-based architecture to embed data analysis capabilities in industrial cyber-physical systems to fulfill the autonomy and dynamic adaptation requirements. In this approach the internal agent architecture is based on several data analysis modules that enable the easy configuration and development of agents to be deployed at the Edge, Fog or Cloud computing layers, according to the application requirements. Moreover, the modules were designed to complement each other in the pipeline of data analysis, aiming to promote and support its decentralization.

The proposed approach was implemented in a smart inspection station for electric motors, where agents embedding different data analysis algorithms were distributed among Edge, Fog and Cloud layers. The case study enabled to show the application of ML techniques to address industrial data analysis requirements, specially regarding the continuous and (near) real-time analysis of streaming of unlabeled time-series data where Autoencoder based on LSTM layers showed to be a suitable approach. The experimental results also illustrated the benefits of distributing the data analysis by different computational layers, particularly performing data analysis at Edge level.

Future work will be devoted to extend the experiments to test the agent interaction strategies towards a distributed and collaborative data analysis, and to explore other ML algorithms in industrial scenarios.

Acknowledgment. This work is part of the GO0D MAN project that has received funding from the European Union's Horizon 2020 research and innovation programme under grant agreement N° 723764.

References

1. Aazam, M., Zeadally, S., Harras, K.A.: Deploying Fog computing in industrial internet of things and industry 4.0. IEEE Trans. Ind. Inform. **14**(10), 4674–4682 (2018)
2. Bonomi, F., Milito, R., Natarajan, P., Zhu, J.: Fog computing: a platform for internet of things and analytics. In: Bessis, N., Dobre, C. (eds.) Big Data and Internet of Things: A Roadmap for Smart Environments. SCI, vol. 546, pp. 169–186. Springer, Cham (2014). https://doi.org/10.1007/978-3-319-05029-4_7
3. Breivold, H., Sandström, K.: Internet of things for industrial automation - challenges and technical solutions. In: 2015 IEEE International Conference on on Data Science and Data Intensive Systems, pp. 532–539, December 2015
4. Chiang, M., Zhang, T.: Fog and IoT: an overview of research opportunities. IEEE Internet Things J. **3**(6), 854–864 (2016)
5. Colombo, A.W., Karnouskos, S., Kaynak, O., Shi, Y., Yin, S.: Industrial cyberphysical systems: a backbone of the fourth industrial revolution. IEEE Ind. Electron. Mag. **11**(1), 6–16 (2017)
6. Fei, X., et al.: CPS data streams analytics based on machine learning for cloud and Fog computing: a survey. Future Gen. Comput. Sys. **90**, 435–450 (2019)
7. Lee, J., Davari, H., Singh, J., Pandhare, V.: Industrial artificial intelligence for industry 4.0-based manufacturing systems. Manuf. Lett. **18**, 20–23 (2018)
8. Leitão, P., Karnouskos, S., Ribeiro, L., Lee, J., Strasser, T., Colombo, A.W.: Smart agents in industrial cyber-physical systems. Proc. IEEE **104**(5), 1086–1101 (2016)
9. Leitão, P., Colombo, A.W., Karnouskos, S.: Industrial automation based on cyber-physical systems technologies: prototype implementations and challenges. Comput. Ind. **81**, 11–25 (2016)
10. Li, L., Ota, K., Dong, M.: Deep learning for smart industry: efficient manufacture inspection system with Fog computing. IEEE Trans. Ind. Inf. **14**(10), 4665–4673 (2018)
11. Lu, Y.: Industry 4.0: a survey on technologies, applications and open research issues. J. Ind. Inf. Integr. **6**, 1–10 (2017)
12. Queiroz, J., Barbosa, J., Dias, J., Leitão, P., Oliveira, E.: Development of a smart electric motor testbed for internet of things and big data technologies. In: 43rd Annual Conference of the IEEE Industrial Electronics Society (IECON 2017), pp. 3435–3440 (2017)
13. Teerapittayanon, S., McDanel, B., Kung, H.: Distributed deep neural networks over the cloud, the edge and end devices. In: 2017 IEEE 37th International Conference on Distributed Computing Systems (ICDCS), pp. 328–339. IEEE (2017)

14. Wang, J., Ma, Y., Zhang, L., Gao, R.X., Wu, D.: Deep learning for smart manufacturing: methods and applications. J. Manuf. Syst. **48**, 144–156 (2018)
15. Wang, S., Wan, J., Zhang, D., Li, D., Zhang, C.: Towards smart factory for industry 4.0: a self-organized multi-agent system with big data based feedback and coordination. Comput. Netw. **101**, 158–168 (2016)
16. Wu, D., et al.: A Fog computing-based framework for process monitoring and prognosis in cyber-manufacturing. J. Manuf. Syst. **43**, 25–34 (2017)

Data Exchange Ontology for Interoperability Facilitation Within Industrial Automation Domain

Václav Jirkovský(✉) and Petr Kadera

Czech Institute of Robotics, Informatics, and Cybernetics,
Czech Technical University in Prague, Zikova 4, 166 36 Prague, Czech Republic
{vaclav.jirkovsky,petr.kadera}@cvut.cz

Abstract. The current gradual digitization emphasizes the needs for easy, faultless, and flexible data exchange. However, the main obstacle is not an exchange of messages but resides in sharing a mutual understanding of the message meaning. Thus, Semantic Web technologies are exploited for facilitation of the data exchange in the approach presented in this paper. Furthermore, the presented solution is based on the modeling of system interfaces and messages instead of designing and implementing clumsy shared not a versatile data model. The proposed solution also benefits from the exploitation of SPARQL and SWRL during the integration of a new component into the system.

Keywords: Ontology · SPARQL · SWRL · Data Exchange

1 Introduction

Data exchange has been an important capability of human beings from ancient time because the data exchange is an integral part of communication. It may be perceived as an essential part of information exchange when we understand information as contextualized, categorized, and calculated data. The data exchange has become crucial in various domains with increasing digitization. The industrial automation domain is not an exception.

Data have to be exchanged among various devices as well as systems. It includes devices and systems located in the lowest level (shop floor), i.e., PLCs[1], Cyber-Physical Systems, etc., and also located at higher levels, e.g., MES[2] or ERP[3]. Data exchange itself is secured by a communication medium together with a transport protocol and a particular format.

However, only "pure" data are valueless in most cases. Thus, the meaning has to be assigned to them to turn data into value. There are several requirements for the assigning meaning to data in a given context—it should be explicitly

[1] https://en.wikipedia.org/wiki/Programmable_logic_controller.
[2] https://en.wikipedia.org/wiki/Manufacturing_execution_system.
[3] https://en.wikipedia.org/wiki/Enterprise_resource_planning.

V. Mařík et al. (Eds.): HoloMAS 2019, LNAI 11710, pp. 145–158, 2019.
https://doi.org/10.1007/978-3-030-27878-6_12

specified (to be machine readable) as well as shared (to be mutually accepted between all involved parties).

For tackling such a challenge, various approaches, standards, and systems were proposed and developed. These approaches are short on their expressivity, flexibility, or user-friendliness.

On the other hand, Semantic Web technologies seem to be suitable for meeting of aforementioned requirements according to the well-known ontology definition from Gruber [5]—"*An ontology is an explicit specification of a conceptualization,*" which was subsequently complemented by the specification of the requirement for a "*shared conceptualization.*"

Data exchange and thus also information exchange is essential within DIGICOR project[4]. The project aims to develop novel collaboration concepts and implements an integrated platform that tries to reduce the burden to setup production networks and collaboration between SMEs. By providing relevant technology support at one place, the DIGICOR Collaboration Platform will shorten the time to jointly respond to business opportunities and simplify the management and control of the production and logistics networks.

In this paper, the approach exploiting Semantic Web technologies (i.e., the ontology in OWL[5] and SWRL[6]) for facilitating data exchange is presented. Most of the already proposed approaches are based on a shared data model which is utilized by all of the platform components. This approach is not suitable within heterogeneous ecosystems such as the DIGICOR platform. The main obstacle is the consistency maintenance. Thus, we proposed to model interfaces and messages between interfaces instead of modeling of components' inner information models. The overall approach is demonstrated by already mentioned DIGICOR project where native project components are integrated using DIGICOR Core Ontology, and external additionally imported components are integrated using Data Exchange Ontology.

The paper is organized as follows: first, Digicor Core Ontology (DCO) is introduced. Then, the motivation and requirements for Data Exchange Ontology (DEO) are presented followed by the description of the ontological model for Application Programming Interface (API) description. Finally, the application of Data Exchange Ontology is presented.

2 DIGICOR Core Ontology

Interconnected industrial automation systems as well as the DIGICOR platform represent complex ecosystems which consist of many loosely or tightly coupled interoperable components. Furthermore, the platform is not intended to be limited to only one domain but aims to be a versatile and flexible system which could be applicable on broad spectrum of diverse domains and also provide interoperability across various suppliers. Thus, the backbone knowledge model of the

[4] https://www.digicor-project.eu/the-project.
[5] https://www.w3.org/OWL/.
[6] https://www.w3.org/Submission/SWRL/.

DIGICOR platform was built using Semantic Web technologies [6] - DIGICOR Core Ontology (DCO).

DCO was proposed for enabling easy incorporation of various aspects of manufacturing (e.g., tendering or scheduling) as well as for easy deployment of the DIGICOR platform in various domains. The main idea is to use DCO as a core knowledge model and a new deployment of DIGICOR to a new domain reside only in the development of a corresponding domain ontology. From the other point of view, the new domain ontology has to be derived from DCO using its general concepts. As prevention of misunderstanding of DCO concepts meaning, DCO exploits DOLCE ontology [1] as its cornerstone, which provides a possibility to clearly define DCO concepts using relations to its more general concepts. Overall schema of DIGICOR Core Ontology architecture is shown in Fig. 1.

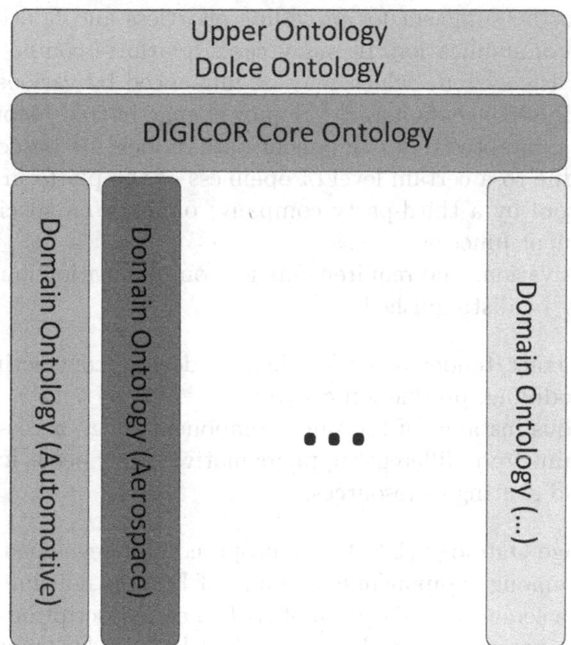

Fig. 1. Architecture of DIGICOR Core Ontology

There may be distinguished two parts within DCO, i.e., the tender-related part and the scheduling-related part. The tender-related part is based on OASIS Standard - Universal Business Language (UBL) [2] and covers concepts together with their relations such as a tender, tenderer, contracting authority, tender requirement, or contract. The scheduling related part is mainly based on ADACOR ontology (ADaptive holonic COntrol aRchitecture for distributed manufacturing systems) [8] and covers concepts and their relations such as a product, recipe, operation, property, job, schedule, or resources. The detailed description of these DCO parts is in the deliverable D3.5. - "Semantic data models specification" of DIGICOR project [4].

3 Data Exchange Ontology

The complex and versatile environment such as the DIGICOR platform has many various components which are focused on solutions of different specialized problems or on providing specific services. These components originate from different designers and developers. Furthermore, this highly heterogeneous nature of the DIGICOR platform is especially caused by the possibility of customization or an extension of DIGICOR tool store by a company needs.

There is an effort for semantic unification of data models within the platform by DIGICOR Core Ontology (see Sect. 2). However, exploitation of the upper ontology may not be sufficient for providing effortless and faultless component integration and communication. In many cases, platform components represent isolated parts of the system, which may be influenced by various subjects, and thus the meaning of concepts may develop or change in time. Moreover, there is no possibility to guarantee that component data models are based on DIGICOR Core Ontology due to a certain level of openness of the platform (e.g., development of a new tool by a third-party company) or due to a specific nature of a platform component function.

Different motivations and requirements for communication among DIGICOR components may be distinguished:

1. Within a contract/tender lifecycle - i.e., tendering, contracting, production planning/scheduling, production control.
2. Between various instance of the same component - e.g., across different data models/domains from different suppliers motivated by needs for flexible manufacturing and sharing of resources.

Data Exchange Ontology (DEO) was proposed and developed for facilitating interoperability among components. The aim of DEO is not unification components' APIs but a semantic description of APIs, i.e., a description of the meaning of API elements, together with their possible relations. DEO exploits DOLCE Ontology (similarly to DCO) as its basis and serves as a complement to DCO. DEO is designed and implemented in OWL similarly to DCO.

In following paragraphs, a way, how to design and implement an ontological model of a message, which is consumed or produced by a service via API, is described followed by an sample implementation of API message models, which correspond to a communication between Tender Decomposition and Matchmaking Service (TDMS) [3] component and Semantic Control and Monitoring (SCM) component. Furthermore, relations between different APIs will be described.

3.1 Ontological Model for API Description

The basic building block is API itself. Items of an API represent a set of information which is required by "surrounding" services for producing or consuming messages. These items may refer to an existing concept or its (data or object) property from data model of a given component or may refer to information which was inferred from component's data model by a certain transformation because of demands of surrounding systems.

There are many different ways how to create an ontological model for API description and depend mainly on the intended exploitation of DEO. DEO OWL model is based on five main concepts - "*System*", "*Tool*", "*Service*", "*Message*", and "*Message Model Element*". These concepts together with their relations are shown in Fig. 2.

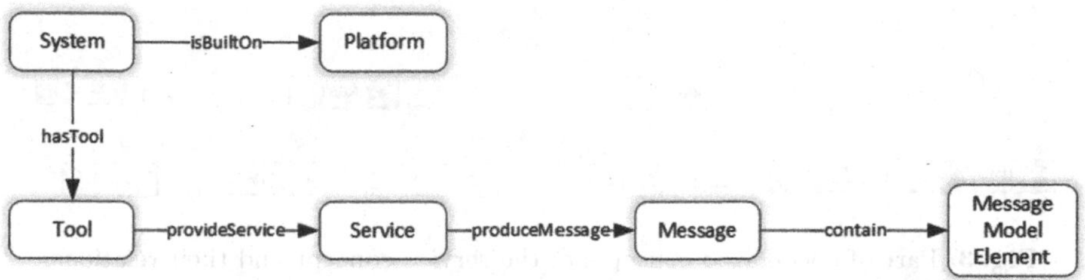

Fig. 2. DEO backbone concepts and their relations

System Concept. The "*System*" concept describes systems or platforms which communicate with each other. The part of the DEO conceptualization related to "*System*" concept is naturally focused on the DIGICOR platform, and therefore the concept specialization is to "*DIGICOR platform*" concept and "*External*" concept. "*External*" concept represents mainly suppliers and manufacturers, i.e., their systems which communicates with the DIGICOR platform.

A general system is composed of various components (sometimes with various names - tools or modules). These parts form a backbone of the overall system architecture and the system ensure platform-relevant operational services for them. The most important properties of the system concept are "*hasName*" (type: String), "*hasTool*" type: Tool, and "*isBuildOn*" (type: Platform).

Tool Concept. The "Tool" concept represents a tool or a component which has a specific purpose and provide services for fulfilling its goal or function. The characteristic feature of tools is they are very often designed and developed by various architectures and designers. Thus, the first difficulties with heterogeneous data models of APIs during communication may be observed at this level. The most important properties of the system concept are "*hasName*" (type: String) and "*provideService*" (type: Service).

Service Concept. Communication and interaction abilities of tools or components are constituted by services. Interactions with a service are possible by messages—incoming and outcoming. From a very general point of view, an incoming message specifies a demanded action or a request for specific data together with data which are required by a service for fulfilling the demanded request. In opposite, an outcoming message contains a result of a requested action or specification of requested data.

Furthermore, services may be categorized by a different architecture on which they are built-up, e.g., Simple Object Access Protocol (SOAP) or Representational State Transfer (ReST). Next, services may also be naturally categorized by a corresponding system or a corresponding component. Figure 3 depicts specialized concepts of the service concept and their relations in DEO.

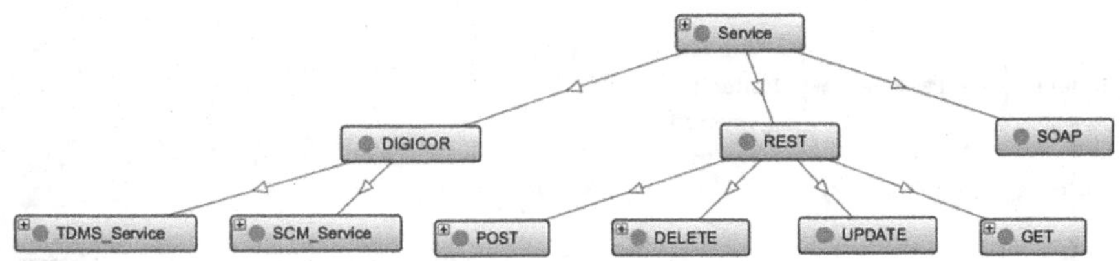

Fig. 3. Part of specialized concepts of the service concept and their relations

One of the benefits resulting from this categorization as well as features of OWL (a service may belong to more than one concept, e.g., semantic controlling and monitoring (SCM) service and get service) is multiple inheritances of properties defined within super-concepts.

Message Concept. The "*Message*" concept serves as an envelope for a message body. Besides a message body represented by "*Message Model Element*" concepts, this concept comprises the id (because of the message traceability) and information about a type of message serialization.

Message Model Element Concept. The "*Message Model Element*" concept is the last of the backbone concepts of DEO. This general concept itself has no specific object or data properties, and all of the properties are defined within its specialized concepts (sub-concepts). Sub-concepts of the "*Message Model Element*" form together with their relations a message body.

The proper specification of the sub-concepts of the "*Message Model Element*" is crucial for DEO because these sub-concepts and their relations represent a previously mentioned ontological model of a service API. The problem of a transformation of one ontological model of API to another is the main problem of data exchange.

4 Application of Data Exchange Ontology: TDMS Component and SCM Component Communication

In this section, the possible description of DIGICOR component (TDMS) services using DEO is introduced. Next, the formulation of a message produced by "*teamById*" service API is presented. Finally, auxiliary approaches for facilitating a new component design or better service API understanding are introduced, i.e., an overview of a given API using the explicit specification of API properties and SPARQL [9], differences of service APIs using SPARQL, and a transformation of a message from one service into a form of another using SWRL [7].

4.1 DEO Model of Tender Decomposition and Matchmaking Service API

Tender Decomposition and Matchmaking Service (TDMS) component is an important tool which provides valuable information for tendering and contracting process. The component can form a team for forming a requested tender based on the specification of the tender, a product decomposition, and a specification of suppliers capabilities. A proposed team (or a list of possible teams) serves as the input for subsequent contracting. On the other hand, the conceptualization presented in the following paragraphs represents the model of TDMS from the perspective of data exchange. The entire TDMS ontology is not needed for the intended purpose of DEO, and even modeling of appropriate services or messages may be impossible.

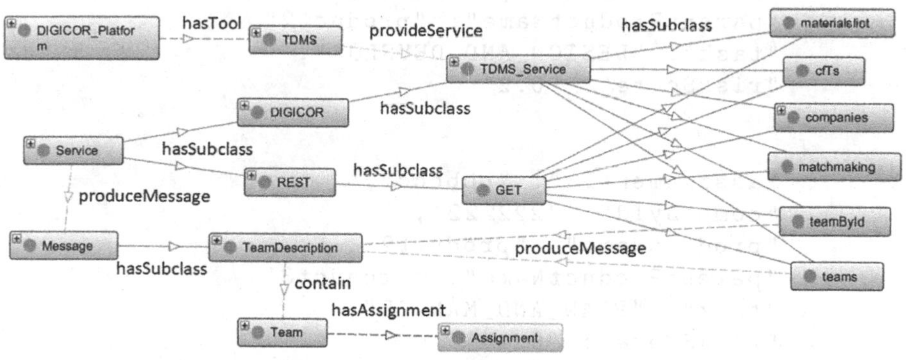

Fig. 4. Part of TDMS conceptualization

TDMS as the native DIGICOR tool complies with REST architecture. In other words, it is possible to categorize TDMS services into four disjoint concepts which correspond to REST methods - GET, POST, UPDATE, DELETE. Every service is characterized within a corresponding concept by its endpoint, path, headers, and query parameters. Next, a concept of a service specifies a message which is produced or consumed by the service according to its type, e.g., GET methods typically only produce messages whereas POST methods typically consume messages. The part of the TDMS conceptualization is illustrated in Fig. 4. Only GET methods, and "*TeamDescription*" message are depicted for better readability.

4.2 Team Description Message

In the following paragraphs, the proposed way, how to model an API, is presented using the "*TeamDescription*" message of DEO and "*teamById*" service of TDMS. The "*teamById*" service (GET method) produces a message where a description of a team is specified related to a given tender. This service has one parameter - Team ID. The original structure of the message is illustrated in Listing 1.1. First, there is stated a header (a team ID and call for tender ID) followed by individual assignments with information about a given task, product, parent product, company (supplier) ID, assignment ID together with a corresponding risk score.


```
{
    "teamid": "aabbccdd",
    "cftid": "12345678",
    "assignments": [
      {
        "assignmentId": "aaabbb",
        "companyId": "111111",
        "productName": "product1",
        "parentProductName": "product2",
        "task": "DESIGN_AND_DEVELOP",
        "riskScore": "0.2"
      },
      {
        "assignmentId": "bbbccc",
        "companyId": "222222",
        "productName": "product2",
        "parentProductName": "product3",
        "task": "PLAN_AND_MANAGE",
        "riskScore": "0.4"
      }
    ]
  }
```


Listing 1.1. Structure of a sample response message from teamById REST service

If this message is converted into the ontological model of DEO, then the message is represented by following concepts - "*TeamDescription*" (subclass of "*Message*" concept), "*Team*" and "*Assignment*" concepts (both as subclasses of "*MessageModelElement*" concept).

The aforementioned concepts provide means for formulating the team description message. Figure 5 demonstrates how individuals "*Message1*", "*Team1*", "*Assignment1*", "*Assignment2*", and "*Assignment3*" formulate a backbone of the message. The corresponding data properties of the individuals are not shown because of better readability.

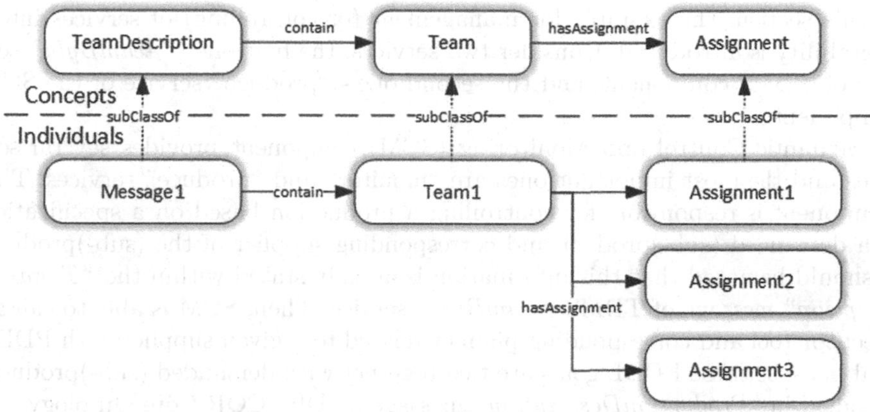

Fig. 5. Model of a message produced by "*teamById*" TDMS service

4.3 Facilitating a Design of a New Component and Service

The design phase and subsequent development of a new component and as well as a new service may be difficult because of an insufficient description of collaborating services and thus complicating understanding of the meaning of particular API items.

A description of APIs and corresponding service messages using DIGICOR Data Exchange Ontology should help to overcome the mentioned obstacles particularly because of the following benefits resulting from the utilization of Semantic Web technologies:

- Explicit specification of API and message properties including message components - often the problem for the proper understanding of an API are implicit knowledge and information of a given model within hardcoded algorithms which produce service messages. On the other hand, ontologies provide a way how to store this information in the explicit form and possibly separated from executing algorithms of services or components.
- Exploitation of a shared vocabulary for a definition of API and message properties which decrease the possible chance for a formation of a heterogeneous and defective environment.
- Easy reuse of previously developed component and algorithms because of proper understanding of their function.

– Overview of API message properties is easily achievable for example by exploitation of SPARQL. A more complex example of the SPARQL utilization for finding out differences of two APIs is presented in the following paragraphs.

4.4 Relations Between Different APIs Using SPARQL

In this section, the example for management (or controlling) of services interoperability is introduced. Consider two services, the first one - "*teamById*" service of TDMS component, and the second one - "produce" service of the SCM component.

Semantic Control and Monitoring (SCM) component provides several services and the most important ones are "monitor" and "produce" services. This component is responsible for controlling a production based on a specification of a demanded (sub-)product and corresponding supplier of the (sub-)product. It should be noted that this information is already stated within the "*TeamDescription*" message of TDMS "*teamById*" service. Then, SCM is able to call an executor tool and corresponding planner related to a given supplier with PDDL goal because these PDDL goals are tied together with demanded (sub-)products specified in "*ProductionDescription*" message by DIGICOR Core Ontology.

The "*ProductionDescription*" concept (representing the message) includes a reference to the message body, i.e., "*DistributedProductionPlan*". The "*DistributedProductionPlan*" CONCEPT contains order ID (from the previously mentioned contracting component) and specification of overall production goal. Next, it contains references to individual operations. The "Operation" concept comprises information about a corresponding product name, a given supplier, and demanded task. In general, the "*TeamDescription*" message and the "*ProductionDescription*" message describes similar thing but from a different perspective - the first one, from team formation perspective, and the second one, from the production perspective. The Fig. 6 illustrates the ontological model of the "*ProductionDescription*" message. Basically, the backbone of the message seems to be similar to the "*TeamDescription*" message, but they differ significantly in concept properties.

There is no direct connection between these two services because (according to the given workflow and a character of the problem) they are connected by the other additional intermediate component. The "*teamById*" service produces a message with a specification of the new team. Next, this information about the new team serves as an input to a contracting component, which processes information about the team and demanded product. Subsequently, a contracting component may trigger a production using the SCM component, namely the "*produce*" service. The "*produce*" service consumes "*ProductionDescription*" message. The mentioned contracting component should transform the message from TDMS in the form of SCM message supplemented by other required information.

A SPARQL query may be exploited for the identification of identical and equivalent properties of corresponding APIs. The query, as well as results of

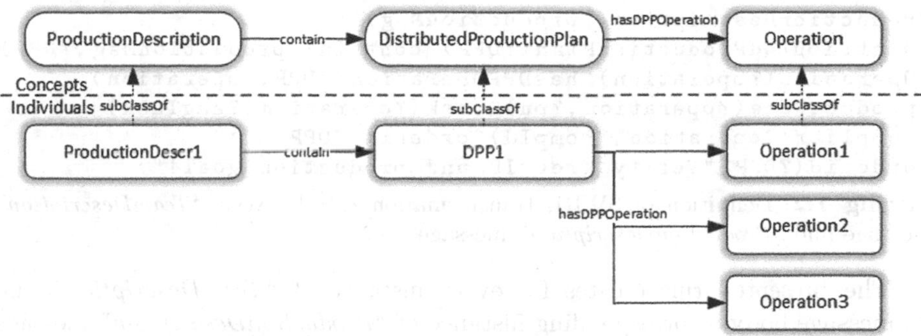

Fig. 6. Model of the "*ProductionDescription*" message

propertyOfAPI1	samePropertyInAPI2	equivalentPropertyInAPI2
supplier		companyId
productName	productName	
task	task	
productionGoal		parentProductName
orderid		

Fig. 7. SPARQL comparison of APIs properties

the query, are shown in Fig. 7. At the bottom, there is shown the list of API1 properties (the distributed production plan properties) together with identical and equivalent properties of API2 (the team properties).

4.5 SWRL Transformation of a Message Between Different APIs

The transformation of a message between different APIs may be facilitated and (semi-)automated using A Semantic Web Rule Language which is based on a combination of the OWL DL with the Unary/Binary Datalog RuleML [1]. This approach resides in a formulation of a transformation SWRL rule for pairs of services where the transformation is required.

In this section, the transformation between "*TeamDescription*" message and "*ProductionDescription*" message will be introduced. Both of these messages and their properties were described in detail in previous paragraphs. The definition of the rule for the transformation is presented in Listing 1.2.

```
TeamDescription(?teamMsg)
^swrlx:makeOWLThing(?productionMsg,?teamMsg)
^contain(?teamMsg,?team)^swrlx:makeOWLThing(?DPP,?team)
^hasAssignment(?team,?assign)
^swrlx:makeOWLThing(?operation,?assign)
^productName(?assign,?pn)^task(?assign,?asgTask)
^companyId(?assign,?compId)
->
```

```
ProductionDescription(?productionMsg)
^DistributedProductionPlan(?DPP)^contain(?productionMsg,?DPP)
^Operation(?operation)^hasDPPOperation(?DPP,?operation)
^productName(?operation,?pn)^task(?operation,?asgTask)
^supplier(?operation,?compId)^orderid(?DPP,"")
^orderid(?DPP,"Verify␣orderID␣and␣production␣goal!")
```

Listing 1.2. Definition of SWRL transformation rule between "*TeamDescription*" message and "*ProductionDescription*" message

The presented rule creates for every instance of "*TeamDescription*" and its message body a corresponding instance of "*ProductionDescription*" message together with its message body according to the implemented rule logic. The last line of the rule specifies the order id of the distributed production plan. This ID as well as precise overall production goal is not specified in the "*TeamDescription*" message and have to be filled in within the contracting component which triggers SCM. Thus, the consistency violation of the distributed production plan concept is used as a user warning because of the order id and production goal verification - the order id has cardinality exactly 1, and therefore the reasoner is able to detect this violation as depicted in Fig. 8.

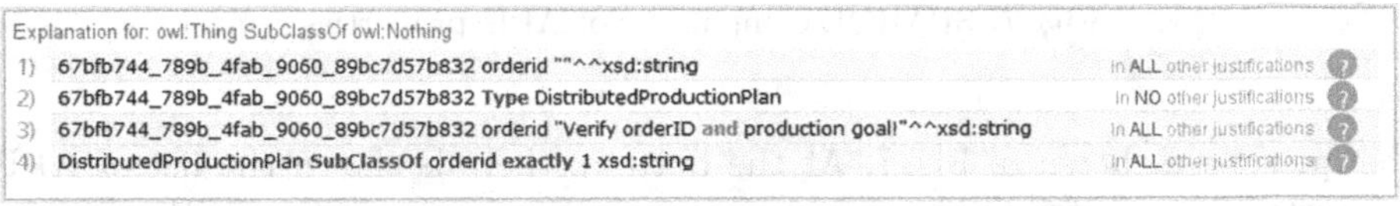

Explanation for: owl:Thing SubClassOf owl:Nothing
1) 67bfb744_789b_4fab_9060_89bc7d57b832 orderid ""^^xsd:string — In ALL other justifications
2) 67bfb744_789b_4fab_9060_89bc7d57b832 Type DistributedProductionPlan — In NO other justifications
3) 67bfb744_789b_4fab_9060_89bc7d57b832 orderid "Verify orderID and production goal!"^^xsd:string — In ALL other justifications
4) DistributedProductionPlan SubClassOf orderid exactly 1 xsd:string — In ALL other justifications

Fig. 8. User warning using reasoner because of order id and production goal verification

The following figures show transformed individuals related to the "*ProductionDescription*" message - Fig. 9(a): "*ProductionDescription*" individual, Fig. 9(b): "*DistributedProductionPlan*" individual, and Fig. 9(c): "*Operation*" individual (only one of the operation individual is shown because of their similarity).

The main benefit of SWRL exploitation for message transformation is the explicit specification of the transformation which may be kept outside a given component. This fact offers easier maintenance of the transformation rule as well as better change management across various services. Moreover, this approach provides consistency maintenance of the outcome message from the transformation using a reasoner.

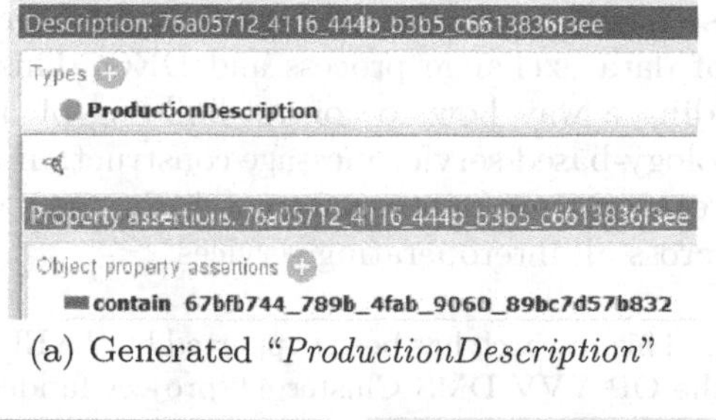

(a) Generated "*ProductionDescription*"

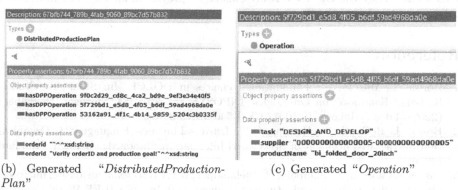

(b) Generated "*DistributedProductionPlan*"

(c) Generated "*Operation*"

Fig. 9. Generated individuals by SWRL transformation rule.

5 Conclusions and Outlook

In this paper, we introduced the solution on how to deal with data exchange within the heterogeneous environment. The main idea resides in the modeling of system interfaces and exchanging messages instead of modeling of a shared model. The shared data model of all system components is not sufficient when the new already implemented component with heterogeneous inner data model has to be implemented.

Therefore, we proposed to overcome this deficiency by the development of introduced Data Exchange Ontology. The ontology is able to facilitate the understanding of messages which are being exchanged within the environment but also provides other means for ensuring successful integration of a new component, i.e., SPARQL and SWRL.

For example, the proposed solution is able to provide (semi-)automatic message transformation using SWRL rules. Moreover, it also facilitates consistency maintenance with the help of a reasoner.

The ontology designed in OWL together with supporting tools was proven to be capable describe and facilitate the data exchange problem because of its good expressivity as well as versatility. On the other hand, there are still several obstacles for full exploitation of OWL and SWRL capabilities mainly because of a lack of suitable and user-friendly tools for the modeling and subsequent testing.

One of the most important subsequent steps in future research is to offer a tight integration of data exchange process and DEO. This integration resides primarily in providing a way how to control building of messages directly by DEO. Such an ontology-based service message construction would provide many benefits including easy change management of APIs not only concerning given services but also across all interoperating services.

Acknowledgment. This research has been supported by the EU Horizon 2020 project DIGICOR and by the OP VVV DMS Cluster 4.0 project funded by The Ministry of Education, Youth and Sports.

References

1. Borgo, S., Masolo, C.: Foundational choices in DOLCE. In: Staab, S., Studer, R. (eds.) Handbook on Ontologies. INFOSYS, pp. 361–381. Springer, Heidelberg (2009). https://doi.org/10.1007/978-3-540-92673-3_16
2. Bosak, J., McGrath, T., Holman, G.K.: Universal business language v2.0. Organization for the Advancement of Structured Information Standards (OASIS), Standard (2006)
3. Cisneros-Cabrera, S., Sampaio, P., Mehandjiev, N.: A B2B team formation microservice for collaborative manufacturing in industry 4.0. In: 2018 IEEE World Congress on Services (SERVICES), pp. 37–38. IEEE (2018)
4. DIGICOR Consorcium: Digicor outcomes (2019). https://www.digicor-project.eu/clients. Accessed 20 Mar 2019
5. Gruber, T.R.: Toward principles for the design of ontologies used for knowledge sharing? Int. J. Hum Comput Stud. **43**(5–6), 907–928 (1995)
6. Hitzler, P., Krotzsch, M., Rudolph, S.: Foundations of Semantic Web Technologies. Chapman and Hall/CRC, Boca Raton (2009)
7. Horrocks, I., Patel-Schneider, P.F., Boley, H., Tabet, S., Grosof, B., Dean, M., et al.: SWRL: a semantic web rule language combining owl and RuleML. W3C Member submission 21(79) (2004)
8. Leitão, P., Restivo, F.: ADACOR: a holonic architecture for agile and adaptive manufacturing control. Comput. Ind. **57**(2), 121–130 (2006)
9. Pérez, J., Arenas, M., Gutierrez, C.: Semantics and complexity of SPARQL. ACM Trans. Database Syst. (TODS) **34**(3), 16 (2009)

Information Exchange and Integration Within Industrial Automation Domain

Václav Jirkovský[1], Marek Obitko[2], and Petr Kadera[1](✉)

[1] Czech Institute of Robotics, Informatics, and Cybernetics, Czech Technical University in Prague, Jugoslávských partyzánů 1580/3, 160 00 Prague, Czech Republic
{vaclav.jirkovsky,petr.kadera}@cvut.cz

[2] Rockwell Automation R&D Center, Argentinská 1610/4, 170 00 Prague, Czech Republic
mobitko@ra.rockwell.com

Abstract. Information exchange and integration are essential in various systems and their interactions across different domains. In this paper, we discuss the core of the information exchange and integration problems together with possible solutions including a description of various standards for information exchange and a description of several wide-spread formalisms for a definition of information models. Finally, information exchange and integration problems used in our Semantic Big Data Historian is described, to illustrate the approach for solving some of the problems.

Keywords: Information exchange · Information integration · Ontology · Industrial automation

1 Introduction

Information exchange and integration are important within and across various areas as well as domains including industrial automation where they are also enablers for Industry 4.0. Their importance is emphasized within the industrial automation domain mainly because of increasing digitization in various systems during various steps as well as levels of manufacturing.

In general, there is no strict boundary between information exchange and integration. However, the difference may be expressed as:

- *Information exchange*—An interoperable system is formed by loosely coupled subsystem, where subsystems are responsible for maintenance of their own information models, and they exchange information for fulfilling demanded or requested goals.
- *Information integration*—An integrated system is composed of tightly coupled components which share a mutual information model, and therefore every component has a full and proper understanding of an information meaning.

V. Mařík et al. (Eds.): HoloMAS 2019, LNAI 11710, pp. 159–170, 2019.
https://doi.org/10.1007/978-3-030-27878-6_13

This perspective is valid when we limit the scope to a particular platform or system. On the other hand, information exchange and integration would be perceived as parts which complement each other. It is obvious in the situation when we refer to a system which is a part of some heterogeneous platform. Every system has its own integrated information model and also requires to exchange information with surrounding platform parts. In other words, information stored in integrated information models has to be shared with its neighborhood and exchanging information has to be subsequently integrated into local information models.

Researchers have been dealing with these problems for many years, and thus there are several solutions for these two different disciplines. In general, the information exchange problem is mainly solved using various communication formats together with corresponding standards (described in Sect. 2) and the information integration problem is solved by the exploitation of some formalisms with sufficient expressivity (described in Sect. 3).

This paper is structured as follows: first, the information exchange problem is introduced together with formats, which facilitate a solution to the problem. Next, the information integration problem is described followed by descriptions of formalisms for a building of information models. Finally, the proposed and implemented solution for the information exchange and integration problems by Semantic Big Data Historian is presented.

2 Information Exchange Problem

Designers, developers, and operators are tackling with the information exchange problem in every industrial information system. Complex engineering problems are typically tackled by various engineering tools, each dealing with a specific sub-problem. For instance, an eCAD tool is used to design electrical wiring, while another tool is used to define the layout of a control system. In this case, an information exchange strategy is needed to export information about physical connection schema into the schema of communication links among automation components (e.g., Programmable Logical Controllers and Input/Output modules).

2.1 Formats for Information Exchange

In this section, various formats for information exchange facilitation will be described. We may distinguish neutral formats as well as specialized formats, which are derived from the specialized formats and have a particular purpose. Many of formats will be skipped in the following paragraphs because of the limited scope of this paper, and only the most wide-spread or the most promising formats are described.

XML. XML is eXtensible Markup Language that is used for transferring data on the Web and has been accepted as a W3C Recommendation in 1998. XML documents are used to store data and information on the Web, and their content is structured in nested tags. An opening and a closing tag delimit a particular content (called an element), and each tag can be supplemented with a set of additional name-value pairs, called attributes.

The XML format is widely accepted and used due to its relatively simple structure and easy processing. Based on these characteristics, XML format could be understood as a universal format for data and information exchange and even for their storage.

The XML format is an important technology which has been used for information exchange in many applications and domains thanks to its simple and powerful syntax which is versatile enough for information sharing among multiple sources. However, XML does not address issues of the explicit, intensive semantic structure of XML documents, i.e., XML files may be shared with many systems, but they are meaningless outside the application.

The importance of XML for information exchange and integration is obvious from the fact that a prevalent part of formats exploits XML for their serialization. From another point of view, the XML-based formats try to add (more or less successfully) some domain-specific vocabulary as well as constructs for expressing relations between concepts.

An XML document can be supplied by a document that specifies the allowed tags and their structure—XML Schema[1]. In other words, XML Schema defines constraints on XML documents. It provides simple vocabulary and predefined constructs for modeling relations among entities.

AutomationML. AutomationML is an XML-based format with the objective to enable seamless automation engineering of production plants [6]. This standard was developed as neutral data and information exchange format of manufacturing systems by a consortium of leading vendors and users of automation technologies.

The AutomationML format is based on the following standards:

- **CAEX** [5] standard is the cornerstone of the hierarchical structure of plant objects.
- **PLCopen** [12] describes plant behavior and control as a sequence of actions.
- **COLLADA** [3] standard is used for geometry and kinematic modeling.

AutomationML provides relatively universal architecture on how to capture information including for example device concepts such as a sensor or an actuator unit class.

OPC UA. The next very interesting way how to model and even exchange information is by means of OPC Unified Architecture (UA) standard [7]. In general, OPC UA is a secure and open mechanism for exchanging data and information between servers and clients in industrial automation. One of the motivations for the OPC UA standard was to overcome the main obstacle of its predecessor (OPC Data Access together with OPC Historical Data Access and OPC

[1] https://www.w3.org/standards/xml/schema.

Alarm&Events)—dependency on COM[2]. Therefore, the OPC UA was designed for the replacement of all existing COM-based specification to be platform independent with extensible modeling capabilities.

OPC UA is built on two main components [11]—transport mechanisms and data modeling. The transport component offers the possibility to communicate via optimized binary TPC protocol for high-performance intranet communication and the next possibility to communicate via Web Services. The data modeling component represents rules and building blocks for the creation and exposing information model. It also defines base types to build a type hierarchy.

In the original OPC standard, only "raw" data is exchanged, i.e., there was not enough information included for understanding the semantics of provided data—a tag name and some information like engineering unit. On the contrary, OPC UA offers more flexible possibility to expose the semantics of the data because of complete object-oriented capabilities including type hierarchies as well as inheritance.

The OPC Foundation has started with standardization of information models of various devices (UA Devices) for the unification of models. Every device vendor may extend these base models with vendor-specific information. This approach is also assumed in other scenarios, e.g., providing data of MES (Manufacturing Execution System) or ERP (Enterprise Resource Planning) systems by exposing the ISA 95 model [4].

There are many interesting features described in OPC UA specification—triggering of methods, variable subscriptions, security, device discovery (local as well as global), etc. Because of these features, OPC UA seems to be one of the most promising frameworks for information modeling and exchange in the automation domain.

ISA-95. ANSI/ISA-95 "Enterprise-Control System Integration" [1], also published as IEC 62264 [2] is an industry standard describing information flows between enterprise and control activities and interfaces between the respective systems. The ISA-95 standard comprises several parts, which contain models focusing on specific integration aspects and terminology to analyze and provide insights into various aspects of manufacturing companies. The three focus areas of the ISA-95 standard are:

- Models of information exchanged between business systems and manufacturing operations systems (parts 1/2/5)
- Models of activities in manufacturing operations systems (part 3)
- Models of information exchanged within manufacturing operations systems (parts 4/6)

The objective of the ISA-95 standard is to reduce costs, errors, and risk associated with implementing interfaces between enterprise and control systems by simplifying their implementation, therefore easing integration. ISA-95 can be utilized as an analysis tool to provide insights into the manufacturing company.

[2] https://www.microsoft.com/com/default.mspx.

The standard can also be used as a basis for developing standardized MES applications that can easily interface with other systems and as a basis for message exchange between ERP and MES systems to achieve vertical integration.

Resource Description Framework. The Resource Description Framework[3] (RDF) developed by World Wide Web Consortium (W3C) represents a standard model for data publishing or exchanging on the Web. Data and their corresponding properties are expressed in the form of RDF statements in the form of triples (s - subject, p - property, o - object) denoting that a resource s has a property p with a certain value o.

For denoting resources including subject, predicate, and object, RDF uses Unique Resource Identifiers (URIs) to allow interoperability on the web. The usage of URIs allows RDF data to be mixed, exposed, and shared across different applications. RDF triples may be serialized in various formats including XML, N3, Turtle. The set of RDF triples may be perceived as an RDF graph consisting of linked nodes.

RDF Schema. RDF Schema[4] (RDFS) provides a data modeling vocabulary for RDF data, and it is used to describe classes and relationships between classes (e.g., inheritance). Next, RDFS specifies also properties and corresponding relationships. Relationships may hold between pairs of properties, or between a class and property. RDFS statements are represented as triples as well, and thus RDFS forms an RDF graph. RDFS triple is called schema triple and other triples data triples.

Web Ontology Language. Web Ontology Language[5] (OWL) is another W3C recommendation. It is built on RDF and RDFS, i.e., it follows the RDF/RDFS meaning of classes and properties and adds primitives added to support the additional expressiveness. On the other hand, RDF and RDFS have very voluminous modeling concepts such as `rdf:Property` and `rdfs:Class`. Their expressive power causes uncontrollable computational complexity, and for some applications a trade-off is needed for efficient reasoning. For this, the OWL defines different levels or profiles[6] to be chosen according to the needs.

2.2 Solutions/Frameworks for Information Exchange

There are a lot of proprietary solutions including OPC UA which provide means not only for information model specification but also means for facilitating communication, for example, the client/server architecture.

Such architectures allow to form a system for information exchange—including "centralized" (with a main central control component) or "decentralized" architecture. The centralized architecture may be built on, for example, OPC UA architecture, where the central component communicates using OPC

[3] https://www.w3.org/RDF/.
[4] https://www.w3.org/TR/rdf-schema/.
[5] https://www.w3.org/OWL/.
[6] https://www.w3.org/TR/owl2-profiles/.

UA (i.e., OPC UA client), and sensors or actuators are connected using OPC UA servers. The example of the "decentralized" architecture could be for example multi-agent systems.

The increasing popularity of Internet of Things emphasized needs for a versatile solution of the information exchange problem. However, a common integration of "things" providing solutions for information exchange relies on ad-hoc solutions and there is no general solution for such integration. These solutions can provide very effective systems. On the other hand, they may bring many drawbacks—difficult system maintenance and malfunction corrections, adding or adjusting components, lower re-usability, etc.

3 Information Integration Problem

When we consider the information integration problem, then we may distinguish two different scenarios—"integration on-the-fly" and "full integration". The first scenario is tightly coupled with the information exchange problem and has no central data storage maintained by the central component. The second scenario represents a common situation with the central component, which handles an information model together with corresponding data storage. The requirement for both of them is an existence of some information model which handles a "schema" comprising all of the participating components. Furthermore, relations between corresponding elements (e.g., concepts with equivalent meaning in a given context) should be included in the "schema" or stated in some explicitly expressed set of mappings.

There are several different aspects of the information integration problem including developing of adapters (how to convert incoming information to a demanded form) and a determination of formalism for expressing information models and their versatility, flexibility, and suitability for subsequent maintenance.

Prevalent part of various adapters is already implemented and also included in many solutions. Therefore, we will discuss various formalisms for information models specification in the following paragraphs.

3.1 Information Models for Integration

In this section, we will present several formalisms for designing information models which are essential for the information integration problem. The most common approaches together with their general description will be described. Key features of these approaches are flexibility and expressivity. Requirements on these features by an application often determine a target formalism.

Relational Database Schema. Relational database management systems (RDBMSs) are widely used for data storage for many years. RDBMS is a data storage with a collection of interrelated data files or structures. According to the name, relational databases were designed to store data. Tables themselves have no information about relations to other tables. Such information in a limited form is stored in a schema. A schema provides information about the relationships between tables and field types. More complex relations among tables have to be stored in queries and many times also in the application implicitly. In other words, RDBMSs provide the solution of the information integration problem which consists of three parts—data storage, a schema, and corresponding application algorithm. Moreover, many of available RDBMS solutions provide implemented adapters to various data sources.

NoSQL Systems. NoSQL (Not only SQL) are systems typically suitable for massive amounts of unstructured data in situations, without the need to clearly define a schema, possibly also relaxing some other RDBMs requirements. Examples of architectures of this wide family of systems are a key-value model, column store, document database, and graph database.

In general, these systems provide greater flexibility. On the other hand, information integration is primarily handled by an application, i.e., also implicitly defined.

Ontologies. Ontologies are tightly coupled with the term conceptualization. A conceptualization is an intensional semantic structure that encodes implicit knowledge constraining the structure of a piece of a domain. An ontology is a (partial) specification of this structure. A conceptualization is a general model of a piece of a domain (which is language independent), but an ontology does not have to express all possible constraint because it depends on the requirements of an intended application.

The exploitation of ontologies for a representation of the information model is connected to Semantic Web Technologies today. Nowadays, a powerful set of formats is available with various expressivity (i.e., RDF, RDFS, OWL) together with complementary technologies - SPARQL, SWRL, reasoners, etc.

From a theoretical point of view, ontologies are the most suitable approach for a solution of the information integration problem as they provide explicit specification of a conceptualization with appropriate expressivity. However, we still see that it is difficult to properly deploy and use them in practial applications today.

4 Information Exchange and Integration: Semantic Big Data Historian

The solution demonstrating dealing with the aforementioned obstacles and challenges is presented in this section. The prototype illustrating the solution is a specific historian software architecture which addresses requirements for information exchange as well as integration. The prototype is named Semantic Big Data Historian (SBDH) and was proposed and developed within long-standing research at Czech Technical University Rockwell Automation Laboratory for Distributed Intelligent Control (RA-DIC).

The core functionality, as well as the main advantage of the historian, is the employment of Semantic Web technologies (more precisely an ontology in

OWL[7]) for explicit definition of knowledge. Thus, specific requirements for a historian architecture stem from the utilization of the ontology. Furthermore, the architecture is influenced by a historian target usage, i.e., gathering data and information from a shop floor and other involved systems as well as controlling a shop floor by appropriate feedback. Thus, the architecture has to be very flexible to process all required data and robust to provide a highly reliable solution. SBDH architecture consists of four layers, and a concept of the overall system is to provide a modular solution which may be adapted according to given needs and requirements for the software. The following listing provides a description of the four SBDH architecture layers:

- Data acquisition and control layer—this layer is responsible for the acquisition of data from relevant sources (e.g., sensors, users via a user interface, and any relevant software from higher levels such as MES/ERP) and providing a feedback to control a given process (e.g., controlling an actuator, calling a relevant services of the 3rd party system, etc.). The preferred way for communication is using previously mentioned OPC UA. Consuming of data streams is solved using Spark Streaming Custom Receivers[8].
- Transformation layer—a transformation to a form of RDF triples according to Cyber-physical system Ontology for Component Integration (COCI) [8]. A very important responsibility of the transformation layer is to resolve semantic heterogeneity and to repair damaged data if possible.
- Data storage layer—transformed data in the form of RDF triples are stored in a triple-store in this layer. The storage respects nature of prevalent part of data, i.e., measurements from sensors. In general, two different file models are used in SBDH to provide more homogeneous data distribution across files in Cassandra—"vertical partitioning" model for data which are not time series (triples are partitioned according to a predicate of the triple) and "hybrid SBDH model" for storage of time series (triples are partitioned according to a triple predicate and a given sensor). More detailed description is available in [9]. It is obvious that this layer is not responsible only for simple data storage but is also responsible for conducting transformations of triples to a corresponding file model.
- Analytic layer—the last layer provides means to access data stored in the triple-store with the help of SPARQL[9] and to implement analytic tasks. Apache Spark MLlib[10] (library with implemented distributed machine learning algorithms) is used as a solution of analytic tasks.

The overall architecture is shown in the Fig. 1 and more details may be found in [10].

[7] Web Ontology Language - https://www.w3.org/OWL/.
[8] https://spark.apache.org/docs/2.2.0/streaming-custom-receivers.html.
[9] https://www.w3.org/TR/rdf-sparql-query/.
[10] https://spark.apache.org/mllib/.

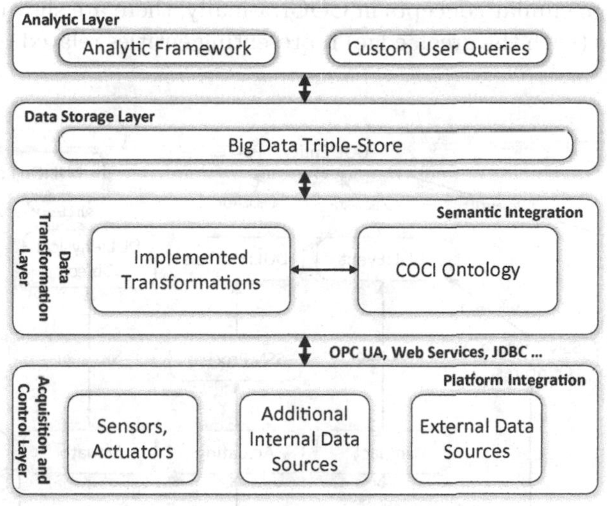

Fig. 1. Semantic Big Data Historian architecture

4.1 SBDH - Information Exchange

Based on our experiments as well as based on increasing adoption of Semantic Web technologies in industry, the exploitation of RDF format for not only data but also for information exchange seems to be a promising approach. On the other hand, comparing only the capabilities of various formats is not enough. Obviously, the adoption of these formats by manufacturers is one of the most important characteristics. Thus, OPC UA was chosen as the primary format for information exchange of SBDH.

The OPC UA information model can be used to express the information about the sensor, provided values, etc. Currently, the information expressed correspondingly to the OWL ontology (in RDF format) is used in OPC UA transferred values.

4.2 SBDH - Information Integration

For dealing with the information integration problem, SBDH exploits developed Cyber-Physical System Ontology for Components Integration (COCI). COCI is not a completely new ontology but is built on the top of Semantic Sensor Network (SSN[11]) ontology, which has Dolce Ultra Light ontology as its cornerstone.

The most important concepts together with their relations are shown in Fig. 2. The concepts with the blue edge are from DOLCE Ultralight Ontology (DUL) and serve as general predecessors of all COCI concepts. There are also several SSN concepts (with the yellow edge) — general concepts from SSN ontology are reused such as SSN:Property, SSN:Process, and SSN:FeatureOfInterest

[11] https://www.w3.org/TR/vocab-ssn/.

instead of design similar concepts in COCI. Finally, there are shown the essential COCI concepts (with the green edge) representing entities related to an actuator.

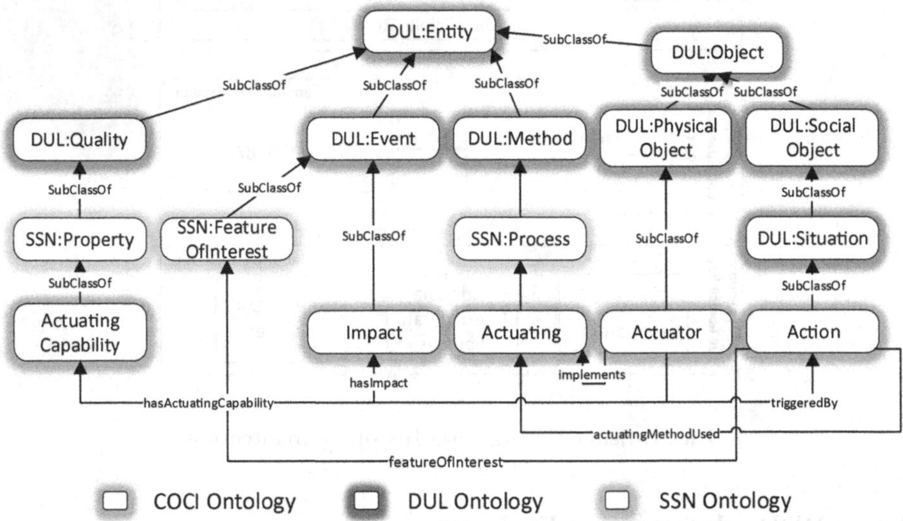

Fig. 2. Part of cyber-physical system ontology for components integration.

The cornerstone of SSN ontology (and of COCI respectively), DUL ontology, provides "a glue" for an integration of various data sources, i.e., the integration of various information. The example of the information integration using SBDH and COCI is presented in [10]. The example presents the integration of sensors from the hydroelectric power plant, information about the weather forecast, and information from the river catchment area.

5 Conclusions

In this paper, we describe the basic challenges and approaches to information exchange and integration problems. The information exchange solutions are primarily based on the exploitation of appropriate formats for communication with sufficient capabilities for given applications—appropriate formats were described. Next, the proper solution of the information integration problem resides in the utilization of suitable formalism for building information model and therefore appropriate formalisms were described with a short overview. Finally, a solution of the exchange and integration problems was demonstrated using Semantic Big Data Historian.

The information exchange problem is challenging primarily because of missing added meaning to exchanged information, i.e., many formats deal with a structure of given messages, not with their meaning. In other words, these solutions are about the data exchange problem but not about the information exchange problem. Moreover, if the formats take a meaning of exchanging data into account, then there is still a big gap between exchanged information and their meaning in a given application.

Based on our experiments, a suitable solution for the information exchange problem is the utilization of Semantic Web technologies which enable to capture not only data or information but also to describe their meaning or relations among particular entities. Furthermore, everything is explicitly specified and thus easy to maintain and reuse. On the other hand, there is a significant impediment of exploitation of these technologies by manufacturing companies, and it is the relative complexity of Semantic Web technologies.

The information integration problem is complex primarily because of various expressivity of given information resources as well as a difficult understanding of the meaning of particular entities in given contexts. The suitable formalism for the solution of this problem seems to be the utilization of ontologies expressed in the Web Ontology Language. OWL is a flexible and versatile format for building information models and therefore is applicable to various problems. However, there is an identical obstacle to the information exchange solution. The OWL is a complex format and using it together with designing an ontology is a complex task. The good news is that there are reusable ontologies available for various domains, as demonstrated in our Semantic Big Data Historian.

Acknowledgment. This research has been supported by Rockwell Automation Laboratory for Distributed Intelligent Control (RA-DIC) and by institutional resources for research by the Czech Technical University in Prague, Czech Republic.

References

1. ANSI/ISA 95: Enterprise-Control System Integration [6 parts] (2000). https://www.isa.org/isa95/
2. IEC 62264: Enterprise-Control System Integration [5 parts] (2003)
3. Arnaud, R., Barnes, M.C.: COLLADA: Sailing the Gulf of 3D Digital Content Creation. CRC Press, Boca Raton (2006)
4. Brandl, D., BR&L Consulting Inc.: What is ISA-95. Industrial Best Practices of Manufacturing Information Technologies with ISA-95 Models. BR&L Consulting (2008)
5. International Electrotechnical Commission (IEC), et al.: IEC 62424. Representation of process control engineering-Requests in P&I diagrams and data exchange between P&ID tools and PCE-CAE tools (2008)
6. Drath, R., Luder, A., Peschke, J., Hundt, L.: AutomationML-the glue for seamless automation engineering. In: 2008 IEEE International Conference on Emerging Technologies and Factory Automation, pp. 616–623. IEEE (2008)
7. OPC Foundation: Unified architecture. https://opcfoundation.org/about/opc-technologies/opc-ua/
8. Jirkovský, V.: Semantic integration in the context of cyber-physical systems. Ph.D. thesis, Czech Technical University in Prague (2017)

9. Jirkovský, V., Obitko, M.: Enabling semantics within industry 4.0. In: Mařík, V., Wahlster, W., Strasser, T., Kadera, P. (eds.) HoloMAS 2017. LNCS (LNAI), vol. 10444, pp. 39–52. Springer, Cham (2017). https://doi.org/10.1007/978-3-319-64635-0_4
10. Jirkovský, V., Obitko, M., Mařík, V.: Understanding data heterogeneity in the context of cyber-physical systems integration. IEEE Trans. Ind. Inform. **13**(2), 660–667 (2016)
11. Mahnke, W., Leitner, S.H.: OPC Unified Architecture. Springer, Heidelberg (2009). https://doi.org/10.1007/978-3-540-68899-0
12. van der Wal, E.: PLCopen. IEEE Ind. Electron. Mag. **3**(4), 25 (2009)

MAS in Various Areas

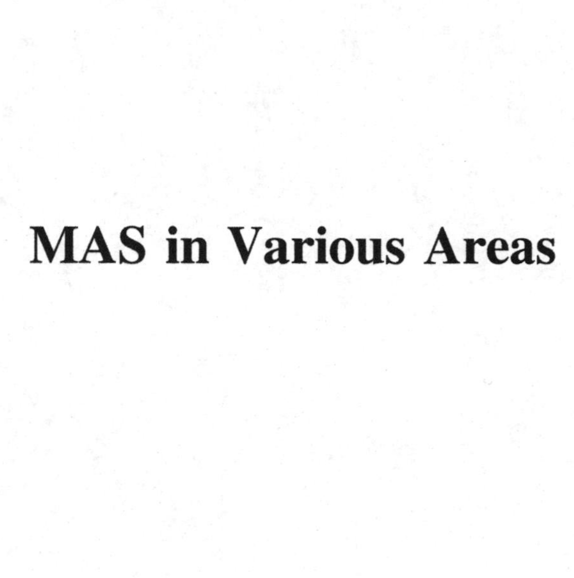

Plant Layout Optimization Using Evolutionary Algorithms

Jiří Kubalík[1(✉)], Petr Kadera[1], Václav Jirkovský[1], Lukáš Kurilla[2], and Šimon Prokop[2]

[1] Czech Institute of Informatics, Robotics, and Cybernetics, Czech Technical University in Prague, Jugoslávských partyzánů 1580/3, 160 00 Prague, Czech Republic
{jiri.kubalik,petr.kadera,vaclav.jirkovsky}@cvut.cz

[2] Faculty of Architecture, Czech Technical University in Prague, Thákurova 9, 166 34 Prague, Czech Republic
{kurilluk,prokosim}@fa.cvut.cz

Abstract. Facility layout problems, i.e., optimal placement of production units in a plant, become an inseparable part of manufacturing systems design and management. They are known to greatly impact the system performance. This paper proposes a new formulation of the facility layout problem where workstations are to be placed into a hall. Within the hall, obstacles and communications can be defined. Each workstation can have multiple handling spaces attached to its sides and oriented links can be defined between workstations. A new evolutionary-based approach to solve this facility layout problem is proposed in single-objective as well as multi-objective variant. The method is experimentally evaluated on a set of standard VLSI floorplanning benchmarks as well as on the data set created specifically for the proposed facility layout problem. Results show the method is both competitive to the state-of-the-art floorplanners on the VLSI benchmarks and produces high-quality solutions to the proposed facility layout problem.

Keywords: Facility layout problem · Evolutionary Algorithms · Optimization

1 Introduction

The facility layout problem (FLP) is concerned with determining an efficient placement of facilities in a plant area. The facilities may have equal or unequal areas and have interactions between them. The aim is to allocate the facilities in the plant based on a given optimization criterion, subjected to the non overlapping restriction imposed on facilities. This problem occurs in various contexts, e.g. arranging machines in a workshop or production lines in a production hall or buildings on a factory premises. Maximizing the utilization of the area available and minimizing the sum of transportation costs between facilities are the most

V. Mařík et al. (Eds.): HoloMAS 2019, LNAI 11710, pp. 173–188, 2019.
https://doi.org/10.1007/978-3-030-27878-6_14

common goals. Various formulations of the FLP have been defined categorized as static, dynamic, multi-objective, multi-floor FLPs with equal or unequal area, etc. [7] and [11].

FLP is known to have a significant impact upon manufacturing costs, work in process, lead times and productivity. A good placement of facilities contributes to the overall efficiency of operations and can reduce between 20% and 50% of the total operating costs [18].

Layout problems are known to be generally NP-hard, thus many recent developments in solving the FLP are based on iterative metaheuristic approaches such as Tabu Search [17], Ant System [13,21], Particle Swarm Optimization [6], Variable Neighborhood Search [9], Simulated Annealing [16] and Evolutionary Algorithms [1,7,8].

An important issue in designing a layout optimization algorithm is the layout representation. Various representations are used in the literature depending on the particular FLP formulation such as discrete representation [20], slicing tree representation [13], sequence-pair representation [15] and flexible bay structure representation [21].

In this work, we solve a layout problem that is given by a set of workstations that have to be optimally placed into a production hall given that all constraints imposed on the generated floorplan are satisfied. One or more optimization criteria can be defined. To solve this problem, we propose an evolutionary algorithm using so-called *priority list* representation. The priority list encodes the order in which the workstations will be added to the floorplan using placement heuristics designed for the problem.

Main contributions of this work are:

- Formulation of a FLP with a realistic definition of the hall and workstations.
- Design of a novel evolutionary-based approach to solving a general class of layout optimization problems in a single-objective and multi-objective variant.

The proposed single- and multi-objective EAs has been experimentally evaluated standard floorplanning benchmark problems as well as on the FLP data set.

The remainder of this paper is organized as follows: Sect. 2 defines the FLP problem solved in this work. In Sect. 3 the proposed method is described. Experimental evaluation of the proposed method is presented in Sect. 4. Section 5 concludes the paper.

2 Problem Definition

In this section we define basic components of the FLP solved in this work. First, a *hall* and a *workstation* will be described.

The hall is defined as a rectangular area with the following attributes and elements:

- *Width* W_h and *height* H_h.
- *Obstacles* – areas composed of rectangular shapes that represent restricted areas that cannot be used by the workstations at all.

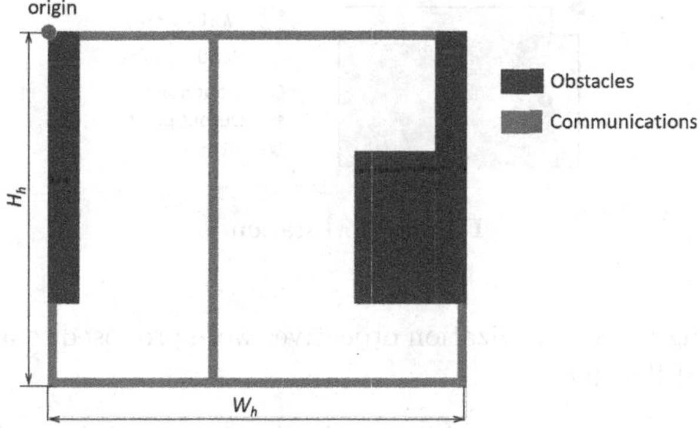

Fig. 1. Hall layout.

- *Communications* – areas composed of rectangular shapes that can be used only by relevant parts of the workstations, see workstation definition below.
- *Origin* – coordinates of the upper-left corner of the minimum bounding box enclosing all above mentioned elements of the hall.

Figure 1 shows an example of the hall. Note, the hall itself has a simple rectangular shape, however rather complex operation area within the hall can effectively be delimited as a set of rectilinear polygons defined using the obstacles and communications.

The workstation is defined as a rectangular object that contains the following elements, see Fig. 2:

- *Working area* – single rectangular area.
- *Handling area* – a rectangular area attached to a side of the working area. Each workstation can have up to four handling areas, each attached to one side of its working area. It represents a part of the workstation that is used for example to transport material and products in and out of the workstation. Workstations can share handling areas, i.e., two workstations can have overlapping handling areas.
- *Input/output points* – these are used to define dependencies between workstations. The output of one workstation can be used as an input to several other workstations. Similarly, the input of a workstation can be linked to the output of several other workstations.
- *Pivot p* – coordinates of the upper-left corner of the workstations's minimum bounding box.
- *Orientation o* – a workstation can appear in the floorplan in one of the following six possible orientations:
  - ∘ workstation is in its original orientation,
  - ∘ workstation is rotated by $-\pi/2$ rad, $\pi/2$ rad or π rad relative to its original orientation,
  - ∘ workstation is flipped horizontally or vertically relative to its original orientation.

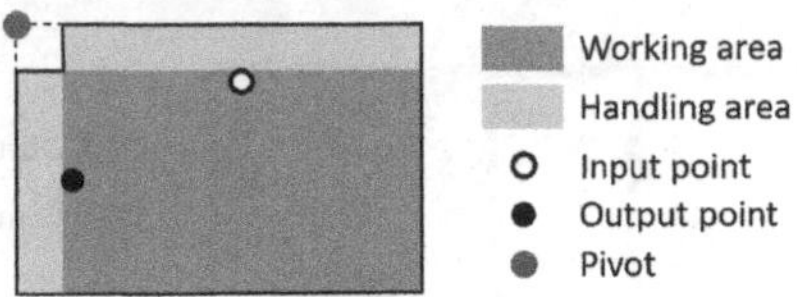

Fig. 2. Workstation.

The following three optimization objectives were proposed to assess a quality of the generated floorplans:

- `minUsedArea` – minimizes the area of the floorplan's minimum bounding box.
- `maxFreeSpace` – maximizes the free space between the bottom edge of the hall and the placed workstations. Using this objective not only maximally compact floorplans are sought, it also prefers floorplans with the remaining space concentrated towards the bottom edge of the hall. Other preferences how the remaining space should be distributed in the floorplan can be specified. This objective is illustrated in Fig. 3 with the yellow area to be maximized. Only segments wide no less than a predefined minimum width count. Here, the minimum segment width is set to 6 m as this is the minimum workstation width observed in the FLP data used in this work.
- `minConnDist` – minimizes the total length of all connections between workstations. The Euclidean distance between input and output point of two interconnected workstations is used in this work. We choose the Euclidean distance just as a proof-of-concept metric that provide a lower bound to the optimal solution. There might be other metrics defined that would describe better the actual distance needed to travel between the two points.

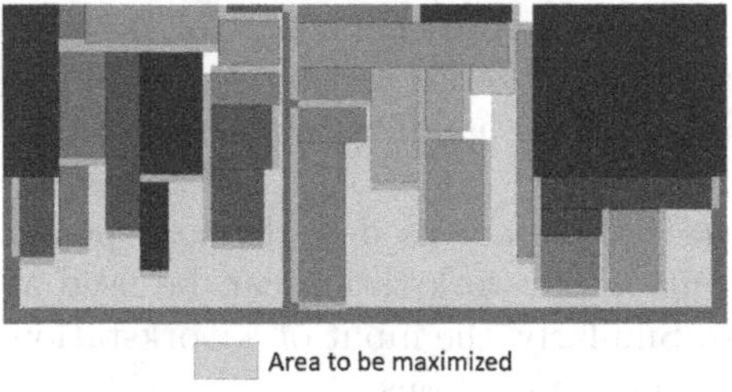

Fig. 3. Illustration of the `maxFreeSpace` optimization objective. (Color figure online)

Let's assume the following functions:

- `overlap(`$area_1$, $area_2$`)` that returns the size of the overlap between $area_1$ and $area_2$.
- `workingArea(`*workstation*`)` that returns working area of the workstation.
- `handlingArea(`*workstation*`)` that returns handling area of the workstation.

- `communications`(*hall*) that returns communications of the hall.
- `obstacles`(*hall*) that returns obstacles of the hall.
- `isInside`(*workstation, hall*) that returns true iff the workstation is entirely enclosed within the hall. Otherwise, false is returned.

Then, we define a *workstation–workstation* constraint for a pair of workstations (w_i, w_j) as

$$\begin{aligned} & \texttt{overlap(workingArea(}w_i\texttt{), workingArea(}w_j\texttt{))} = 0 \\ \wedge\ & \texttt{overlap(workingArea(}w_i\texttt{), handlingArea(}w_j\texttt{))} = 0 \\ \wedge\ & \texttt{overlap(handlingArea(}w_i\texttt{), workingArea(}w_j\texttt{))} = 0 \end{aligned} \tag{1}$$

a *workstations–hall* constraint for workstation w and hall h as

$$\begin{aligned} & \texttt{overlap(workingArea(}w\texttt{), communications(}h\texttt{))} = 0 \\ \wedge\ & \texttt{overlap(workingArea(}w\texttt{), obstacles(}h\texttt{))} = 0 \end{aligned} \tag{2}$$

and a *size* constraint for workstation w and hall h as

$$\texttt{isInside(}w, h\texttt{)} \tag{3}$$

The FLP solved in this work is given by a particular specification of the hall $\mathcal{H}$, a set of N workstations $\mathcal{W} = \{w_1, \ldots, w_N\}$ and an optimization objective or multiple objectives. A *floorplan*, i.e., the particular assignment of the pivot and orientation for all workstations $w \in \mathcal{W}$, is *feasible* if and only if it satisfies constraint (1) for all pairs (w_i, w_j), where $w_i, w_j \in \mathcal{W}$ and $w_i \neq w_j$ and constraints (2)–(3) for all workstations $w \in \mathcal{W}$ and the hall $h = \mathcal{H}$. The goal is to find a feasible floorplan that is optimal w.r.t. the given optimization objective(s).

3 Method

3.1 Indirect Representation

The proposed evolutionary algorithm uses an indirect representation of the evolved floorplans as a sequence of elements of the form of tuples (`id`, `orientation`, `heuristic`), called a priority list, with the following meaning of the attributes:

- `id` – An identifier of the workstation.
- `orientation` – A particular orientation of the workstation in which it will be added to the floorplan. One out of the six possible orientations listed in the workstation description above is chosen.
- `heuristic` – A particular placement heuristic that is to be used to place the workstation into the floorplan. Two possible heuristics are defined in this work, see below.

Each workstation is represented by exactly one element of the priority list. The order of elements determines the order in which the workstations will be added into the developed floorplan.

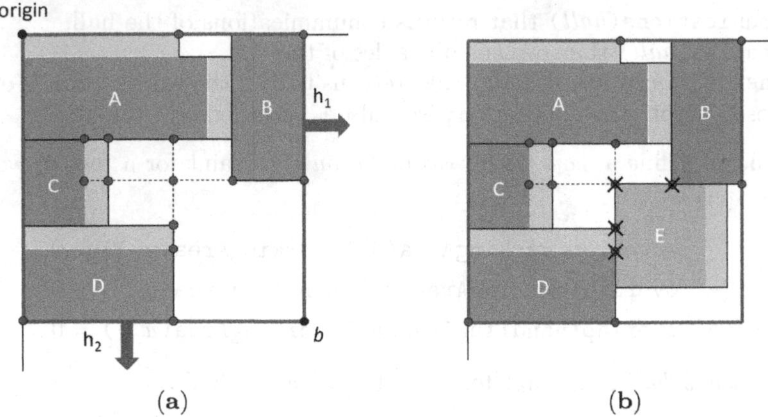

Fig. 4. Candidate placement points. (a) A situation after four workstations have been placed into the floorplan. (b) Elimination of candidate points after the workstation has been added to the floorplan. (Color figure online)

3.2 Mapping of Priority List to Floorplan

Each priority list maps to one floorplan through an iterative process. Input of the mapping process is a specification of the hall and workstations and the priority list. Moreover, either the maximum floorplan width $W_f > W_h$ or the maximum floorplan height $H_f > H_h$ can be specified. This provides an extra operational space for the placement heuristics as described below. Output of the mapping process is the floorplan $\mathcal{F}$ constructed according to the priority list. The floorplan is represented as a list of workstations, where each workstation has its orientation set according to the information stored in the respective element of the priority list and the pivot coordinates calculated using a placement heuristic.

First, we describe important components of the mapping algorithm, particularly the candidate placement points and their management, floorplan minimum bounding box and the placement heuristics.

Placement heuristics work with a set of candidate placement points $\mathcal{P}$. When a new workstation is to be placed into the floorplan, first its orientation is set according to the information stored in the respective element of the $priorityList$. Then, a position of its pivot is chosen among the points in $\mathcal{P}$ using a placement heuristic. At the beginning, $\mathcal{P}$ is initialized with the hall origin and gets updated whenever a new workstation has been added to the developed floorplan. Points are sorted in the upper-to-bottom and left-to-right manner. Figure 4 shows an example of $\mathcal{P}$ for one particular situation with four workstations in the floorplan.

Always, the upper-right, lower-left and lower-right corners of the newly added workstation are added to $\mathcal{P}$. In addition to that, other candidate points are generated with respect to the lower-left corner (we denote it LLC) and upper-right corner (we denote it URC) of the workstation. The rationale behind this candidate point generation strategy is that when a workstation is added to the

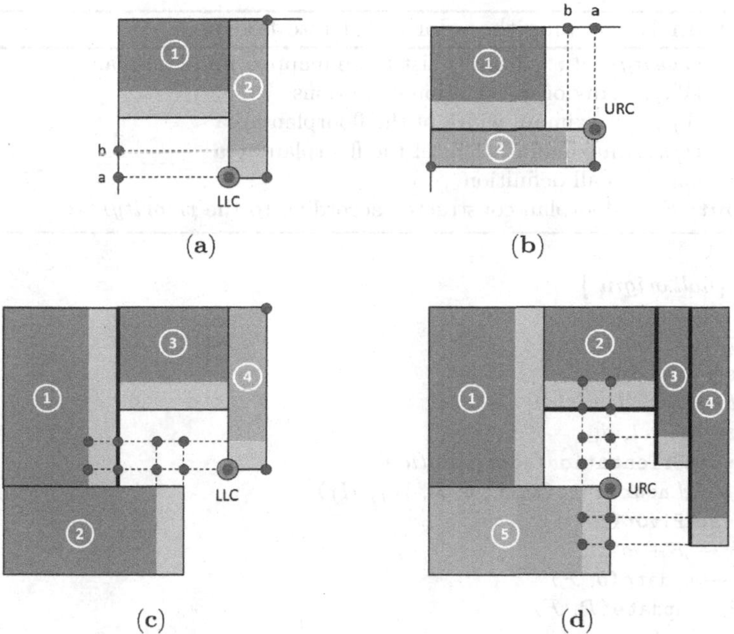

Fig. 5. Four situations when new candidate placement points can be generated. New points are generated with respect to the upper-right and lower-left corner of the newly added workstation (marked as red dot with green ring), respectively. Red dots represent newly generated candidate placement points. Workstation numbers indicate the order in which they were added to the floorplan. (Color figure online)

floorplan, some other workstations might still fit to the space which is to the lower left of this workstation's LLC and to the upper right of its URC, respectively.

Figure 5 illustrates four distinct situations when the new candidate points are generated. Figure 5(a) shows the case when there is no other workstation to the left of the LLC. Then, a new candidate point is generated with coordinates [0,LLC.x] (i.e., the point labelled with 'a'). The same procedure is applied to the LLC of the working area of the newly added workstation yielding another candidate point (the one labelled with 'b'). Similarly, when there is no other workstation above the URC, then a new point with coordinates [URC.x, 0] is generated, see Fig. 5(b). And another point generated in the same way for the URC of the working area of the newly added workstation. Figures 5(c)–(d) illustrate situations analogous to the previous two when there are other workstations to the left of LLC and to the upper right of URC, respectively. Note, the above described node generation strategy does not produce a complete set of candidate placement points that would guarantee the optimal solution can be constructed. It can happen that the optimal solution might be missed. However, the experiments presented in Sect. 4 clearly demonstrate the proposed candidate points generation allows to generate high-quality solutions.

Algorithm 1. Mapping the priority list into floorplan.

Input: *priorityList* ... priority list to be mapped into floorplan
$\mathcal{W}$ ... array of workstation definitions
W_f ... maximum width of the floorplan area
H_f ... maximum height of the floorplan area
hall ... hall definition
Output: $\mathcal{F}$ ... floorplan constructed according to the *priorityList*

```
F ← {}
P ← {hall.origin }
b ← hall.origin
i ← 0
while i < N do
    el ← priorityList [i]
    w ← W [el.id]
    w.setOrientation(el.orientation)
    p ← el.heuristic(w, F, b, P, W_f, H_f)
    w.setPivot(p)
    F ← F + w
    b ← update(b, F)
    P ← update(P, F)
    i ← i + 1
return F
```

When a new workstation is added to the floorplan, some placement points become useless and are removed from $\mathcal{P}$. Those are all the points where a pivot of any other workstation (a pivot is always the upper-left corner of the workstation) cannot be placed any more. Figure 4(b) illustrates such a node elimination.

A minimum bounding box of the floorplan is another structure that is used by the placement heuristics, see the red rectangle in Fig. 4. The bounding box is represented just by its lower-right corner, b, and is initialized with the hall origin (i.e., the bounding box is initialized with zero width and height). It is also updated after adding each workstation to the floorplan.

Two heuristics for placing workstation w into the floorplan $\mathcal{F}$ are used in this work, though other heuristics can be proposed as well. They choose a position for the workstation w such that the following conditions hold:

1. The resulting floorplan satisfies constraint (1) for all workstation pairs (w, w_i), where $w_i \in \mathcal{F}$.
2. The resulting floorplan satisfies constraint (2) for the workstation w and the hall $\mathcal{H}$.

First, a point p from $\mathcal{P}$ is sought such that the workstation w placed with its pivot at the point p entirely fits into the current floorplan bounding box. The first point that satisfies this condition is taken. If no such point is found, then the heuristics h_1 and h_2 choose a position $p \in \mathcal{P}$ that leads to a floorplan entirely fits into the maximum floorplan area $[W_f \times H_f]$ as follows

- h_1 chooses p such that $(p.y < p_i.y)$ for all $p_i \in \mathcal{P}$, $p \neq p_i$,
- h_2 chooses p such that $(p.x < p_i.x)$ for all $p_i \in \mathcal{P}$, $p \neq p_i$.

Generally, h_1 and h_2 leads to extending the floorplan bounding box width and height, respectively, as indicated in Fig. 4.

The mapping algorithm, see Algorithm 1, starts with an initialization of $\mathcal{F}$, $\mathcal{P}$ and b, lines 1–3. Then, it takes elements of the priority list one by one and adds the corresponding workstations into the floorplan as follows. First, the workstation's orientation is set according to the orientation stored in the element, line 8. Then, a placement position of the workstation is found using the heuristic assigned to the workstation and the workstation is placed at the chosen position, lines 9–10. The workstation is added to the floorplan, line 11. Finally, the floorplan's bounding box and candidate placement points are updated, lines 12–13. Once all workstations have been placed into the floorplan, the floorplan is returned.

Note, not necessarily just feasible floorplans are produced. Constraints (1) and (2) are always satisfied. However, constraint (3) might get violated as the placement heuristics applied according to the priority list may produce a floorplan that does not entirely fit within the hall area $[W_h \times H_h]$.

Another important aspect of this representation is that several priority lists can map to the same floorplan. Such a redundancy of the representation can be good for optimization algorithms as there can exists multiple basins of attraction in the representation space for the optimal floorplan.

3.3 Evolutionary Algorithm

The evolutionary algorithm, see Algorithm 2, takes five parameters on its input, namely the population size, maximum number of generations, probability of crossover and mutation and size of the elite set. Output of the algorithm is the layout represented by the best individual in the final population.

The algorithm starts with a random initialization and evaluation of the population of individuals, each represented by a priority list. Then, it iterates through generations, lines 4–20, in each generation a new population being created as follows. A population *tempPop* is created through a evolutionary standard process using selection, crossover and mutation. We use a tournament selection and a 2-point crossover. Mutation is a variation operator that modifies a randomly chosen element of the priority list so that it changes either its position within the priority list, or its `wsOrientation` or `heuristic`. When the *tempPop* of size *PopSize* has been generated, a number of *EliteSize* top best unique individuals from the previous generation are added to *tempPop*, line 18. Finally, the best *PopSize* unique individuals from *tempPop* are selected to the new *population*, line 19. In the end, a floorplan represented by the best-fit individual of the population is returned.

Besides the single-objective evolutionary algorithm described above, a multi-objective evolutionary algorithm working with the indirect representation can be used as well. Here, we implemented the NSGA-II algorithm

[5]. The multi-objective algorithm returns a set of non-dominated solutions from which one can choose the final solution based on his/her preferences.

Algorithm 2. Single-objective evolutionary algorithm for FLOP.

Input: *PopSize* ... population size
MaxGenerations ... maximum number of generations
P_C ... crossover rate
P_M ... mutation rate
EliteSize ... number of elite individuals
Output: Floorplan represented by the best individual

```
init(population)
evaluate(population)
generations ← 0
while generations < MaxGenerations do
    tempPop ← {}
    while |tempPop| < PopSize do
        par1 ← select(population)
        if rand() < P_C then
            par2 ← select(population)
            child ← crossover(par1, par2)
            if rand() < P_M then
                mutate(child)
        else
            child ← par1
            mutate(child)
        evaluate(child)
        tempPop ← tempPop + child
    tempPop ← tempPop ∪ elite(population, EliteSize)
    population ← getUnique(tempPop, PopSize)
    generations ← generations +1
return getBest(population)
```

4 Experiments

We have carried out the following series of experiments to validate the proposed method:

1. Single-objective EA on standard floorplanning benchmarks – these proof-of-concept experiments were carried out on the MCNC and GSRC benchmarks circuits – ami33, ami49, n100a, n100b and n100c. This represents a pure floorplanning problem with the goal to pack simple rectangular objects as compact as possible. We compared our method with several other state-of-the-art floorplanning algorithms, namely the Variable-Order Ant System (VOAS) [10], Moving Block Sequence-Organizational Evolutionary Algorithm (MBS-OEA) [14], Multi-agent Evolutionary Algorithm-Moving Block Sequence (MAEA-MBS) [19], Evolutionary Search (ES) [3], Greedy Insertion

Table 1. Characteristics of the problems from MCNC and GSRC benchmarks.

Problem	# Modules	Total area of all modules (mm^2)
ami33	33	1.1564
ami49	49	35.4454
n100a	100	17.9501
n100b	100	16.0126
n100c	200	17.1966

Technique (GIT) [12], Discrete Particle Swarm Optimization (DPSO) [4] and Blockpacking with Branch-and-Bound (BloBB) [2].

2. Single- and multi-objective EA on FLP data – these experiments were carried out on synthetic data specifically created to evaluate our approach under a realistic scenario with our proposed representation of the production hall and workstations, see below.

4.1 Data

MCNC and GSRC Benchmarks. We selected several circuits from the MCNC and GSRC benchmarks that belong among the most frequently used floorplanning problems in literature. Their characteristics are shown in Table 1.

FLP Data. In order to validate an ability of the proposed approach to solve FLP problems with the realistic specification of the facility and the workstations to be placed in it, as described Sect. 2, we created the FLP data set with the hall of the same layout as shown in Fig. 1 and the following characteristics:

- $W_h = 276$ m, $H_h = 236$ m, total hall area is 65.136 m^2,
- total area of the obstacles is 12.955 m^2,
- total area of communications is 4.992 m^2,
- total free space is 47.189 m^2.

The set of workstations has the following characteristics:

- number of workstations and inter-workstation links 58,
- total area of all workstations is 41.276 m^2,
- total working area of the workstations is 34.013 m^2,
- total handling area of the workstations is 7.263 m^2.

The workflow topology determined by the workstation dependencies is shown in Fig. 6. The ratio of the total area occupied by the workstations to the free space of the hall is 0.87 that together with the above listed characteristics render the data set an interesting FLP benchmark.

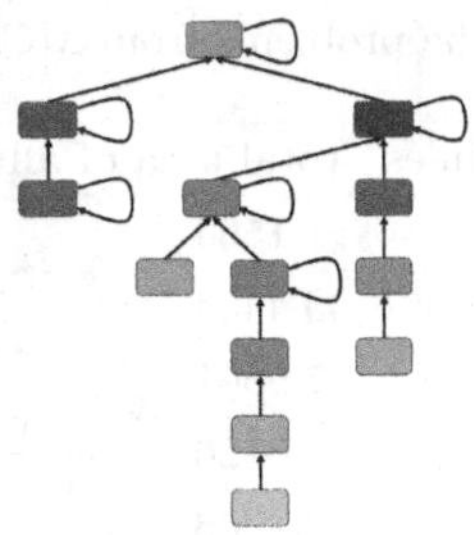

Fig. 6. Dependencies between workstations.

4.2 Experiment Setup

Experiments on the MCNC and GSRC benchmarks were carried out with the following setting of the evolutionary algorithm's parameters: $PopSize = 500$, $MaxGenerations = 300$, $P_C = 0.8$, $P_M = 0.1$, `minUsedArea` used as fitness. These benchmarks involve just simple rectangular objects, so the workstations have only working area and no handling space. Moreover, no limits are imposed on the floorplan area, so all size parameters W_h, H_h, W_f and H_f were set to a large value calculated as $\sum_{w \in \mathcal{W}} \max(w.width, w.height)$.

Experiments on the FLP data set were carried out with almost the same setting of the evolutionary algorithm's parameters but the fitness function used was the `maxFreeSpace` in the single-objective EA plus the `minConnDist` in the multi-objective EA. Moreover, the size of the maximum floorplan area is set as $W_f = W_h$ and $H_f = 2 * H_h$. Thus, the placement heuristics can use extra space below the hall if needed.

For each experiment a series of 30 independent runs have been executed. The median and the best solutions are presented in the tables.

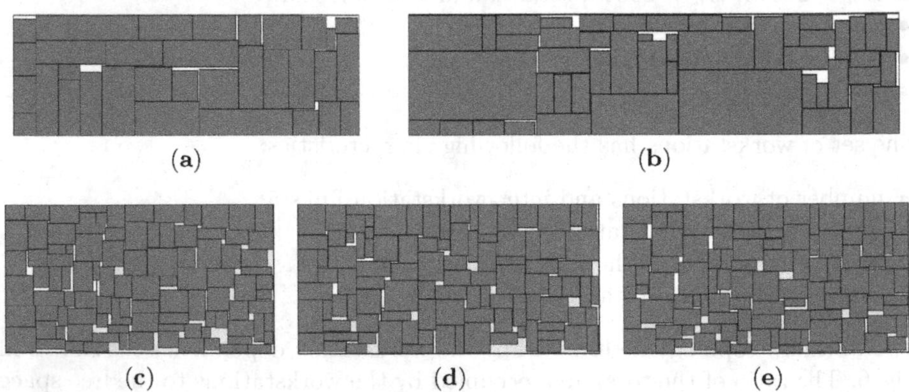

Fig. 7. Best floorplans obtained with the proposed method on the standard floorplanning benchmark circuits – (a) ami33, (b) ami49, (c) n100a, (d) n100b, (e) n100c. The floorplans' areas are listed in Table 2.

4.3 Results

Table 2 presents a comparison of the proposed method with the state-of-the-art floorplanners on the MCNC and GSRC benchmark problems. It shows that our method is competitive with the compared ones. Moreover, it found the overall best solution out of all compared floorplanners on the n100a benchmark. Figure 7 shows the best floorplans generated with the proposed method on the benchmark circuits.

Table 2. Comparisons on MCNC and GSRC benchmarks. An area in (mm^2) of the minimum bounding box surrounding the packed workstations is shown. Results obtained with the proposed single-objective EA are in the last column.

Problem	MAEA-MBS	MBS-OEA	ES	GIT	DPSO	BloBB	VOAS	This work
ami33	1.19	**1.175**	1.19	1.28	1.25	1.28	1.18	1.18
ami49	36.75	36.35	36.30	36.88	38.18	38.80	**36.24**	36.40
n100a	19.40	18.98	18.96	19.45	19.22	–	18.87	**18.86**
n100b	17.05	16.98	–	–	17.53	–	**16.84**	16.96
n100c	18.28	18.27	–	–	–	–	**18.05**	18.23

Table 3 presents results obtained with the proposed single- and multi-objective EA on the FLP data set. The third and fourth column show results obtained with the single-objective EA with the `maxFreeSpace` and `minConnDist` optimization objective, respectively. Values in the median rows are the median values of the corresponding objective value over the set of final solutions of the 20 runs. The best value rows represent the objective values of the overall best solution evolved w.r.t. the corresponding optimization objective.

We see that solutions optimized w.r.t. one objective have a very good value of that objective while the other objective value is rather poor. This is in agreement with our expectations. See Fig. 8 where the best floorplans evolved with individual optimization objectives are shown. Note that when optimizing w.r.t. `minConnDist` objective, the final solutions might be, and in fact most of the time are, infeasible. Simply, the `minConnDist` objective itself does not make a sufficient pressure towards the maximally compact floorplans.

Last two columns of Table 3 show results of the multi-objective EA. Note, the multi-objective EA returns a set of non-dominated solutions from which one chooses the final solution(s) according to his/her preferences. Here, we take the extreme non-dominated solutions, i.e., the one with the best value of the `maxFreeSpace` objective and the `minConnDist` objective, respectively, see Fig. 9(a). The third and fourth column of Table 3 presents performance statistics of the best non-dominated solutions w.r.t. the `maxFreeSpace` and the `minConnDist`, respectively. Importantly, every run of the multi-objective EA produces feasible floorplans that are good in both objectives. Examples of the best floorplans are in Fig. 9(b) and (c).

Table 3. Results obtained on the FLP data set. The last two columns present performance statistics calculated from the non-dominated solutions with the best value of the optimization objective marked with an asterisk.

Performance		Optimization objective(s)			
		`maxFreeSpace`	`minConnDist`	`maxFreeSpace`* `minConnDist`	`maxFreeSpace` `minConnDist`*
`maxFreeSpace` (m^2)	Median	7933	4319	7759	5493
	Best	9106	4478	9617	6807
`minConnDist` (m)	Median	7155	3214	4722	3396
	Best	7627	3021	4723	3078

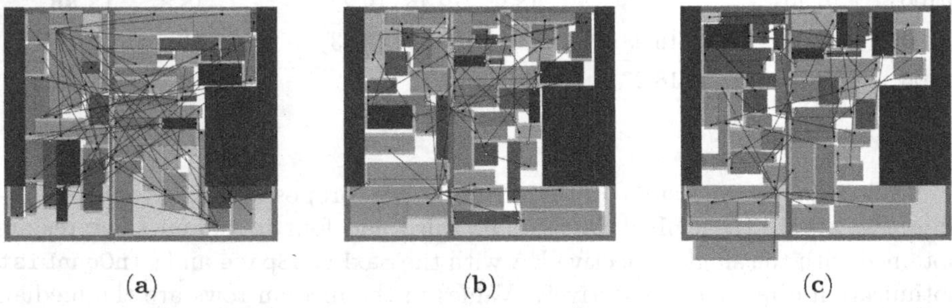

Fig. 8. Results obtained with a single-objective evolutionary algorithm. (a) The best floorplan evolved with the `maxFreeSpace` fitness. (b) The best feasible floorplan evolved with the `minConnDist` fitness. (c) An infeasible floorplan with the overall best `minConnDist` fitness value.

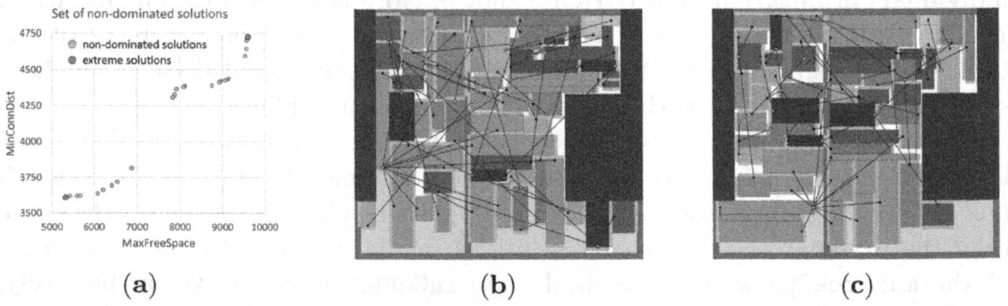

Fig. 9. Results obtained with a multi-objective evolutionary algorithm. (a) The final set of non-dominated solutions. (b) The extreme solution with the best `maxFreeSpace` value. (c) The extreme solution with the best `minConnDist` value.

5 Conclusions

New FLP problem has been defined and two variants, single-objective and multi-objective, of an evolutionary algorithm to solve it has been proposed. Proof-of-concept experiments on standard VLSI floorplanning benchmark problems proved an ability of the algorithm to generate floorplans competitive to state-of-the-art floorplanners. Experiments on the FLP data set specifically created for the proposed problem shown an ability of the algorithm to generate well-performing layouts with respect to the used criteria.

Future research will focus on extending this approach towards an optimization framework providing a user with an ability to guide the layout optimization process using a prior knowledge about the problem. In the envisioned framework a user will be able to interact with the optimizer so that for example certain parts of the current best solutions will constitute higher-level blocks for next stage of the layout optimization process.

We will also investigate alternative definitions of the inter-workstation communication objectives. With the `minConnDist` objective used in this work it can happen, that some workstation can be surrounded by other workstations so that its handling area and input/output points get inaccessible. We will investigate possibilities to calculate distances between workstations using the A* algorithm that would introduce a pressure towards feasible solutions with perfect workstations' accessibility.

Acknowledgment. This work was funded by Ministry of Education, Youth and Sport of the Czech Republic within the project Cluster 4.0 number CZ.02.1.01/0.0/0.0/16_026/0008432.

References

1. Aiello, G., Scalia, G.L., Enea, M.: A multi objective genetic algorithm for the facility layout problem based upon slicing structure encoding. Expert Syst. Appl. **39**(12), 10352–10358 (2012)
2. Chan, H.H., Markov, I.L.: Practical slicing and non-slicing block-packing without simulated annealing. In: Proceedings of the 14th ACM Great Lakes Symposium on VLSI, GLSVLSI 2004, pp. 282–287. ACM, New York (2004)
3. Chen, D.S., Lin, C.T., Wang, Y.W., Cheng, C.H.: Fixed-outline floorplanning using robust evolutionary search. Eng. Appl. Artif. Intell. **20**(6), 821–830 (2007)
4. Chen, G., Guo, W., Chen, Y.: A PSO-based intelligent decision algorithm for VLSI floorplanning. Soft. Comput. **14**(12), 1329–1337 (2010)
5. Deb, K., Pratap, A., Agarwal, S., Meyarivan, T.: A fast and elitist multiobjective genetic algorithm: NSGA-II. IEEE Trans. Evol. Comput. **6**(2), 182–197 (2002)
6. Derakhshan Asl, A., Wong, K.Y.: Solving unequal-area static and dynamic facility layout problems using modified particle swarm optimization. J. Intell. Manuf. **28**(6), 1317–1336 (2017)
7. Drira, A., Pierreval, H., Hajri-Gabouj, S.: Facility layout problems: a survey. Annual Reviews in Control **31**, 255–267 (2007)

8. García-Hernández, L., Arauzo-Azofra, A., Salas-Morera, L., Pierreval, H., Corchado, E.: Facility layout design using a multi-objective interactive genetic algorithm to support the DM. Expert Sys.: J. Knowl. Eng. **32**(1), 94–107 (2015)
9. Guan, J., Lin, G.: Hybridizing variable neighborhood search with ant colony optimization for solving the single row facility layout problem. Eur. J. Oper. Res. **248**(3), 899–909 (2016)
10. Hoo, C.S., Jeevan, K., Ganapathy, V., Ramiah, H.: Variable-order ant system for VLSI multiobjective floorplanning. Appl. Soft Comput. **13**(7), 3285–3297 (2013)
11. Hosseini-Nasab, H., Fereidouni, S., Ghomi, S.M.T.F., Fakhrzad, M.B.: Classification of facility layout problems: a review study. Int. J. Adv. Manuf. Technol. **94**(1–4), 957–977 (2017). https://doi.org/10.1007/s00170-017-0895-8
12. Janiak, A., Kozik, A., Lichtenstein, M.: New perspectives in VLSI design automation: deterministic packing by sequence pair. Ann. Oper. Res. **179**(1), 35–56 (2010)
13. Komarudin, K., Wong, K.Y.: Applying ant system for solving unequal area facility layout problems. Eur. J. Oper. Res. **202**(3), 730–746 (2010)
14. Liu, J., Zhong, W., Jiao, L., Li, X.: Moving block sequence and organizational evolutionary algorithm for general floorplanning with arbitrarily shaped rectilinear blocks. IEEE Trans. Evol. Comput. **12**(5), 630–646 (2008)
15. Meller, R.D., Chen, W., Sherali, H.D.: Applying the sequence-pair representation to optimal facility layout designs. Oper. Res. Lett. **35**(5), 651–659 (2007)
16. Saraswat, A., Venkatadri, U., Castillo, I.: A framework for multi-objective facility layout design. Comput. Ind. Eng. **90**, 167–176 (2015)
17. Scholz, D., Petrick, A., Domschke, W.: STaTS: a slicing tree and tabu search based heuristic for the unequal area facility layout problem. Eur. J. Oper. Res. **197**(1), 166–178 (2009)
18. Tompkins, J., White, J., Bozer, Y., Tanchoco, J.: Facilities Planning. Wiley, New York (2010)
19. Wang, H., Hu, K., Liu, J., Jiao, L.: Multiagent evolutionary algorithm for floorplanning using moving block sequence. In: 2007 IEEE Congress on Evolutionary Computation, pp. 4372–4377, September 2007
20. Wang, M.J., Hu, M.H., Ku, M.Y.: A solution to the unequal area facilities layout problem by genetic algorithm. Comput. Ind. **56**(2), 207–220 (2005). Applications of Genetic Algorithms in Industry
21. Wong, K.Y., Komarudin, K.: Solving facility layout problems using flexible bay structure representation and ant system algorithm. Expert Syst. Appl. **37**(7), 5523–5527 (2010)

Experimentation of Negotiation Protocols for Consensus Problems in Smart Parking Systems

Bruno Rafael Alves[1(✉)], Gleifer Vaz Alves[1], André Pinz Borges[1], and Paulo Leitão[2]

[1] UTFPR - Federal University of Paraná (UTFPR), Câmpus Ponta Grossa, Ponta Grossa, Brazil
brunoa@alunos.utfpr.edu.br, {gleifer,apborges}@utfpr.edu.br
[2] Research Centre in Digitalization and Intelligent Robotics (CeDRI), Instituto Politécnico de Bragança, Campus de Santa Apolónia, 5300-253 Bragança, Portugal
pleitao@ipb.pt

Abstract. A smart city uses emergent technologies for improving the services that will contribute to make the citizens' daily life more comfortable and convenient. Among several strand offered by a smart city, the smart parking systems focus the transportation and parking of vehicles problems, providing intelligent solutions based on ICT technologies, and particularly artificial intelligence techniques. In this context, a cyber-physical system, based on multi-agent systems, was developed for an intelligent parking system for car and bicycles. This multi-agent based system consists of a community of distributed, intelligent and autonomous agents, representing the parking spots and drivers, which cooperate to reach their objectives. In such systems, the global system behaviour emerges from the interaction between these individual entities, being crucial the adoption of the proper cooperation protocols. This paper studies and compares possible approaches to solve consensus problems in such distributed smart parking systems, and particularly addressing the negotiation strategies. For this purpose, the Contract Net Protocol, the English auction and the Dutch auction negotiation strategies were implemented in an agent-based smart parking system using the JADE framework. The experimental results allowed to perform a comparative analysis, considering the satisfaction levels of the actors, the scalability and the negotiation time to decide which approach better fits with the smart parking problem.

Keywords: Multi-agent systems · Negotiation protocols · Smart parking systems

1 Introduction

Nowadays, the cities are becoming very large, with the number of urban residents expanding by nearly 60 million every year, and more than 60% of the world's

V. Mařík et al. (Eds.): HoloMAS 2019, LNAI 11710, pp. 189–202, 2019.
https://doi.org/10.1007/978-3-030-27878-6_15

population expecting to be living in cities by 2050, leading to the emergence of some problems, namely pollution, waste and traffic. A Smart City [9] aims to make the citizens' daily life more comfortable and convenient by using emergent technologies to provide accessibility to public information and services [2]. Particularly, citizens will get access to advanced facilities like smart transportation facilities, smart electricity systems and smart applications for governance.

In terms of traffic, the parking problem can be crucial for the improvement of the smart city concept, since 40% of the traffic in New York is generated by drivers trying to find a spot to park their cars [8]. In this way, a parking that uses advanced technologies to improve its management and the provided services can contribute for a reduction of the traffic [8]. Additionally, a best management of the available parking spots allows to achieve a better profit for the parking and best prices for the drivers.

On the other hand, smart parking systems are not easy to build due to their dynamic and sometimes chaotic environments. In fact, the system needs to be able to deal with a significant amount of drivers asking and receiving offers for parking spots, and at the same time, the parking needs to decide which requests will satisfy more. Due to its dynamics, large-scale and often chaotic nature, the use of distributed systems can be helpful, being easier to divide the entire complex process into simpler micro processes than having a single entity encharged by the entire process [15].

In particular, multi-agent systems (MAS) [10] offers an alternative way to design such systems by distributing the intelligence and control over a community of autonomous and cooperative agents that will cooperate to achieve their objectives. In the smart parking problem, the agents will represent the drivers of cars, bikes and trucks, and the parking spots available in the system. The use of MAS solutions provide scalability, i.e. the system continues operating under condition even with the increase of the number of agents, and flexibility, i.e. the system can be adapted for different use cases, such as a car parking, a bicycle parking or considering bike and cars at the same time.

Traditionally, the smart parking system is approached using a centralized monolithic solution, but recently the adoption of MAS is being reported in the literature (see for example, [5] and [16]). However, in these works, the negotiation among the agents follows a centralized approach, which simplifies its implementation but limits the use of the MAS potentialities. In fact, during the negotiation among the agents to find a consensus, each type of agent has its own objectives that usually are in conflict: drivers want to pay as less as possible and the parking spots want to receive as much as possible.

The huge number of agents interacting with each other may affect the negotiation strategy and consequently the system performance. The negotiation needs to be simple and fast enough and yet show a good balance for both the driver and the parking perspectives. Also, aiming to be competitive, the parking system needs to have the capability to understand the environment and adapts the prices depending of the amount of requests for parking spots and the amount of vehicles nearby.

The objective of this paper is to study negotiation protocols for consensus problems in smart parking systems. In particular, the Contract Net Protocol (CNP), the English auction and the Dutch auction strategies were implemented using the JADE agent-based framework under the agent-based smart parking system [3]. These strategies were implemented using the interaction protocols defined by the Foundation for Intelligent Physical Agents (FIPA) [1], and tested according to different scenarios. The evaluation has considered the level of satisfaction of the actors in the system, the scalability and the negotiation time.

The remainder of this paper is organized as follows. Section 2 overviews the agent-based architecture for the smart parking system and highlights the importance of negotiation protocols to address the consensus problems in such distributed systems. Section 3 analyses several existing negotiation protocols found in literature and Sect. 4 describes the implementation of three negotiation protocols using the JADE framework. Section 5 analyses the achieved experimental results under the smart parking context perspective, and finally, Sect. 6 rounds up the paper with the conclusions and points out the future work.

2 Multi-agent System Architecture for Smart Parking

In order to solve the smart-parking problem, an agent-based model was adopted due its capability to distributed intelligence and processing power, as well as the offered scalability. The system architecture establishes two types of agents: the *driver agent* representing the person that drives the vehicle and the *spot agent* representing a specific place to park a vehicle. In such agent-based cyber-physical system, the system components combine cyber and physical parts, e.g., a spot agent being the cyber part and the parking spot being the physical asset.

A parking spot can have different levels of granularity, i.e. can represent the entire car park, a floor of the park, a sector or only a single spot. The design of such feature can be performed by using the holonic principles [7], where holarchies can be used to organize the agents and the recursivity property can be explored, simplifying the design of such large-scale and complex parking systems. A useful example is given by a parking organized in sectors, where each sector comprises a set of spots. With this approach the sectors only negotiate with the inner spots to offer a parking spot to the driver, instead to have a completely flat negotiation among drivers and parking spots.

Figure 1 illustrates the use cases for the smart parking system, being possible to see the interactions among the system entities. In such model, it is possible to verify its flexibility since one driver can have and administrate more than one vehicle, which can be a car or a bike. Another feature of this model is the "admSpot" that represents the parking, which can create the desired number of spot agents, that will work separately. As a consequence, the system will be robust, preventing the system to break no mater how many agents fails, until all of them fails.

The most important part of the system is related to the *"Negotiate Parking Spot"* case, involving the interaction between the spot and driver agents.

This use case assumes a crucial importance because in MAS, the overall behaviour emerges from the interaction among individual agents, and in this case the negotiation is between two type of actors that presents different interests: driver agents want to get parking spots at the lowest prices and the spot agents wants to offer their services at the highest prices. For this purpose, a proper negotiation strategy should be adopted in order to maximize the efficiency of the MAS-based parking system.

In this work, three different negotiation protocols are studied, implemented and compared in order to evaluate which one better fits the smart parking requirements.

3 Analysis of Negotiation Protocols

In distributed systems, the cooperation assumes a crucial issue, being presented in different forms, like collaboration, negotiation and competition, depending of the objective of the participants in the cooperation schema. Since in the parking system, the driver and spot agents have opposite interests, the cooperation in such system will be in terms of a negotiation to find a consensus, pleasing both parts.

Negotiation can be defined as the effort made by two or more entities to achieve an agreement benefiting themselves [17]. The complexity of the negotiation is mainly dependent of the following parameters:

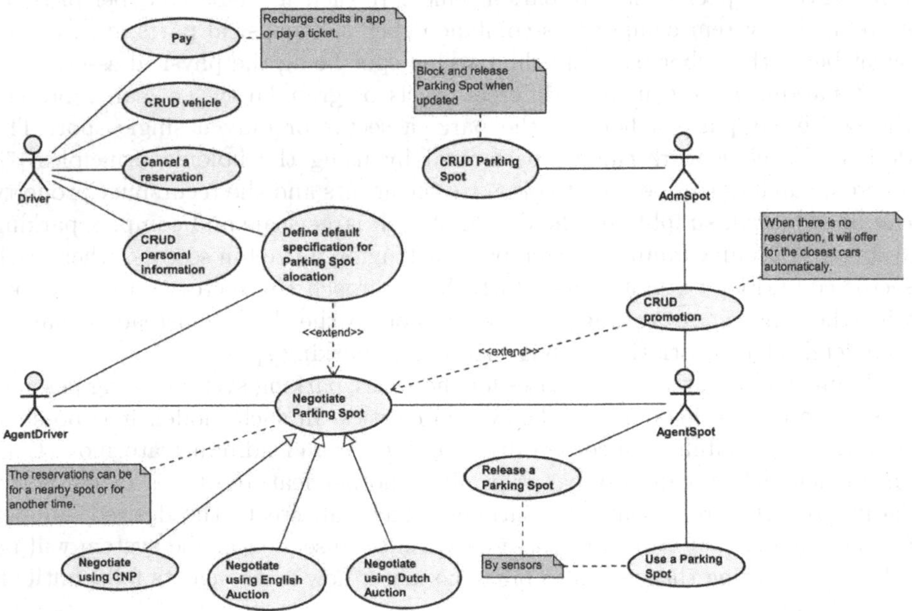

Fig. 1. Use cases for the smart parking system.

- Goals: each entity (agent) or community of entities have specific goals, which cannot be compatible.
- Dependencies of tasks: the execution of tasks is inter-related and in the negotiation process should be considered the dependencies and precedences between tasks.
- Incomplete information: in some cases, it is necessary to negotiate without to know all information about one problem.

In the literature, several negotiation strategies can be found, namely the English auction, the Dutch auction and the CNP. These three mechanisms have different characteristics and the selection of the best one is dependent of the system requirements and application scenario. The next subsections will detail the principles of these three negotiation strategies and describe how they can be adopted in the smart parking problem.

3.1 Contract Net Protocol (CNP)

The CNP is a well-known negotiation protocol and widely used to implement the co-operation process [14]. Basically, this negotiation process works like a bidding process, where the agents exchange messages according to the pattern illustrated in Fig. 2.

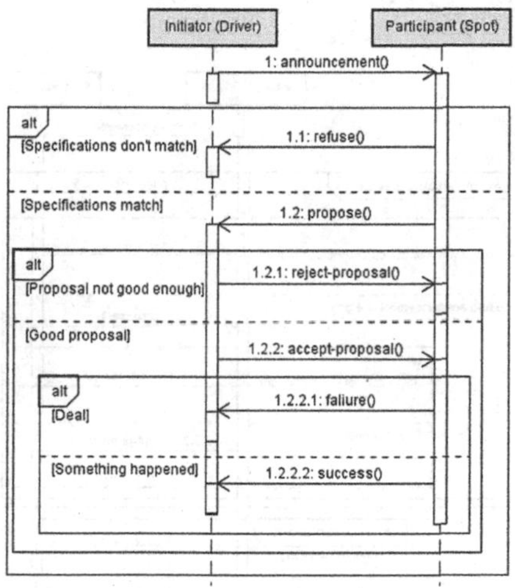

Fig. 2. Interaction diagram for the Contract Net Protocol [1].

Initially, the *Initiator* agent initiates the negotiation by announcing the auction to the *Participant* agents. This announcement message will contain the eligibility specifications that the participant agents will have to satisfy in order to participate in the auction, the specification of the task and the deadline to respond. When a participant agent receives an announcement message, it verifies if the required specifications can be satisfied by itself, and in affirmative case it sends a bid proposal indicating its capacities and conditions to participate in the auction. After receiving the replies, the *Initiator* evaluates all arrived bid proposals and decides which one is accepted according to its selection criteria. If none satisfies the *Initiator*, a new iteration will start with new specifications.

The CNP approach leads to sub-optimal solutions due to its spatial and temporal myopic. Spatial myopia means that the information of the state of others initiator agents is not used during the construction of a bid proposal, while the temporal myopia means that the information of sub-sequent tasks is not used either in the bidding or in the award selection [13]. As the communication process is slower than the computation process, the CNP intends to have reduced communication between the entities, modular and highly independent problems, and no centralized control. However, it presents a problem related to the renegotiation, which may occurs when a deviation occurs, e.g., the non-compliance of the specifications of the task by the awarded entity.

3.2 English Auction

The English auction tries to achieve the consensus between the agents by changing the price over each turn, starting with a bad price for the initiator until none of the participant agents accepts more changes in the price [11]. In this auction, the sequence of messages is represented in Fig. 3.

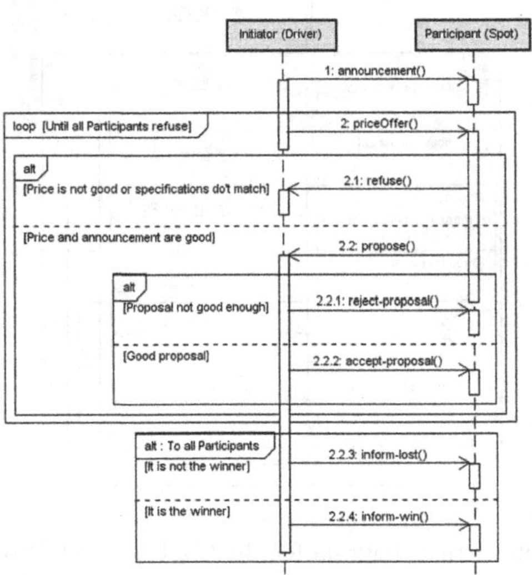

Fig. 3. Interaction diagram for the English auction [1].

Simmilarly to the CNP schema, the *Initiator* agent initiates the negotiation by announcing the auction to the other agents, which contains the eligibility specifications, the task specification and the deadline to respond. In parallel, the *Initiator* sends an offer with the price to all participant agents. When an participant agent receives an auction announcement message, the requested specifications, and particularly the price, are verified, and if they can be satisfied a proposal is sent. Otherwise, the announcement is rejected.

If at least one agent accepts the offer, the previous process will be repeated until no agent accepts the new offer. The expectation is that the price can be improved with the new offer and one agent might accept the offer. After no agent agrees with the offer, the *Initiator* sends a message to the selected entity according to its selection criteria.

The main problem of this auction is the amount of messages exchanged, which means that the increase of the number of participants will significantly increase the number of messages and consequently require more time to achieve the consensus.

3.3 Dutch Auction

Similarly to the English auction, the Dutch auction tries to achieve the consensus between the agents by changing the price over each turn. But instead of starting with a bad price for itself, the initiator starts with a very good price, and iterativelly, the price will be decreased until some participant agent accepts it. The pattern for this auction is represented in Fig. 4.

Initially, the *Initiator* agent sends a message to the other agents announcing the start of the auction, which includes the eligibility specifications that the agents will have to satisfy to participate the auction and the deadline to respond. After, the *Initiator* agent sends an offer with the expected price to all participant

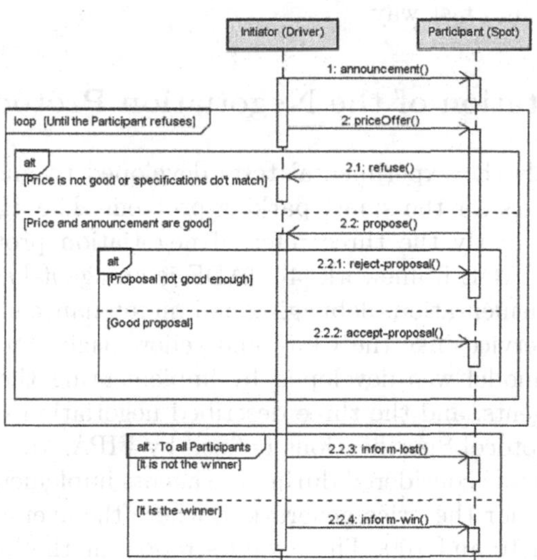

Fig. 4. Interaction diagram for the dutch auction [1].

agents, and waits that one participant accepts the price and makes a propose. When a participant agent receives an auction announcement message, it verifies if the required specifications can be satisfied by itself, and particularly the price, and in affirmative case, it will make a proposal with that price.

If some participant agent accepts the offer, the *Initiator* sends a message to the selected agent confirming the agreement. Otherwise, it means that the price is not good enough for the participant agents, so it repeats the procedure until one agent accepts the price, the price reaches a value that is not anymore interesting for the *Initiator* or the negotiation reaches the time limit.

3.4 Comparative Analysis

The English and the Dutch auctions are very similar, with both implementing an interactive process with the objective to get the best price over each interaction. However, the amount of exchanged messages can be a problem, especially for a large number of participants. If the system is not prepared to support a huge amount of communication at once, it may cause some agents to stop working. In contrast, the CNP mechanism consumes less resources and might be a good alternative protocol in scenarios where a large number of agents negotiate at the same time. However, the myopia is a problem exhibited by the CNP protocol. Aiming to overcome some CNP limitations, other approaches that extends its principles were proposed in the literature, namely the Extended Contract Net Protocol (ECNP) [6] and the B-Contract Net [12].

Since, the main objective of this paper is to test these negotiation strategies, it will be possible to verify if there is a significant difference between the performance achieved by the Dutch and the English auctions (i.e. price and distance), and also, to verify if the resources consumption is really needed for achieving better agreements in a fast way.

4 Implementation of the Negotiation Protocols

This section details the experimental tests developed to analyze the different negotiation protocols for the smart parking problem. The agent-based parking system, and particularly the three referred negotiation protocols, was implemented using the JADE framework [4]. JADE is an agent-base framework that facilitates the implementation, debugging and maintenance of agent-based solutions by offering services like the white and yellow pages and the sniffer agent. The agent-based model was developed by implementing the behaviour of the driver and spot agents, and the three described negotiation strategies following the Interaction Protocol Specifications defined by FIPA [1].

An important issue considered during the agents implementation was related to the mechanisms for the price generation, where the average price is selected randomly between 10 and 100. These values represent the highest price that a driver can pay for a spot and the lowest value the spot will accept.

4.1 Scenarios

The behaviour of each negotiation protocol was tested taking into consideration 9 scenarios build up the variation of the number of available parking spots and drivers, considering three sets: small (50), normal (175) and large (300). These scenarios, ranging from 50 drivers and 50 parking spots, to the 300 drivers and 300 parking spots, were experimentally tested 40 times each one.

Since the parking system is a dynamic system, it was considered that the parking spots are available from the beginning, but the driver agents are not created all at the same time, each one having a possibility of 10% to be created. The parking time can range from 1ms to 100 ms, and the searched area for parking by a driver is at maximum 50% of the whole parking.

The profile of the driver and spot agents follows one of three categories reflecting its role in the negotiation process:

- *Conservative*, which in terms of the driver agent means that the maximum value that it is willing to pay is 40, and the increasing price step in each negotiation iteration is 5. For the spot agent, the minimal accepted price is 5% below the average price.
- *Moderate*, which in terms of the driver agent means that the maximum value that it is willing to pay is 70, and the increasing price step in each negotiation iteration is 10. For the spot agent, the minimal accepted price is 10% below the average price.
- *Aggressive*, which in terms of the driver agent means that the maximum value that it is willing to pay is 100, and the increasing price step in each negotiation iteration is 15. For the spot agent, the minimal accepted price is 15% below the average price.

The distribution of profiles in the agents follows a normal distribution, with the system having 30% of conservative agents, 40% of moderated agents and 30% of aggressive agents.

These simulations intends to get all the possible scenarios to see how the system will react with each one of the negotiation strategies. The covered scenarios are very embracing, allowing at the end to conclude about the best negotiation approaches for each scenario. However, an important remark should be considered: these scenarios consider that at the beginning, the parking is empty, with no cars at any parking spot. This means that a 24 h parking is not considered in this work.

4.2 Metrics

The metrics defined to evaluate the negotiation protocols are mainly related to the price paid by the driver to reserve a parking spot and the distance between the desired parking place and the parking spot got by the driver. The achieved results will be evaluated under these two parameters considering the previously described scenarios.

Additionally, the three negotiation strategies are also evaluated taking into consideration the number of messages exchanged during the negotiation process and the time required to conclude the negotiation.

5 Analysis of Experimental Results

This section analyses the results from the experimental testing of the three implemented negotiation protocols, namely the CNP, English auction and Dutch auction, considering the scenarios previously described. Initially, the average values for the price paid and the distance to the desired parking place are analyzed, and finally, other parameters are also compared, namely the number of exchanged messages and the negotiation time.

The agent-based smart parking was running in an Aspire F5-573G, Intel core i5 7200U, 8 GB RAM DDR4, SSD and NVIDEA GeForce 940MX with 2 GB RAM in a Windows 10.

5.1 Analysis of the Price Paid by the Driver

The results for the price paid by the driver for the three negotiation protocols are illustrated in Fig. 5. The achieved results for the three strategies follow the same behaviour, with the price remaining stable between 50 and 175 parking spots in the system, and then drooping for scenarios considering more than 175 parking spots, which means that when the driver agents are competing for a limited amount of parking spots, the price they need to paid is slightly higher. In fact, since there is more options for the driver to choose the parking spot, the driver prefers the cheapest one (i.e. the selection function tries to minimize to price to pay), with the spot agents needing to reduce the proposal prices to remain competitive.

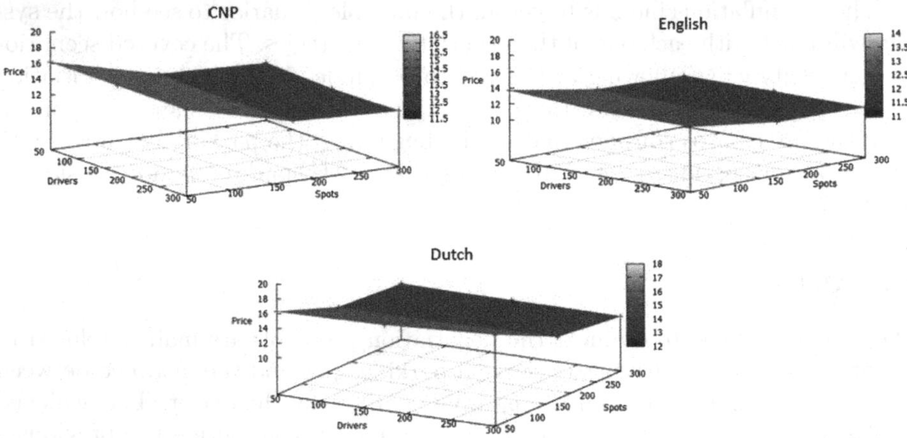

Fig. 5. Results of the price paid by the driver for the three negotiation protocols.

The price values for the CNP and English auction strategies seem to be dependent only from the number of the spot agents, while in the case of the Dutch auction, the values are dependent of the number of drivers and spot agents. The English auction reached the lowest prices from the three tested strategies. The price values reached for the CNP are approximately 2% worst, being similar for scenarios with a high number of parking spots. From the three negotiation protocols, the Dutch auction is clearly the one that presents the worst results.

5.2 Analysis of the Distance to the Desired Parking Place

The results of the distance of the assigned parking spot to the desired parking place for the three negotiation protocols are illustrated in Fig. 6. The observation of these results shows a quite similar behaviour for the three strategies. This distance is mainly dependent of the variation of the number of the parking spots, being higher as higher is the number of parking spots. On the other hand, the distance almost does not change with the variation of the number of drivers in the system.

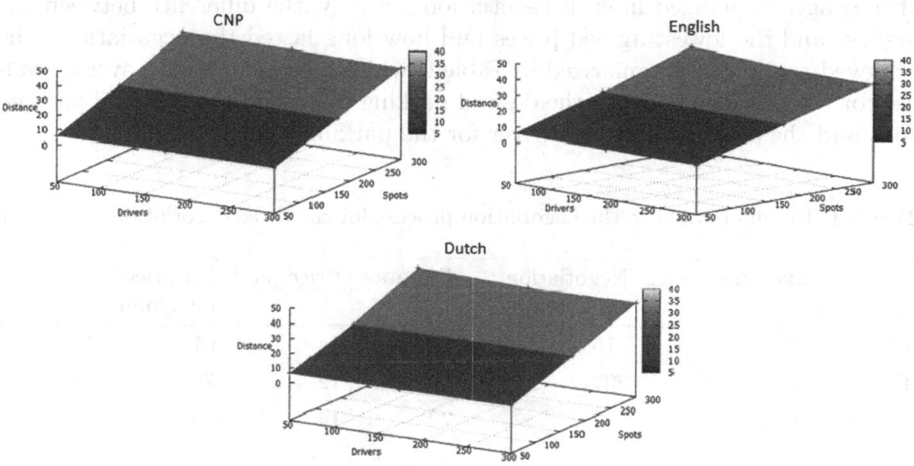

Fig. 6. Results of the distance to the desired parking place for the three negotiation protocols.

The correlation between the number of parking spots and the distance values is quite surprising, but occurs because with more options to park the car, the probability to park far from the desired parking spot is higher (note that the decision function tries to minimize the price to be paid by the driver). However, if the decision function used in the negotiation strategy considers not the minimization of the price but instead the distance, the results are completely different, being less dependent of the number of drivers and parking spots, as well as are smaller for a higher number of parking spots, as illustrated in Fig. 7 for the CNP strategy.

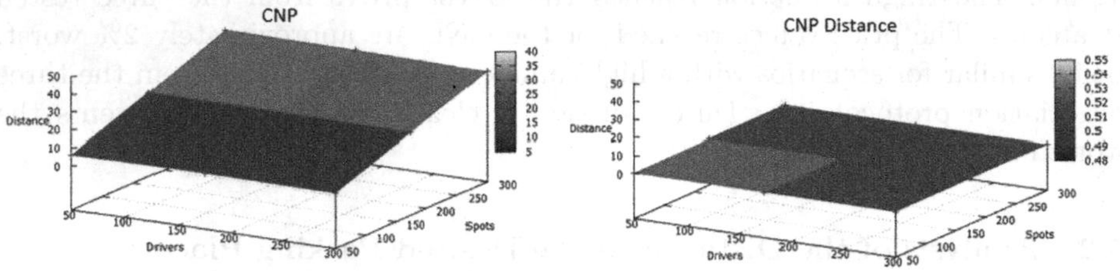

Fig. 7. Results for the CNP negotiation strategy considering the minimization of the price or the minimization of the distance.

5.3 Analysis of Operating Parameters

In addition to the analysis of the price and distance parameters, the average of some other parameters is also performed in this section, namely the amount of messages exchanged in each negotiation strategy, the difference between the highest and the lowest agreed prices and how long lasted the negotiation. The achieved results are summarized in Table 1, which also includes the average values for the distance between the desired parking place and the assigned parking spot and the price paid by the driver for the parking spot.

Table 1. Results related to the negotiation process for the three negotiation strategies.

	Exchanged msg	Negotiation time (ms)	Distance	Price paid	Dif price max/min
CNP	224	15	22	14	61
English	1340	207	22	12	78
Dutch	520	42	22	14	76

As observed, the number of exchanged messages between the agents during a negotiation process was significantly different between the CNP protocol and the English and the Dutch strategies, in favour of CNP. In fact, the number of exchanged messages in the CNP strategy is approximately only 17% of the number presented by the English auction and 43% of the value presented by the Dutch auction. Consequently, the CNP strategy presents the lowest average time to obtain a parking spot, as initially expected. Surprisingly, the number of exchanged messages in the Dutch auction is significantly lower than in the English auction, which occurs since the convergence point is much closer to the initial price value established by the Dutch strategy than in the English strategy (note that the starting point in the Dutch auction is 10, in the English auction is 100, and the convergence value is 14, as illustrated in Table 1).

In spite of presenting the lowest average price, the English auction has the highest difference between agreed prices (i.e. between the highest and lowest price for the several experimental scenarios), being the CNP the most deterministic negotiation strategy.

Summarizing, the English auction reached the best results regarding the agreed prices, but in opposite requires more resources to reach a solution for the negotiation process, expressed in the highest number of the exchanged messages and the requested time to conclude the negotiation. The option for one negotiation strategy may be dependent of the requirements, but the capability to conclude the negotiation faster can be in favour of the CNP strategy, since the difference in terms of price paid by the drivers is very reduced.

6 Conclusions and Future Work

This paper aims to analyze several negotiation strategies for consensus problems in smart parking systems, since the negotiation assumes a crucial issue in such distributed systems. For this purpose, the CNP, the English auction and the Dutch auction strategies were implemented using the JADE framework under the agent-based smart parking system, tested according to different scenarios and evaluated taking into consideration, among others, the level of satisfaction of the actors in the system, the scalability and the negotiation time.

The achieved results show that the Dutch auction strategy presents the worst results, the English auction reached the best results regarding the agreed prices, even with a slightly difference to the others, and the CNP requires much less resources to reach a solution for the negotiation process, expressed in the lowest number of the exchanged messages and the time to conclude the negotiation. In this way, it seems that the CNP protocol is the most suitable strategy to implement the negotiation process in smart parking systems, since it is able to conclude the negotiation faster and the difference in terms of price paid by the drivers is very reduced to the best one.

The future work will be devoted to testing the three negotiation strategies for the agent-based parking system designed by using the holonic principles, e.g., considering holarchies of drivers or spots, which may influence the performance of the negotiation process. Furthermore, comparisons should be made between this work and others approaches, like other branches of this work, which may reveals differents best approaches for differents scenarios. Also, the analysis of a 24 h parking scenario should be considered, discarding the initial results and running the systems for a longer period of time.

References

1. Foundation for Intelligent Physical Agents (FIPA). http://www.fipa.org/index.html
2. Anthopoulos, L., Fitsilis, P.: Digital cities: towards connected citizens and governance. In: Politics, Democracy and E-Government, pp. 275–291 (2010)
3. Bellifemine, F., Caire, G., Greenwood, D.: Developing Multi-Agent Systems with JADE. Wiley, Chichester (2007)
4. Bellifemine, F., Poggi, A., Rimassa, G.: JADE-a FIPA-compliant agent framework. In: Proceedings of the Practical Applications of Intelligent Agents (PAAM 1999), pp. 97–108 (1999)
5. Di Napoli, C., Di Nocera, D., Rossi, S.: Agent negotiation for different needs in smart parking allocation. In: Demazeau, Y., Zambonelli, F., Corchado, J.M., Bajo, J. (eds.) PAAMS 2014. LNCS (LNAI), vol. 8473, pp. 98–109. Springer, Cham (2014). https://doi.org/10.1007/978-3-319-07551-8_9
6. Fischer, K., Müller, J., Pischel, M., Schier, D.: A model for co-operative transportation scheduling. In: Proceedings of the 1st International Conference on Multi-Agents Systems (ICMAS 1995), pp. 109–116 (1995)
7. Fischer, K.: Agent-based design of holonic manufacturing systems. Robot. Auton. Syst. **27**, 3–13 (1999)
8. Koster, A., Koch, F., Bazzan, A.L.C.: Incentivising crowdsourced parking solutions. In: Nin, J., Villatoro, D. (eds.) CitiSens 2013. LNCS (LNAI), vol. 8313, pp. 36–43. Springer, Cham (2014). https://doi.org/10.1007/978-3-319-04178-0_4
9. Neirottia, P., Marcob, A.D., Caglianoc, A.C., Manganod, G., Scorranoe, F.: Current trends in smart city initiatives: some stylised facts. Cities **38**, 25–36 (2014)
10. Olfati-Saber, R., Fax, J.A., Murray, R.M.: Consensus and cooperation in networked multi-agent systems. IEEE **95**(1), 215–233 (2007)
11. Omote, K., Miyaji, A.: A practical English auction with one-time registration. In: Varadharajan, V., Mu, Y. (eds.) ACISP 2001. LNCS, vol. 2119, pp. 221–234. Springer, Heidelberg (2001). https://doi.org/10.1007/3-540-47719-5_19
12. Scalabrin, E.: Conception et Réalisation d'environment de développment de systàmes cognitifs. Ph.D. thesis, CNRS UMR Hendiasyc, Université de Technologie de Compiàgne (1996)
13. Seilonen, I.: Distributed and collaborative production management systems in discrete part manufacturing: a review of research and technology. VTT Research Notes, Espoo (1997)
14. Smith, R.G.: The contract net protocol: high-level communication and control in a distributed problem solver. Trans. Comput. **C-29**(12), 1104–1113 (1980)
15. Tanenbaum, A.S., Steen, M.V.: Distributed Systems Principles and Paradigms. Createspace Independent Publishing Platform, Scotts Valley (2016)
16. Wang, H.: A reservation-based smart parking system. Ph.D. thesis, University of Nebraska - Lincoln (2011)
17. Young, H.P.: Negotiation Analysis. The University of Michigan Press, Ann Arbor (1991)

Development of Resource-Demand Networks for Smart Cities 5.0

Sergey Kozhevnikov[1(✉)], Petr Skobelev[2,3], Ondrej Pribyl[4], and Miroslav Svítek[4]

[1] Czech Institute of Informatics, Robotics and Cybernetics, Czech Technical University in Prague, Jugoslávských Partyzánů 1580/3, 160 00 Prague 6, Czech Republic
koz@kg.ru

[2] Samara State Technical University, Molodogvardeyskaya Street 244, 443100 Samara, Russian Federation

[3] ICCS RAS, Sadovaya Street 61, 443020 Samara, Russian Federation

[4] Faculty of Transportation Sciences, Czech Technical University in Prague, Konviktska 20, 110 00 Prague 1, Czech Republic

Abstract. In the paper, the new vision of "Smart City 5.0" is presented. It is based on a previously developed model of Smart City 4.0 and implementing the concept of the complex adaptive system for balancing conflict interests of different city actors. These actors can include business, transport, energy and water supply providers, entertainment and other services and can be unified based on resource and demand model.

The paper describes the general principals, functionality and the architecture of the digital multi-agent platform for creating eco-system of "Smart City 5.0". It is designed as holonic p2p network of smart services and technological components for supporting demand-resource relations.

It is shown that in proposed eco-system smart services can interact both vertically and horizontally supporting competition and cooperation behavior on the basis of specialized protocols of p2p network. In the future, each smart service is considered as an autonomous cyber-physical multi-agent system which can be decomposed on a lower level of smaller services recursively.

The first prototypes of smart services and their interaction are presented, the next steps for future research work are outlined.

Keywords: Smart City 5.0 · Holonic system · Digital eco-system · Smart services · Multi-agent technology · Artificial intelligence

1 Introduction

Smart Cities are constantly growing, both in the number of inhabitants and the number of smart services provided for citizens. One of the major problems of vast growing is a lack of interoperability [1]. The majority of smart services (SmtS) solve local tasks working on a certain small amount of data provided by the city government. It is difficult to find good examples of cooperative or better - co-evolution work of SmtS as one smart system.

V. Mařík et al. (Eds.): HoloMAS 2019, LNAI 11710, pp. 203–217, 2019.
https://doi.org/10.1007/978-3-030-27878-6_16

On the technological level, we can see the current trend for open standards and frameworks for SmartCity (SC) data use. For example, the EU Synchronicity program proposing to collect data from SC sources to be operated in one market place. The project targeting to create standard IOT protocols and organizational principals for semantic descriptions of data collected from various systems, making it more accessible for computer processing in different applications [2].

Another important trend in SC is digital ecosystems (Apple, Yandex) with integrated and unified information space of hardware, devices and software where users can easily switch from ordering food, to analyzing traffic jams, navigation, checking or planning sports activities and other cases.

On the methodology level, there is a trend for universal programs, frameworks and action plans to achieve a better quality of living, for example, the Green Cities Programme Methodology prepared by European Bank for Reconstruction and Development (www.ebrd.com).

Taking into account all current trends we make the first attempt to define Smart city as an open complex system, alive and constantly developing adaptive system that self-organizes and evolves in all its spheres with set of different Key Performance Indicators (KPI) like business, recreation, comfort, transport, environment, goods availability, medical care, education and prices for services, etc. It is obvious that such a system will have various actors and players sometimes with contradictory interests. The problem we want to solve is the overall integration at both the functional and technological level through creating an open platform architecture that allows adding different services and easily integrate them into a SC environment.

In the first and the second section of the paper, the problem is defined and the existing architecture solutions are evaluated. The third part describes the Smart cities 5.0 concept (compare with predefined SmartCity 4.0) based on the intelligent platform. It consists of two levels: the level of technologies and the level of services. In the fourth part of the paper, the Resource and Demand (RD) model as the core of every SmtS is presented. The concept of RD model is not new and has already been used in various MAT systems, but this article proposes to use it for the first time for interaction not only within one service but also between several services. In this new approach, a request created in one service can be satisfied by a comprehensive solution of multiple agents of different services. This RD model will help to build interaction between services both on the horizontal and on the vertical level of the platform. In the fifth section, we show several examples of SC services and models implementation based on RD model and examples of services co-evolution.

2 State of the Art

Smart city development is now considered a complex problem. But not so many researchers explore SC as a complex adaptive system, where "complex system" is used in prof. Prigogine meaning [3]. There are many efforts to create one universal architecture that can be applied to all modern cities. Usually, they meet difficulties because of too many actors, relations, diversities, etc. To overcome those difficulties, the novel approaches are trying to introduce distributed architectures and put knowledge about actors in the heart of SC development.

Zygiaris in [4] describes his vision of the Smart City Reference Model. He opposes virtual gated communities and corporate enclaves at the heart of SC. In his opinion, Smart cities should be built and developed as public-controlled integrated urban operating systems. In addition, Zygiaris relies on the work of Belissent [5], emphasizing that the Smart city project should take into account the context of a particular city. As a result of his reasoning Zygiaris proposes a multi-level architecture of a SC, includes the following levels: The City Layer, The Green City Layer, The Interconnection Layer, The Instrumentation Layer, The Open Integration Layer, The Application Layer and The Innovation Layer. Significant development of the upper levels of the model is impossible without the development of the lower levels. Urban systems form the playing field on which an open integrated Smart City system can be built.

Hancke [6] defines a Smart city as an integrated model of all its infrastructure and citizen services and to the use of intelligent devices for monitoring and control. Based on this definition, in Chamoso et al. [7] note in their work that designing individual smart systems is not enough to build a SC. A Smart city should function as a single organic ensemble. This model inevitably contains a huge number of interrelated elements (M2M concept). To implement this concept, mechanisms are needed to support the volume of connections and the type of communication. Chamoso et al. refer to technologies ZigBee, Bluetooth, Wi-Fi, WiMax, PLC, GSM/GPRS, 6LoWPAN, EnOcean and Z-Wave to build M2M models.

Chamoso et al. [7] note in his review that more and more sensors are needed to build a SC based on the IoT. Therefore, they propose the model sensing as a service to Smart City design. Perera et al. [8] provide a comprehensive overview of sensing as a service model. They note the stability, scalability and power of the model. Chamoso et al. [7] analyze the functionality of the platforms Sentilo, IBM Intelligent Operation Center, CitySDK, Open Cities, i-SCOPE, People and IoTOpenplatforms. They come to the conclusion that at the moment there is no universal and open platform for encapsulating information and knowledge about the city.

Therefore, Chamoso et al. offer their own architecture consisting of a set of technological solutions for Autonomous information management and a distributed system providing analysis and services. The advantage of the architecture is a modular design that allows adapting the system to the needs of new cities.

Almeida et al. [9] consider the problem of the handle a large number of mobile sensors/devices, with high heterogeneity and unpredictable mobility. They propose the Multi-Technology Communication Platform for Urban Mobile Sensing. This architecture is based on the unified and extremely heterogeneous network uniting cars, aerial and aquatic drones, bicycles, and fixed sensors stations. The main elements of the system are monitoring sensors, mobile nodes, gateways, and a server. Experiments have shown that the described architecture has reduced the overhead of the network.

Krylovskiy et al. [10] note the complexity of the creation in practice large-scale Smart City IoT platforms that can scale and evolve over time adopting new technologies and requirements. They describe their early experience of applying the microservice architecture style to design a Smart City IoT platform. Krylovskiy et al. propose a microservice architecture which allows working on individual parts independently, maintaining its integrity and efficiency. In this case, different parts of the system can be implemented in different ways. In their architecture, there is no complex technology middleware. They use simple communication protocols and APIs. This has resulted in a significant reduction in coordination work. They come to the conclusion that at the current stage the proposed architecture is a compromise between simplifies the design and implementation of individual services and the complexity of distributed systems.

The most promising approach is presented by Roscia et al. [11]. Authors proved that the transformation of cities in smart systems should be based on different subsets that communicate and interact, in order to make the concrete realization of a smart city. They analyze and design the approach that simulates a dynamic infrastructure within the broader context of the envisioned Smart City. With full understanding that the final solution should be based on integration and finding the balance between SmtS the authors explore the idea of the Smart City Grid that should be intelligent, distributed and autonomous and based on smart agents that move the grid beyond central control to a collaborative network of almost biological complexity. They present IDASC model (Intelligent Distributed Autonomous Smart City) as a grid-wide computing network. This approach still does not consider of semantic interoperability of Smart Services, and provide more technical realization and universal agent model and also do not provide the answer of heterogeneous services collaboration.

Analysis of different existing Smart City services standards and frameworks shows the trend for open frameworks and flexible distributed structures, with step to the digitization of knowledge and the automation of decision making process.

3 Description of the New Smart City 5.0 Vision

In this paper, we present one of the possible future models of the Smart City - as a complex adaptive system is able to work under conditions of high uncertainty and dynamics of events.

In comparison with predefined approach of Smart City 4.0 [12] - model based on adoption and of Industry 4.0 concept principles, characteristics and integration of computing technologies, we offer a model that can be characterized as a fully distributed autonomous cyber-physical system for resource management. It will allow to support of different KPIs of many actors, continuous growing and evolution of the system as a whole when some autonomous parts can be replaced "on-the-fly". The platform will provide open access for all participants in real time. This advantage will help to create SC when it is difficult to characterize from the very beginning all parties who will be involved [13].

The developed vision of SmartCity 5.0 is based on the concept of a digital platform for creating eco-system of smart services. The architecture of the new SC platform includes the following main layers: technology level and service level (see Fig. 1). The technology level can have several instruments: data management instruments, decision making engine, intelligent/AI technologies, big data, simulation tools, etc. The service level consists of different Smart Services of various kind of managing resources.

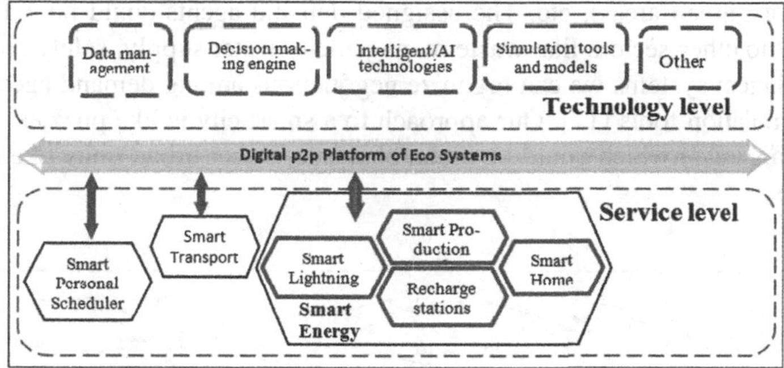

Fig. 1. Smart City 5.0 system architecture.

Every service in this platform can be functionally unique but common in the core architecture and created on the same basic principles. The core of every service is a Resource and Demand model and open access to collective data space. This allows services to solve their internal task, but also be part of bigger services (holons) [14].

In this concept each smart service is presented by an autonomous agent. They can compete or cooperate with each other through a service bus, interacting both vertically and horizontally on the basis of specialized protocols. Top-level services are constructed as autonomous multi-agent systems of a lower level, where any agent of such a system can recursively reveal a new service for itself.

The proposed solution also requires Peer-to-Peer Network (p2p network) of planners on a platform layer, which unites heterogeneous systems and allows them to communicate with each other in order to achieve coordinated and close to optimal results.

4 Development of Resource Demand Model for Smart Services Interactions

The basic approach for supporting the interaction of SmtS is a resource and demand (RD) model which advanced by new types of agents, satisfaction functions and bonus-penalties and compensations [15]. This means that every problem solved by the SmtS can be described as a combination of resource and demand interactions [16].

Let us define the basic ontology model tailored-made for a smart city. Practically, we can simulate different city sectors as it is shown in Fig. 2 using different simulation software for transport, energy, land use, environment, or other segments.

Energy demands are connected with nodes of energy consumption, production or storage. Transport demands are represented by a set of the origin-destination (O-D) lines to which are assigned typically two parameters: the number of vehicles in both directions in given time and the quality of transportation such as travel-time (the number of parameters can be extended based on applications). Land use is defined as the domain (geometrical shape) with a lot of attributes like square meters, reason of use (parking slots, green areas), etc. The assigned demand agents could be extended in a similar way to other sectors like waste management, water supply, safety and security.

In multiagent systems we can organize negotiations among demand agents through different simulation tools [17]. Our approach to a smart city is like puzzles of different pieces (urban areas) which could be assembled into higher urban units like districts or whole cities.

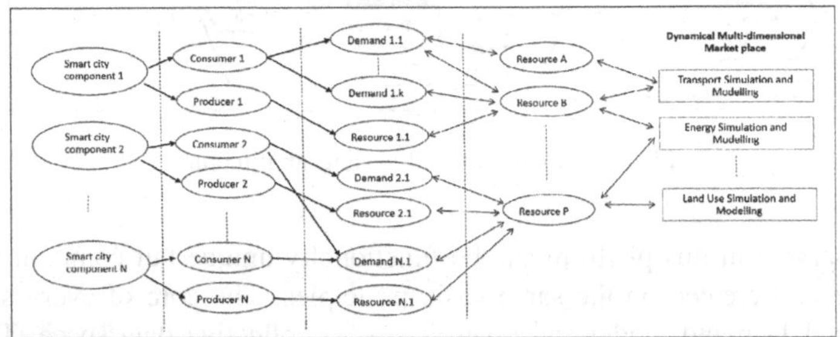

Fig. 2. System architecture of resource-demand model for smart cities

Each technical component (building, street light, charging station, etc.) or different users (citizen, municipality, group of people) requires limited resources (energy, transport, parking slot, land, etc.) in given time interval t (dynamical demand requirements). These requirements are represented by Demands Agents which are able to negotiate among themselves [17].

The SC simulation model can be understood as the virtual market place for MAS that represents available infrastructure together with their parameters (limited energy resources in the given node, maximal traffic flow in selected roads, maximal environmental parameters in the district, etc.).

Negotiation among Demand agents with city simulation model will yield into dynamical resources assignments represented by Resources agents that offer the best possible service to each consumer. In case one consumer does not accept the assigned resources it must change their demands. The negotiation can be repeated once again under new conditions.

The negotiation process among agents should result in the time schedule of customers' assigned resources (energy, transportation, parking slots, etc.). In future, we can enlarge our approach to take into account also the energy, traffic and parking control strategies.

The resulting approach as a user interface between aggregated demand agents assigned into different smart city components and aggregated urban sustainability parameters (economic, environmental and social) is depicted in Fig. 3. The decision-makers, typically municipality, should specify the sustainability parameters (KPIs) for the whole urban area. The demand and resource agents mutually negotiate with a city simulation model to propose to each smart city component the reduced comfort to fulfill the requested KPI.

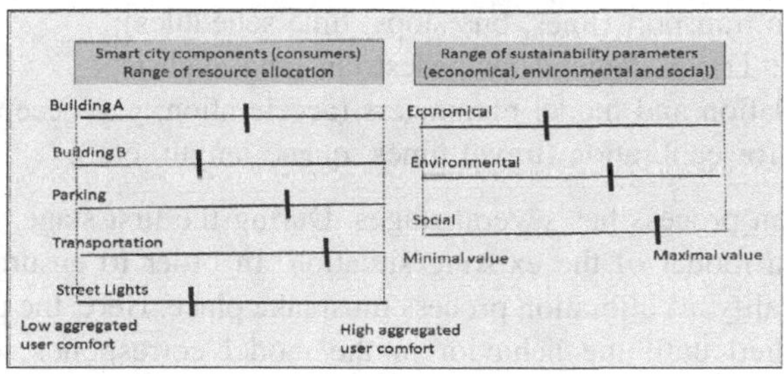

Fig. 3. Smart city "equalizer"

With respect to the presented system architecture we can define the following illustrative services for different users:

- strategical planning of green areas (modeling of the urban ecosystem together with its optimized future evolution);
- strategical planning of resource consumptions in different areas;
- recommendation of apartments'/residents' number in an urban area with respect to transportation, energy, etc.;
- recommendation for advanced building operation (category, consumption, transport);
- change of time schedule of public transport (time tables, transport services);
- change from the fuel to electric buses in public transport (environmental and economic impact);
- change of traffic control strategy (green lines, environmental impact);
- recommendation of active intervention during rush hours;
- recommendation of better reaction to unexpected events (accidents, disasters, blackout, crises management, etc.).

5 Smart City Services Implementation Based on Resource and Demand Model

Below we present several Smart Services and models as part of the Smart City 5.0 concept.

5.1 Transportation Service

Transportation system (TS) is the core element of every city. Within the overall system, we can perceive it as a subsystem with certain input values and output KPIs [18].

Inputs cover:

- (IP) RG: Road geometry (incl. nodes, sections, parking, etc.);
- (P) TD: Travel demand (incl. origin-destination (OD) matrices for particular vehicle classes);
- (IP/P) TC: Traffic control (signal plans, traffic signs, etc.);

- (P) PT: Public transport (lines, bus stops, time schedules);
- (P) TD_VRU: Travel demand for pedestrians and cyclists;
- (P) SP: Simulation and model parameters (acceleration, gap acceptance, etc.); and
- (-) CD: Data for calibration (travel times, queue length, etc.).

The simulation process has several stages. During the first stage, a basic model is created. This is a model of the existing situation. In order to ensure that the model corresponds to reality, a calibration process must take place. Here, the parameters of the model are modified until the behavior in the model corresponds to the real work situation. Typically, travel times or for example queue length is used for this comparison. After we have a calibrated model, different alternative scenarios can be evaluated.

The list of inputs above also consists of specification whether the given group of parameters is implicit (denoted - IP), or whether they can be used as parameters (denoted - P). Some scenarios require implicit changes in the model (typically changes in road geometry such as different number of traffic lanes, changes from signal control to roundabout, etc.), some just changes in input parameters (for example changes in travel demand as a result of certain policies, changes in public transport, changes in the number of pedestrians, time shift of the demand and others). Using different policies (for example support of car sharing etc.) has a direct influence on the OD matrices. This is a way how different subsystems can influence each other.

With all of this said, the transportation model is addressed by the remaining agents (sub-systems) in the following way:

$$O_i^S = TM(t,\ p, ip) \tag{1}$$

The output of a certain scenario, *S*, depends on the inputs, *p*, and input parameters, *ip*, at a given time *t*.

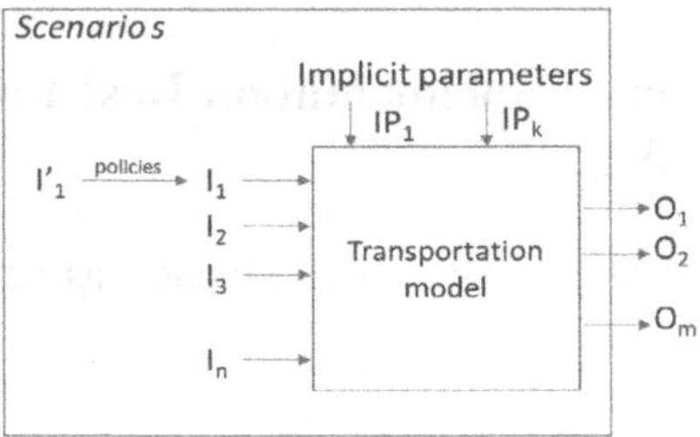

Fig. 4. Scenario oriented transportation model

Typically, the performance of the system (i.e. output or KPIs) cover the cost of a given situation (scenario) and its influence on the environment (emissions, fuel consumed, and others), but also for example characteristics such as travel time or the delay of the vehicles in the network (Fig. 4).

With respect to the energy, the model can be perceived as a black box with input and output variables. The other subsystems must not know about its internal behavior. There are however some issues that cannot be dealt with on an aggregated level. The two most important are discussed below:

Dynamic behavior – transportation is rather a complex system with many dependencies. For example, simple variables such as travel time (TT) are not constant. This is a dynamic parameter and its value depends on several parameters, but mainly the actual travel demand, D.

$$TT(t) = f(t, D) \tag{2}$$

Interactions among different elements – several approaches (such as highway capacity manual) allow the analytical description of the behavior on a single network element, for example, road segment or an intersection. They, however, do not offer to model of interactions among such elements. For example, unsuitable control algorithm or too high travel demand can lead to a situation that a queue caused by the first intersection influences not only speed on the given road section, but can cause the fact that vehicles cannot clear the adjacent intersection.

In order to provide a sufficient level of details and realistic behavior, a microscopic simulation model is the preferred solution for MAS. It is able to deal with the first two challenges described above, but they do not allow the modeling of human decisions. Changes in the destinations are not part of the model and must be dealt with prior to the simulation. It does not react to changes in the attractiveness of certain parts of the network etc.

5.2 Smart Energy Service as Part of Smart City Concept

In many cities lack of energy and other resources are becoming stop factor for future growth and intensive development of the economy and social infrastructure. Almost all Smart cities are characterized with a constantly growing need for energy resources that identify the number of existing constraints (infrastructure, network, the difficulty to predict consumption, etc.). Every city is characterized by unique energy, gas, heat and water supply network model. The task of the Smart energy service is to find the optimal balance between reasonable consuming and smart sufficient production.

To solve this problem, the Smart Energy Service prototype based on the principles of Smart grid [19] was developed (see Fig. 5). It allows automating the process of adaptive dynamic distribution of requests for resources, taking into account various criteria. The system can also simulate devices and sensors for collecting information from the bottom level, the state of networks, the capacity of suppliers.

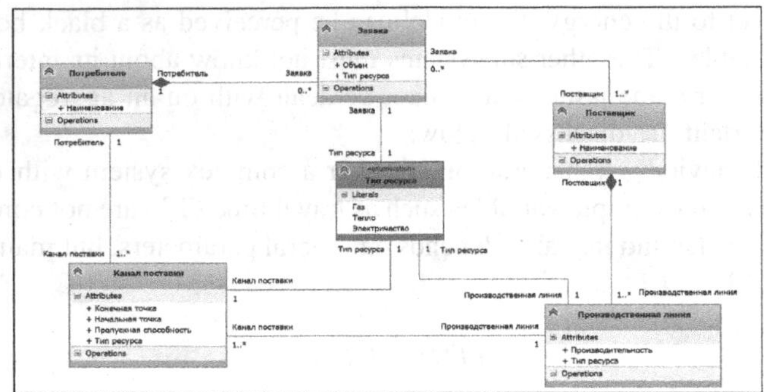

Fig. 5. E-R diagram of the entities of the Smart Energy service

The developed model will allow performing the following functions:

1. Set the initial configuration of the network, including consumers and suppliers of resources and communication lines with their parameters.
2. Set the required performance indicators of the network (cost, equal load, etc.).
3. Set the list of events with time, coming to the network as input.
4. Simulate the process of (re)distribution of requests for resources in the network.
5. Create unexpected events: for example, the unexpected rise of consumption, the breakdown of any resource or implementing of a new resource to the system, changing the parameters of the resource, etc.

As a method of solving optimization task, we used resource and demand model based on multi-agent technology and the market approach of optimization.

In the simulation model of the system, we have many resources producing water, heat and electricity designed to meet different needs, with different performance and cost parameters. They all are connected by a network with different capacity parameters. At random time, the system receives events, for example, new orders (demand) in a certain place of the network. New demands can be consolidated into larger orders for a certain time horizon. Time and amount characteristics of orders may be unknown until the arrival. Every provider of water, electricity and gas has its own tariff price, as well as each communication line has its own capacity and cost.

Every order (demand) and opportunity (resource) in the network will receive its agent. Resource agent primarily evaluates the possibility to execute the order. If it is impossible, the resource agent requests neighboring resources for assistance. As a result, the agents of resources and demands negotiate with each other, knowing their requirements and deadlines. In this case, a flexible resource allocation plan is built adaptively, determining who will execute which order. Agents not only form but also control the execution plan and the maximum possible load. The plan can be adjusted as new orders arrive or new resources are connected or disconnected.

Network agents evaluate and try to find the most appropriate route. It is assumed that the agent of any node has all the necessary information about the neighboring nodes (with possible interference and delays), and any node is reachable during the sequence of negotiations. Negotiations are made with the aim of redistribution of load in the network. The most open capacity "attract" the load from other capacities and, as a result, the load is distributed evenly over the network or moves where it is cheaper. If resource breaks orders reallocate to other resources.

Every agent of the consumer (demand) object has the ability to plan its work on the time horizon, building a schedule of consumption and respectively resource agents can plan production. The system can work both on a microservice level collecting the orders from a smart apartment or smart house, or on the macro level to analyze the vast growing demand (for example, a new house or a new industrial factory is planned to be connected to the network).

Characteristics of resource demand model:

- the expression of all optimization parameters: time, volume, characteristics of the network bandwidth, is considered through the universal cost characteristics represented in internal currency;
- setting the rules of agent's negotiations aimed to increase the local profit of every agent by reducing costs in the internal currency, that leads to a dynamic improvement of the network parameters;
- the automatic finding of the optimal dynamic balance of a multi-agent system by exchanging virtual money;
- use of the component-by-component change of parameters of optimization of the modeling system for the purpose of alignment of indicators.

It is obvious that the complexity of such a model will not allow creating one centralized system for the whole city, suitable for all levels: from a separate apartment – to the whole city. In this regard, this project proposes to create such a system as a holonic and network-centric, built as an adaptive p2p network of individual planners capable to coordinate their decisions both vertically (top – down and bottom – up) and horizontally among themselves [20].

Holonic, in this case, means that the system can act autonomously at the level of a smart apartment for example, but act together as a bigger more generic system at the level of a smart house or district. It provides higher openness, flexibility, performance, scalability, reliability and survivability of the system.

5.3 Smart Personal Scheduler as a Part of Smart City Concept

Smart Service for personal tasks scheduling is focused on providing a flexible dynamic real time planning with a capability to automatically improve the plan according to changing environment and events. All existing software applications used for this purposes show major limitations in real time (re)scheduling, semantic descriptions of events and p2p dependencies between users [21]. As a result, scheduling now is very time-consuming and becomes a challenge - users spend more time for planning and tracking daily tasks.

For solving this problem, Smart Personal Scheduler based on RD model and extended market-based reasoning mechanisms is proposed. In a virtual market agents of orders and resources recognize conflicts and try to re-allocate orders between resources using negotiations and taking in account not only their current states, given goals and preferences but also special kind of virtual money, which they get proportionally as the profit and which works as the energy for creating and revising developed links between agents. In this case, there are no needs to stop or restart scheduling manually it works continuously in real time.

This approach will provide the capability to develop a model for managing virtual market by the amount of accumulated money, level of satisfaction of agents, factors based on a number of communications between different agents in different parts of schedule and strength of agent links which will show the stability of scheduling.

Self-organization in our approach means the ability of scheduling system to revise and change links between agents of demands and resources, tasks and operations, which are triggered by different events or started proactively [22].

The key elements of the model:

- the advanced virtual market mechanism based on resource demand model;
- self-regulation and self-adaptation for managing quality and efficiency of scheduling;
- level of satisfaction and virtual money for agents;
- trade-offs for balancing decisions between different criteria;
- support p2p interactions of intelligent schedulers in adaptive networks;
- pro-active interaction with users.

The personal scheduler can work not only reactively and pro-actively but also can be triggered by entering external events from other planners. The development of multi-swarm schedulers will not only provide a number of new benefits including open architecture, high scalability and performance (every swarm runs on its hardware), reliability but also will help to test the designed approach applicable for "Smart City 5.0".

5.4 Examples of Coevolution of Services

Examples of coevolution of services are demonstrated in two cases. The first case presents the negotiation between Smart Energy Service and Smart Transport Service. The optimized consumption plan of energy resources in the real world is easily ruined by the transport system. Delay in trams schedule can ruin the energy plan and can cause a tremendous rise in consumption. As a solution we offer change of time schedule of public transport (time tables, transport services), change the type of transport - bus instead of the tram (cab be negotiated with Smart Environment Service), change of traffic control strategy (green lights).

The second, more complicated case is based on Smart Personal Scheduler. Smart City 5.0 model, can evolve as a user-centric concept we intelligent personal schedules as the main access instrument to Smart services.

Personal plan can be renegotiated several times through the connection to different Smart Services. As an example - a lingered meeting can be the reason for the whole day or week rescheduling as the result of automatic conflict-driven reasoning in the intelligent scheduler. This event will trigger for example the cancellation of lunch with a friend or its reallocation to another day, the shift of the other meetings. But with respect to the late trip to the airport intelligent personal scheduler can check current traffic situation and traffic model and recommend to use the train instead of personal electro car. In that case, the next recharge of the car is rescheduled. This example shows different Smart services cooperation: Smart Personal Schedulers, Smart Food Service, Smart Transport Model, Smart Energy Service.

In this view, the advanced intellectualization of future smart services becomes possible because of bringing new reach operational context of users into consideration. This approach gives new opportunity for SME to build shared networks of clients aggregating services [23]. The personal scheduler unites separate people into one dynamic collaborative group that quickly reacts to upcoming events, performs adaptive scheduling in real time and efficiently carries out coordinated plans. But, the most advanced innovation will take place when intelligent schedulers described above will start working together demonstrating co-evolution of self-organized systems.

6 Conclusion

The Smart City 4.0 model [12] based on Industry 4.0 principals shows integrating ICT and computing technologies throughout whole production enterprise enable to share data, information, and instructions between all agents during all phases of the production value chain. The presented concept of Smart City 5.0 provides a new vision of a city as a digital platform and eco-system of smart services where agents of people, things, documents, robots and other entities can directly negotiate with each other providing the best possible solution for formed demand.

The proposed concept of digital eco-systems will allow these services to interact and coordinate decisions and achieve consensus (balance of interests), instead of a simple transfer of data from one service to another. In this concept agents of services will compete or cooperate with each other, interacting on the basis of specialized protocols - both vertically and horizontally. Top-level services will be constructed as autonomous multi-agent systems of a lower level, where any agent of such a system can recursively reveal a new system for itself.

All smart services in this concept are created based on resource demand model. This approach is not fundamentally new, but in this article we propose to use it for the first time for a Smart city. The second contributed result is the use of RD model for interaction not only within one service but also within several services and models to increase flexibility, efficiency, scalability and high performance and reliability of the solution.

The proposed concept of RD model allows creating a new generation of Smart City applications that can show co-evolution of self-organization of systems.

Acknowledgment. This work was supported by the European Regional Development Fund under the project AI&Reasoning (reg. no. CZ.02.1.01/0.0/0.0/15_003/0000466).

References

1. Bastidas, V., Bezbradica, M., Helfert, M.: Cities as enterprises: a comparison of smart city frameworks based on enterprise architecture requirements. In: Alba, E., Chicano, F., Luque, G. (eds.) Smart-CT 2017. LNCS, vol. 10268, pp. 20–28. Springer, Cham (2017). https://doi.org/10.1007/978-3-319-59513-9_3

2. Synchronicity (2019). https://synchronicity-iot.eu/. Accessed 11 Jan 2019
3. Nicolis, G., Prigogine, I.: Exploring Complexity: An Introduction. W.H. Freeman, New York (1989)
4. Zygiaris, S.: Smart city reference model: assisting planners to conceptualize the building of smart city innovation ecosystems. J. Knowl. Econ. **4**, 217–231 (2012). https://doi.org/10.1007/s13132-012-0089-4
5. Belissent, J.: Getting clever about smart cities: new opportunities require new business models. Forester (2010)
6. Hancke, G.P., de Silva, B.D.C., Hancke Jr., G.P.: The role of advanced sensing in smart cities. Sensors **13**(1), 393–425 (2013)
7. Chamoso, P., González-Briones, A., Rodríguez, S., Corchado, J.M.: Tendencies of technologies and platforms in smart cities: a state-of-the-art review. Wirel. Commun. Mob. Comput. **2018**, Article ID 3086854, 17 p. (2018). https://doi.org/10.1155/2018/3086854
8. Perera, C., Zaslavsky, A., Christen, P., Georgakopoulos, D.: Sensing as a service model for smart cities supported by internet of things. Eur. Trans. Telecommun. **25**(1), 81–93 (2014). https://doi.org/10.1002/ett.2704
9. Almeida, R., Oliveira, R., Luis, M., Senna, C., Sargento, S.: A multi-technology communication platform for urban mobile sensing. Sensors **18**, 1184 (2018). https://doi.org/10.3390/s18041184
10. Krylovskiy, A., Jahn, M., Patti, E.: Designing a smart city internet of things platform with microservice architecture. In: 2015 3rd International Conference on Future Internet of Things and Cloud, Rome, pp. 25–30 (2015). https://doi.org/10.1109/ficloud.2015.55
11. Roscia, M., Longo, M., Lazaroiu, G.C.: Smart city by multi-agent systems. In: 2013 International Conference on Renewable Energy Research and Applications (ICRERA), pp. 371–376 (2013). https://doi.org/10.1109/ICRERA.2013.6749783
12. Postránecký, M., Svítek, M.: Conceptual model of complex multi-agent system smart city 4.0. In: Mařík, V., Wahlster, W., Strasser, T., Kadera, P. (eds.) HoloMAS 2017. LNCS (LNAI), vol. 10444, pp. 215–226. Springer, Cham (2017). https://doi.org/10.1007/978-3-319-64635-0_16
13. Rzevski, G., Skobelev, P.O.: Managing Complexity. WIT Press, Boston (2014)
14. Valckenaers, P., Van Brussel, H.: Fundamental insights into holonic systems design. In: Mařík, V., William Brennan, R., Pěchouček, M. (eds.) HoloMAS 2005. LNCS (LNAI), vol. 3593, pp. 11–22. Springer, Heidelberg (2005). https://doi.org/10.1007/11537847_2
15. Skobelev, P.: Towards autonomous AI systems for resource management: applications in industry and lessons learned. In: Demazeau, Y., An, B., Bajo, J., Fernández-Caballero, A. (eds.) PAAMS 2018. LNCS (LNAI), vol. 10978, pp. 12–25. Springer, Cham (2018). https://doi.org/10.1007/978-3-319-94580-4_2
16. Skobelev, P.: Multi-agent systems for real time adaptive resource management. In: Leitão, P., Karnouskos, S. (ed.) Industrial Agents: Emerging Applications of Software Agents in Industry, pp. 207–230. Elsevier (2015)
17. Gorodetsky, V.: Internet of agents: from set of autonomous agents - to network object. In: Lutzenberger, M. (eds.) Topics in Internet of Agents, 16th International Conference on Autonomous Agents and Multiagent Systems, Sao Paulo, May 2017, pp. 1–17. Springer (2017)
18. Pribyl, O., Pribyl, P., Lom, M., Svitek, M.: Modeling of smart cities based on ITS architecture. IEEE Intell. Transp. Syst. Mag. 1 (2018). https://doi.org/10.1109/mits.2018.2876553
19. Smart Grid. http://www.oe.energy.gov/smartgrid.htm

20. Bukhvalov, O., Gorodetsky, V.: P2P self-organizing agent system: GRID resource management case. In: Omatu, S., et al. (eds.) Distributed Computing and Artificial Intelligence, 12th International Conference. AISC, vol. 373, pp. 259–267. Springer, Cham (2015). https://doi.org/10.1007/978-3-319-19638-1_30
21. Skobelev, P.O., Kozhevnikov, S.S., Mayorov, I.V., Poludov, D.P., Simonova, E.V.: Smart projects: multi-agent solution for aerospace applications. Int. J. Des. Nat. Ecodynamics **12**, 492–504 (2017). https://doi.org/10.2495/dne-v12-n4-492-504
22. Skobelev, P., Mayorov, I., Kozhevnikov, S., Tsarev, A., Simonova, E.: Measuring adaptability of "swarm intelligence" for resource scheduling and optimization in real time. In: Loiseau, S., Filipe, J., Duval, B., Herik, J. (eds.) 7th International Conference on Agents and Artificial Intelligence, Lisbon, January 2015, vol. 2, pp. 517–522. SCITEPRESS, Portugal (2015)
23. Kozhevnikov, S., Larukhin, V., Skobelev, P.: Smart enterprise: multi-agent solution for holonic enterprise resource management. In: Matsuo, T., Lee, R., Ishii, N. (eds.) 12th International Conference on Computer and Information Science 2013, Niigata, June 2013, pp. 111–116. IEEE Computer Society, Piscataway (2013)

Author Index

Printed in the United States
By Bookmasters